PUBLICATIONS IN ARCHAEOLOGY
Patrice A. Teltser, Director of Publications

Also in this series

Center for Archaeological Investigations
Southern Illinois University at Carbondale

Tracing Archaeology's Past

The Historiography of Archaeology

Edited by Andrew L. Christenson

Southern Illinois University Press
Carbondale and Edwardsville

Library of Congress Cataloging-in-Publication Data

Tracing archaeology's past : the historiography of archaeology /
edited by Andrew L. Christenson.
    p. cm.—(Publications in archaeology)
    At head of title: Center for Archaeological Investigations,
Southern Illinois University at Carbondale.
    Bibliography: p.
    Includes index.
    1. Archaeology—Historiography.   2. Archaeology—History.
I. Christenson, Andrew L.   II. Southern Illinois University at
Carbondale. Center for Archaeological Investigations.   III. Title:
Tracing archaeology's past.   IV. Series: Publications in archaeology
(Southern Illinois University at Carbondale. Center for
Archaeological Investigations)
CC100.T73   1989
930'.1'072—dc19   88-27278
ISBN 0-8093-1523-8   CIP

Contents

Figures and Tables

Figures

Tables

Preface

Archaeology as a professional discipline began between the 1840s and the 1860s with the work of people like J. J. A. Worsaae and Jeffries Wyman, who devoted much of their time to and derived their livelihood from archaeology. As one might expect, publications on the history of archaeological research were scarce in this early period, Samuel Haven's (1856) overview of American archaeology being a notable exception. It took nearly a century for major studies on this topic to become commonplace.

Prior to the books by Stanley Casson (1934, 1939), there were no broad-scope histories of archaeology and Glyn Daniel's *Hundred Years of Archaeology* (1950) was the first study to treat the subject in a systematic manner. Based upon references in Kemper and Phinney (1977), Trigger (1985), and my own library, I estimate that the output of books on the history of archaeology has been doubling about every decade through the century. This growth rate parallels that of archaeology as a whole, at least from the 1930s to the 1970s, and although the growth of the discipline seems to have stopped, at least in the United States (Rogge 1983), the increase in history of archaeology literature does not seem to be slowing.

The increased interest in archaeology's past is part of a trend in archaeology toward recognizing history and historical perspectives as subjects of interest and even of critical importance in understanding the prehistoric past (e.g., Deetz 1988; Hodder 1986). A strong dichotomy had been made between history and science, with archaeology being strongly tied to science, by many "new archaeologists" of the previous two decades (e.g., Dunnell 1971:20–21; Spaulding 1968), but there has been a realization that such a dichotomy is false and dangerous. Michael Schiffer has amply demonstrated in a recent volume that "the behavior of the archaeologist is the greatest source of variability in the archaeological record" (1987:362), thus elevating historical studies to a major place in archaeological research.

My initiation into historical research on archaeology came first in constructing bibliographies and overviews of topics that I was currently studying (e.g., Christenson 1980) and later in writing historic overviews for cultural resource management projects. My first foray into history for history's sake came as a specific reaction to erroneous statements in the literature about the early recognition of North American shell middens (Christenson 1986).

My involvement with the history of archaeology deepened during my tenure as curator of the archaeological collections at the University of California, Los Angeles, which included those of the Rainbow Bridge–Monument Valley Expedition. This multidisciplinary project involved major archaeological research on the Colorado Plateau during the 1930s and included many individuals who were then or who later became prominent archaeologists or anthropologists. My research on the history of this project, which involved oral history, archival research, analysis of photographs, and so on, made me aware of the difficulty of interpreting archaeology's past, even when the evidence is abundant (Christenson 1983).

My next historic project was a study of archaeological research in the Kayenta Anasazi region of northern Arizona. This nine-month study involved archival research, interviews, and systematic reading of all the published literature in the region through 1968 (Christenson 1988). Early in this project I began to think seriously about the problems of interpreting the history of archaeology and to question my qualifications and the qualifications of any archaeologist to do historic research.

A review of the literature revealed little concern among archaeologists for the methods of historical research or for the theoretical biases that archaeologists may bring to their interpretation of archaeology's past (Schuyler 1971 is unique in this respect). It appeared that the history of archaeology had not yet reached the introspective stage. When the opportunity arose to suggest a conference for the 1986–1987 visiting scholar position at the Center for Archaeological Investigations, Southern Illinois University, Carbondale, this topic seemed to me to be much in need of discussion. I proposed to bring together scholars active in the history of archaeology to examine critically how accounts of archaeology's past are produced and how these accounts are used by archaeologists. My proposal was accepted and the conference, "Explaining Archaeology's Past: The Method and Theory of the History of Archaeology," was held 1–2 May 1987 at Southern Illinois University.

All but two of the papers presented at the conference are included in revised chapter form in this volume. The chapters have three different but overlapping themes—the uses of the history of archaeology; the contexts of the history of archaeology; and the processes and problems of researching, documenting, and presenting the history of archaeology.

History as a method of study is as broad as human life itself, and so it is impossible in a volume of 17 papers to cover more than a fraction of the relevant issues. The volume should be considered a sampler of the problems and issues that researchers currently active in the history of archaeology deem important. Most of the papers do not provide concrete answers to particular questions of historical method and theory—that would be too much to expect of an area of study so early in its development. Rather, the volume provides ideas and perspectives for those working in or considering working in the history of archaeology. If this volume causes such individuals to examine seriously why they are writing about the history of archaeology, to think more carefully about the sociopolitical contexts within which their subjects lived, or to see that an archival collection is preserved or made accessible to researchers, then it will have served its purpose.

Acknowledgments

Numerous individuals helped make the conference a success and guided the production of this volume. George J. Gumerman and the other members of the visiting scholar committee, Brian Butler, and Jon Muller, deserve special thanks for making the visiting scholar conference possible.

Barbara Emil and the staff of the Division of Continuing Education at Southern Illinois University handled much of the organization of the conference, and their efficiency made my task much easier.

Douglas R. Givens gave major support to the conference by having the conference announcement and the cover of the final program printed at St. Louis Community College. Christopher Chippindale, Brian M. Fagan, Curtis M. Hinsley, Jr., Nancy J. Parezo, and Gordon R. Willey gave useful advice and encouragement in the early phases of planning. Don D. Fowler served as a discussant and Douglas R. Givens, Alice B. Kehoe, Edwin Lyon, Charles R. McGimsey, III, David R. Wilcox, and Stephen Williams served as session moderators. Michael Tarabulski gave a special showing of his video "Reliving the Past," and the Alabama Museum of Natural History loaned historic films for viewing. Christopher Chippindale graciously said a few words in memory of Glyn Daniel, who did so much to make the history of archaeology a respectable field of study.

The volume was edited by Kathryn Koldehoff and Ruth Strack, and word processing was done by Brenda Wells.

Part I

Uses of the History
of Archaeology

Introduction

The history of archaeology, like history in general, serves a variety of functions (Vaughn 1985). As the history of archaeology is written primarily by archaeologists for archaeologists, its range of purposes is somewhat narrower than the range of purposes for many other types of history. The most common forms taken by the history of archaeology are commemorations or obituaries and reviews of past work from an intellectual perspective as background for discussions of current research. These historical forms usually have a narrow perspective, which requires leaving out many aspects of the past. Obituaries and commemorations by their nature are positive and place little emphasis upon conflict, competition, and other aspects of human behavior that are an important part of any discipline (Greene 1986:98–99).

Historical forms of more relevance to this volume are writings that look in detail at the origin and evolution of archaeological ideas and that attempt to place current archaeology in a historic context. It has been suggested that such "critical historiography" is evidence of disciplinary maturity and is necessary for development (McVicar 1984:4–5; see also Fahnestock 1984). As several authors of this volume indicate, historical studies of archaeology can have a major influence upon research (cp. Kuhn 1968:120). Meltzer (chapter 1) argues that many deeply held beliefs about the archaeological record and about the past are based upon shaky historical foundations and that a careful examination of how such ideas were passed from generation to generation may help archaeologists be more critical of such accepted interpretations. By considering the early failure of archaeologists to use the fluorine test on the Piltdown frauds, Meltzer also questions the idea that the history of archaeology should have as its major goal the retrieval of lost ideas and techniques from the past for solving current problems.

The need to have intellectual ancestors and to found current ideas in the past is an urge that drives disciplinary history (cf. Graham et al. 1983). Such "ascription of paternity" attempts to legitimize ideas by rooting them in an intellectual tradition (Merton 1979:9). Chippindale (chapter 2) argues that such quests are often doomed to failure because they attempt to find specific modern ideas in past work that was done in a different context. He recounts his search for a "social archaeology" in mid-nineteenth-century Great Britain. Although he found no such early ancestry for the idea, he did discover that looking at the past with a specific modern starting point places one in a position to see intellectual patterns that would not have been apparent otherwise.

A good example of history done for present archaeological purposes is provided by Willey and Sabloff's *History of American Archaeology* (1974, 1980). Presented in an evolutionary format, the volume illustrates the origin of archaeological concepts and methods used today and explicitly aims to influence the direction of the field (1980:xiii). It is one of the few histories of archaeology to undergo revision, and the junior author discusses some of the intellectual factors in his own career that influenced the changes in the second edition (chapter 3). Sabloff emphasizes that history can be used to evaluate the validity and likely success of new ideas in the field by examining the relative success of similar ideas in the past.

Perhaps the most significant use of the history of archaeology is in historical research on past archaeological work to solve current research questions on the same sites or in the same region. This approach falls generally into the category of collections or archival research intended to make past data suitable for modern research questions. Such historical research has become an increasingly important part of archaeology as fieldwork becomes more expensive and politically difficult and as the vast research potential of museum collections is recognized (see Cantwell et al. 1981). Reyman (chapter 4) provides an example of how historical research on previous archaeological work in Chaco Canyon, New Mexico, helped identify remains that were unexplained or unnoticed. Reyman also illustrates how the failure to study and to understand previous archaeological work in an area can lead to erroneous interpretations of the archaeological record. Later in the volume, Jeter (chapter 15) provides additional examples of such research.

A small but growing audience for the history of archaeology exists outside the discipline, and scholarly studies of archaeology's past have even hit the mass paperback market (e.g., Fagan 1975, 1977; Silverberg 1974). Because it has a broad interdisciplinary perspective, archaeology can provide not only entertainment but also examples of method, data, and worldview in science that are useful for teaching students to think critically. Bender (chapter 5) discusses how events in the history of archaeology can be used to illustrate the interplay between evidence and interpretation in a social context.

Scholarly disciplines other than archaeology are also interested in the history of archaeology. There are several nonarchaeologist historians working on the topic (e.g., Brunhouse 1971, 1975, 1976; Hinsley 1981; Mark 1980), one of whom is represented in this volume (Hinsley, chapter 7).

Embree (chapter 6) comes from philosophy, a discipline that one might not expect to be too interested in the history of archaeology (as opposed to its epistomological structure [e.g., Salmon 1982]). As a phenomenologist, however, Embree is interested in how archaeology, "the most basic science of all" (1987a), is actually conducted. He discusses a variety of ethnographic, sociological, and historical methods that he has used in a study of an intellectual tradition that blossomed in the 1960s as "new archaeology," but that has expanded almost into a subdiscipline, which he calls "theoretical archaeology."

1

A Question of Relevance

David J. Meltzer

> Advocates of the history of science have occasionally described their
> field as a rich repository of forgotten ideas and methods, a few of
> which might well dissolve contemporary scientific dilemmas.
> —Thomas S. Kuhn, *The Essential Tension: Selected*
> *Studies in Scientific Tradition and Change*

A Parable

In introducing a volume of essays on the history of archaeology, Glyn
Daniel asked, "Why should we bother to do this? Is it merely an amusing
and sentimental exercise in past history, like collecting pictures of Copen-
hagen and French megaliths in 1800?" Not at all, he answered, for in his
mind "the history of archaeology needs studying not only as an interesting
and exciting story in itself . . . but because without an historical perspective
we can at the present day forget, at our peril, or even repeat, past errors"
(1981a:10). Daniel cited the controversy and the subsequent resolution of
the Piltdown forgery in support of his argument.

You will recall the story. In 1912, Charles Dawson, a lawyer and
amateur archaeologist from Sussex, brought several cranial fragments to Arthur Smith Woodward, keeper of geology at the British Museum. The bones,
including a skull and mandible, appeared deeply stained and derived from
a geological context that was apparently late Pliocene to early Pleistocene
in age (Dawson and Woodward 1913). It was a puzzling association of
skeletal elements, for the skull was nearly that of a modern human, while
the jaw was very apish, thus apparently quite primitive.

Piltdown was greeted enthusiastically by English paleontologists and
physical anthropologists. After decades of being mired in the backwater of
prehistory, with early stone tools but never fossil human remains to rival the
discoveries on the European continent, English paleoanthropology suddenly
found itself in sole possession of a fossil form that not only might predate
Neanderthals but also looked decidedly more human (Gould 1979). Piltdown seemed to confirm the pre-sapiens theory of Marcellin Boule and a
host of other scientific luminaries (including G. Elliot Smith, Arthur Smith

Woodward, and Arthur Keith) that the sapiens lineage could be traced independently of Neanderthals to an earlier period (Spencer and Smith 1981:436). Even better, *The Earliest Englishman,* to borrow the title bestowed by Woodward (1948), corroborated what many anatomists had long suspected: "in the evolution of man the development of the brain must have led the way" (Smith 1913:131).

There were, however, those who argued that Piltdown was anatomically impossible. The American physical anthropologist Aleš Hrdlička, for one, doubted its great age and was skeptical about an essentially modern human skull with an apelike jaw. They did not fit literally: the articular surfaces on the ascending ramus of the mandible were missing, making it impossible to check the join of mandible to skull. They did not fit theoretically: the fossils were completely at variance with Hrdlička's understanding of biomechanics and the evolution of human craniofacial morphology (Spencer and Smith 1981:442). Hrdlička, unlike most of his contemporaries, placed Neanderthals in the mainstream of human evolution (1927; Spencer and Smith 1981:443); Piltdown was phylogenetically unacceptable.

Hrdlička submitted a set of casts of the Piltdown fossils to Gerrit Miller, a Smithsonian Institution mammalogist, with the suggestion that Miller compare them with the jaws of *Pongidae* in the collections of the United States National Museum. From his examination Miller concluded that "a single individual cannot be supposed to have carried this jaw and skull" (1915:2). It was more logical to attribute the skull and mandible to two separate species, human and ape, and then determine how the elements from these two separate species became associated (see also Waterston 1913). At the time neither Miller nor anyone else suggested the bones were a plant (Hooton 1954:288). In a comment that now takes on unintended irony, Miller observed that "deliberate malice could hardly have been more successful than the hazards of deposition in so breaking the fossils as to give free scope to individual judgement in fitting the parts together" (1915:1).

The pre-sapiens theory and the plausibility of Piltdown remained intact until well after World War II (Spencer and Smith 1981:442), this despite no further discoveries of Piltdown material and an ever-growing list of fossil forms that included australopithecines and other early hominid forms. Then in 1949 Kenneth Oakley of the British Museum reexamined the Piltdown remains—this time working with the original fossils. Application of the fluorine test demonstrated that the Piltdown cranium and mandible were considerably younger than the Lower- and Middle-Pleistocene-age fauna said to have been found at the site (Oakley and Hoskins 1950). Further examination revealed that the jaw was from an ape and had been altered to give the appearance of great antiquity and human affinities. Radiocarbon dating showed that these fossils were no more than 600 years old (de Vries and Oakley 1959); DNA sequencing has now demonstrated that the jaw and teeth were from an orangutan (Lowenstein et al. 1982).

After Oakley published his results, he and others went on to document that the technique of fluorine dating had actually been discovered and applied to archaeological problems in the nineteenth century (Oakley 1953:51; Stewart 1951:391).

The most remarkable of those applications was by Thomas Wilson, a curator at the United States National Museum. In the early 1890s Wilson conducted separate examinations of various chemical constituents of the Calaveras, California, skull and of the Natchez, Mississippi, pelvis (1892, 1895) to determine whether these allegedly ancient human remains and the associated mammalian fossils were contemporaneous. Using the fluorine test Wilson demonstrated that the Natchez human pelvis had amounts of fluorine similar to those recorded in the bones of the extinct *Mylodon* (syn. *Glossotherium*) found in the same deposit. The result seemed to indicate that the human and the sloth were "substantially of the same antiquity" (1895:725), clear evidence for a Pleistocene human occupation in North America. Wilson was well impressed by the power of the fluorine test: "I consider this to be a valuable discovery, and one which may afford large opportunities for determining the antiquity of man in America, thereby aiding to settle some of those disputed questions about which the dogmatism of certain scientists has had such free rein" (Wilson to G. Goode, 21 June 1895, United States National Museum, Letters Received, Box 13, Folder 10, Smithsonian Institution Archives).

It was the rediscovery of this prior knowledge, not so much the Piltdown affair itself, that so troubled Glyn Daniel, for this meant that the fluorine technique could have been used on the Piltdown remains in 1912–1914, if only someone had remembered it (a similar argument is implied by Heizer and Cook [1954]). But they "had all forgotten about it" for they were "historically ignorant" (Daniel 1981a:12). Here, Daniel sees the true relevance of the history of archaeology:

> If there had been an adequate history of scientific techniques in physical anthropology available in the early years of this century we would not have had to go through the nonsense of Piltdown Man, which I regard as one of the most embarrassing and distressing incidents in British Archaeology. . . . This is why the study of the history of archaeology is so valuable: the past is what we make it and we made it hideously wrong at . . . Piltdown—and may do so again [Daniel 1981a:12].

But consider that, unknown to Daniel, after Hrdlička died, T. Dale Stewart found in his files a reprint of Thomas Wilson's 1895 paper on the fluorine test (Stewart, personal communication 1981). While Hrdlička had Wilson's paper, he had not, to my knowledge, cited it in any of his discussions about human antiquity in the Americas. His published remarks on the Natchez pelvis, moreover, fail to mention Wilson's analysis and conclusions (1907:16–19). Hrdlička avoided comment on the age of the Natchez fossil by remarking that any speculation on the matter would be "quite useless" (Hrdlička 1907:19). Hrdlička, as is well known, was unwilling to accept this or any other skeletal material that indicated a deep human antiquity in the Americas (Meltzer 1983a:25–34).

This is not to say, however, that Hrdlička was unaware of the potential role of chemical tests in determining fossil age and association. Indeed, he had used analogous tests (which included analysis of fluorine content) on fossil bones in his own work (e.g., 1907:56–57, 1912:296–297, 1918:61–63). Certainly at the time of Piltdown he knew such chemical tests existed. This being the case, it casts Daniel's argument in a whole new light.

Consider the implications of Hrdlička's knowledge of chemical tests, including the fluorine test, for the analysis of fossil bones. Daniel's argument implies that Hrdlička should have advocated such tests to resolve the Piltdown controversy. But he did not—despite a profound skepticism about the veracity of the Piltdown find. Why?

Hrdlička may have wanted to avoid jeopardizing his long-established and well-publicized stand on human antiquity in North America. A call on his part for the application of the fluorine test would have indicated that he believed the test had some validity, which might have been construed by critics as tacit admission that he agreed with Wilson's conclusion that humans were contemporaries of an extinct form of sloth found in North America in Pleistocene times. Hrdlička obviously could have countered that argument by agreeing that such tests worked well in theory, but then he could have attacked their specific application at Natchez (or Piltdown, if the results were not to his liking). But in any case, there was a safer alternative.

If Hrdlička quietly ignored the fluorine test, he could continue to argue on evolutionary and anatomical principles that the Piltdown material is an incongruous mix of ape jaw and human skull. He could continue to criticize the pre-sapiens theory as unacceptable and push for his views on the Neanderthal phase of human prehistory (1927:270). He could maintain his stance on human antiquity in the New World. This strategy would not so neatly solve the Piltdown controversy as would, and did, the application of the fluorine test, but he did not stand to lose anything in adopting it.

Yet, it might be that Hrdlička's unwillingness to advocate the fluorine test was not motivated by such deep, paradigmatic concerns, but simply by doubts about the reliability or the validity of such tests. In 1907 Hrdlička applied a variety of chemical analyses to alleged Pleistocene human skeletal material from western Florida. Those analyses left "no doubt that the bones in question are fossilized to a considerable degree, a condition which has been very generally regarded as an important indication of antiquity" (1907:57). The results, however, contradicted the "somatological examination," which had indicated no great antiquity (1907:60). The contradiction was resolved to Hrdlička's satisfaction by a trip to the site in February

1906, where he discovered that the local environment seemed to favor fossilization (1907 : 64).

Hrdlička had a similar experience five years later with Ameghino's *Homo pampaeus* from Argentina. Limited chemical analyses of bone mineralization, which were intended to gauge bone age, were inconclusive, showing that the process of fossilization "is far more a question of environment than of time" (Hrdlička 1912 : 297).

In these and in all other cases of alleged fossil or ancient human remains, Hrdlička depended far more on morphological evidence than on analytical tests, geological evidence, or context to determine the antiquity of human remains (Meltzer 1983a : 30–33). Chemical tests were peripheral to the discussion. He relegated the chemical analyses of the controversial Vero skeletal material, which included a measure of fluorine content, to a minor addendum in his report (Hrdlička 1918 : 61–63). If the chemical tests agreed with the morphological interpretation of skeletal age or context, they were cited as supplementary evidence; if the chemical tests disagreed, the results were noted, then dismissed. He viewed these tests as suggestive not as crucial.

The Lessons of the Parable

It is not my intent to account fully for whether Hrdlička's "failure" to advocate the fluorine test in the Piltdown controversy was motivated by a desire to protect a paradigm, or, more likely, by a lack of confidence in these tests. Instead, let me use the parable to convey a few lessons about the history of archaeology.

First, our disciplinary past is not a vast plundering ground where search and seizure missions will produce practical solutions to contemporary problems of archaeology and anthropology. Granted one can discover, after a new technique, concept, or theory is invented and used, a historical precedent. But, as Kuhn asks, would attention to history have accelerated that innovation? "Almost certainly . . . the answer is no. The quantity of material to be searched, the absence of appropriate indexing categories, and the subtle but usually vast differences between the anticipation and the effective innovation, all combine to suggest that reinvention rather than rediscovery will remain the most efficient source of scientific novelty" (1977 : 121). Second, the rediscovery of a technique, concept, or theory hardly guarantees its application—witness the Piltdown affair. Believing that rediscovery will lead to application assumes that a technique, concept, or theory is understood in similar ways by different people at different times. In this case, it assumes that those who knew of the fluorine test in 1912 had the same understanding of its power and potential for resolving the controversy as did those who actually applied the test in the 1950s. But clearly Hrdlička in 1912 perceived the value of the test differently than did Wilson in the 1890s, than Oakley did in 1950, or than Daniel did in 1981.

Believing that rediscovery will lead to application also assumes an ideal, if not slightly naive, view of scientific behavior. Yet, while history does not always live up to our expectations, Hrdlička's failure to behave as Daniel believed he should have behaved is ultimately far more instructive about the Piltdown episode than the object lesson of "false archaeology" (Daniel 1981a:10). Science is practiced by scientists; their actions are embedded in a cultural constellation of belief, motivation, learning, and thinking. Understanding how Hrdlička actually responded to Piltdown provides a more meaningful glimpse into the structure of scientific thinking than does the observation that he failed to respond as he should have responded.

Finally, for all the reasons just given, it is unlikely that the study of the history of archaeology can be justified by its immediate practical value to the contemporary science (Stocking 1968:2). It cannot always be counted on to "expose, if not answer, some vital issues about the name and nature of man himself" (Daniel 1981a:13).

Two questions arise. First, must the history of archaeology be relevant at all? Not necessarily. Archaeologists study the history of archaeology for the same reason they study archaeology: because it is there. Equally true, studying the history of archaeology is really nothing more than studying the anthropology of archaeology, and as such, it should require no further justification for a group who are, at least nominally, anthropologists (Gruber 1975:3). That being the case, I would then ask the second question: Why does Daniel, who did so much to make the study of the history of archaeology a viable endeavor and whose work in that field warrants no justification, feel compelled to raise the issue of the relevance of the history of archaeology within the narrow confines of its "necessity" as a problem-solving tool in contemporary archaeology? My guess, and it is nothing more than that, is that he was spurred on by the observation that, when it comes to its own past, archaeology is one of the more ahistorical of the historical disciplines. Its history is the incidental pursuit of a limited number of scholars primarily engaged in archaeological field and laboratory research. For the majority of archaeologists, the history of archaeology is what one does in those brief sections of dissertations, reports, or monographs labeled, as Flannery put it, "Previous (Bad) Work in the Region" (1973:373). Thinking thus, Daniel's effort to identify areas where the history of archaeology had apparent practical utility can be seen as a sincere, though flawed, strategy for attracting converts to the field.

A Narrow View of Relevance

If asking whether the history of archaeology must be relevant is irrelevant and if pursuing relevance in immediate problem-solving terms is fruitless, it would seem there is little left to say on the subject. There I would leave the matter of relevance, were it not for one thing: I cannot shake the feeling that studying the history of archaeology might be surprisingly relevant to contemporary archaeology.

I have long been puzzled by the fact that so few archaeologists are curious about the history of their field. My mystification is not because I am so naive as to believe that everyone would be as fascinated by history for history's sake as I, but because this indifference to history is in stark contrast to the interest in history intrinsic to so many other fields. For example, in paleontology and evolutionary biology, historical sciences that are structurally similar to archaeology (Mayr 1976:14), the history of science, the study of Darwin alone, is a major, multinational industry involving practicing scientists and researchers (see, for example, Kohn 1985). That the works of Darwin and those of his contemporaries do actively figure in the dialogue of modern evolutionary biology prompts the question, What do biologists and paleontologists see in the history of their sciences that we are missing by neglecting our own?

The answer is twofold. First, they recognize that the study of a field's history is the best way of acquiring an understanding of its concepts (Mayr 1982:20). As Ghiselin put it: "To learn the facts, one reads the latest journals. To understand biology, one reads Darwin" (1969:232). The history of biology in this regard is not only meaningful, it is useful. Obviously archaeology differs insofar as it lacks an extant body of theory like evolution by natural selection that, though derived over 100 years ago, is still viable today.

Second, and in more general terms, they recognize that the reasons we do what we do are embedded in what and how we think, which is in large part a function of what and how those before us have thought (Mayr 1982:6; see also Gruber 1975:6). Science, like politics, economics, and the arts, has a history. But more so than the history of those endeavors, the history of science (and archaeology) is deterministic and progressive. What we know today builds upon, is constrained by, or is in reaction to past knowledge. There is a paradox here. The epistemic continuity between the present and the past goes a long way toward explaining why "the essential questions of a discipline are usually specified by the first competent thinkers to enter it," why most of what follows is just "so many variations on a set of themes" (Gould 1977a:1; see also Mayr 1982:6), and why attention to history provides a deeper understanding of the contemporary science. But the very essence of science insures that scientific works cannot be "timeless" classics, in the sense of a work by Plato, Shakespeare, or Twain (Knight 1987:5–6). Sooner or later, all science is superseded.

Put into an archaeological context, ideas of the past change with some regularity, but change cannot be attributed simply to increases in knowledge about the past, although to a certain extent this is true. Nor can this be attributed to the past itself changing. It does not. Instead, what changes is our perception of the past, a perception rooted in ideas about the external world, perception that is the historical and cultural frame of reference the practitioners bring to experience (Binford 1981:23, 1986:460; Gruber 1975:6−7).

It follows from this argument that archaeologists do not study the past, they create models of it (Binford 1986:473; see also Leone 1986:419). This does not imply that, as is fashionable in some circles today, archaeology is somehow arbitrary or that it must dissolve into a Boasian nightmare of "pointless relativism" (Leone 1986:419) in which everyone is encouraged to develop his or her own past (Hodder 1984:31). Instead, it suggests that archaeology must involve constant critical self-reflection to understand the cultural basis of scientific knowledge of its created past. Such does not "deny our ability to learn [or] modify the limiting effects that our culture places on our understanding of external reality" (Binford 1986:471); it only means we gain a better understanding and appreciation of what we think and why we think it.

Here is where the history of archaeology becomes important, for it helps reveal why the past looks the way it does and shows the context in which ideas have developed and are embedded (Binford and Sabloff 1982). The best way to understand why we do what we do is to unfold the beliefs that have structured, and continue to structure, our work. It is extremely difficult to extract such beliefs from contemporary work, owing to the "immediacy" problem (see chapter 14). It is much easier to do so to past work, because the luxury of the distance between ourselves and the subject makes the context more readily available and much more accessible (Meltzer 1983b:68). It is, of course, precisely that work that has determined how we approach issues today. The history of archaeology reveals theoretical and intellectual (internal), as well as social, political, and economic (external) contexts of views of the past. These views contribute to the current "state of the art" and condition the character of many problems facing archaeologists (Binford 1981:4). Two examples follow; first, of the manner in which interpretive frames are embedded in historical precedent and, then, of the manner in which collection techniques are likewise embedded in beliefs about the nature of the record or questions concerning that record.

The confirmation, in 1927 at Folsom, New Mexico, that human groups and an extinct species of bison were contemporaneous (Figgins 1927) resolved the long-standing controversy over human antiquity in North America (Meltzer 1983a). Here at last was unequivocal proof that ancient North Americans had first arrived during the Pleistocene.

In the decade following Folsom a battery of older, Clovis-age sites with associated megafauna were discovered on the western High Plains and in the Southwest. As detailed earlier (Meltzer 1988:2−3), virtually all of these archaeological sites were initially paleontological, not archaeological, discoveries. Large bones (generally of mammoth or bison) were found first. Only after the more detailed attention to the deposits that followed were fluted points found. Clovis Paleo-Indian sites without large mammal bones were then, as they are now, extremely rare.

The repeated association of fluted points with the bones of extinct megafauna and the scarcity of nonkill sites led quite naturally to the inference that the "first migrants were unquestionably hunters" (Roberts 1940:104). A continentwide distribution of Clovis fluted points was soon documented, and this led in turn to the inference that these groups were highly mobile, specialized hunters.

Fifty years later the claim is still made that across the continent, Clovis Paleo-Indians relied on specialized big-game hunting for their subsistence strategy (Haynes 1982:390–393; Stoltman and Baerreis 1983:254); gathering of plant foods and exploitation of small mammals is thought to have played an inconsequential role in their diet. Given the tremendous amount of archaeological research over that intervening period, one would expect that this conclusion is now fortified by an abundant record of fluted point kill sites. It is not. In eastern North America, for example, there is an abundant record of fluted point localities, but extremely few even equivocal instances of "kill" sites (Meltzer 1988:22–24). This is not for want of opportunities: many hundreds of terminal Pleistocene sites with extinct megafauna remains have been found, but only a very few show any sign of human association, much less a kill (Meltzer 1986, 1988).

The lack of empirical support for specialized hunting is wholly understandable in theory, given the limited conditions under which subsistence specialization occurs (Meltzer and Smith 1986). Yet the notion of pancontinental specialized "big-game" hunting, though lacking empirical and theoretical support, is still very much alive. It is still asserted, for example, that "a big-game hunting life-style analogous to that of Plains fluted-point makers was characteristic of the East at the same time" (Stoltman 1978:712).

The tenacity of the big-game hunting image results from historical inertia. An idea, once set in motion, stays its course and is only dislodged with the great force of accumulated anomalies (Bailey 1968). Historical inertia is a very powerful thing in science; it is one of the properties Kuhn ascribed to a paradigm (1962), though the property may have been lost in the wide latitude allowed that word. Inertia creates archaeological "myths," incorrect pictures of the past with unquestioned veracity that guide interpretation (Binford 1981:4). Archaeologists are often "unaware of how their traditionally held paradigms [these myths] influence their views of the past" (Binford and Sabloff 1982:139).

Awareness can be heightened by increased attention to the historical origins and context in which those myths developed. Kidder (1936) is an early and masterful example of this: he explained how important were changing myths of chronology and the ramifications of Folsom on apparently unrelated issues such as the origin of the New World civilizations. More recent illustrations of this heightened awareness through attention to historical context and myth include Binford and Sabloff (1982; Sabloff et al. 1987) and Grayson (1986).

From a practical standpoint, such myths or interpretive frames also condition the character of research, techniques of data collection, and interpretive principles. Archaeologists are aware that observation is a theory-laden process. From this it follows that the recognition of archaeological facts is influenced by current theoretical and conceptual contexts.

Let me return to the 1927 Folsom discovery. With the demonstration of an Ice Age human occupation in North America, American archaeologists suddenly found themselves faced with a massive "void" in their prehistory (Kidder 1936:114) between the late Pleistocene and the late Prehistoric (the chronological details of the latter having been worked out using the direct historical approach). To fill that void and to detail the chronological skeleton on which North American prehistory would be built, archaeologists turned their attention to fundamental issues of chronology. Culture history, which dominated the field from the 1930s to the 1960s to a degree difficult to appreciate today and which seemed so pedestrian and arbitrary to the New Archaeologists of the 1960s, was a quite legitimate response to the gap wrought by Folsom.

Culture history was not a monolithic enterprise, but one can legitimately characterize the venture as a series of fugues whose central theme was time. Its principal concern was the identification of the major culture types in a region and the placement of those types in their correct chronological positions—"behavioral inferences and other niceties were not forbidden, but they were decidedly a second order of business" (Spaulding 1985:301), much to the consternation of those with more anthropological interests (e.g., Bennett 1943; Kluckhohn 1940; Steward and Setzler 1938; Taylor 1948). Explanation was to be addressed after the data were in, following the construction of time-space frameworks (Kluckhohn 1940; Spaulding 1985:301; Steward 1949).

Archaeological ignorance, in this context, was the result of sites that had not been dug or places and times uninvestigated (Binford 1986:459). Certain criteria, ease of access, site size, presence of unusual features (such as mounds), presence of stratified deposits (to provide a chronology), or presence of material from a particular time period, were the essential determinants of field research (Binford 1964:427).

Underlying the cultural-historical approach was an assumption that archaeological data are not continuously variable but occur in natural, homogenous packages, which was the basis of the later charge that culture historians employed a "normative" view of culture. Such an assumption helps explain why sampling played a minor role in culture history: if spatial units were homogenous, sampling was unnecessary.

Excavation and not surface data constituted the main source of data. Surface remains were useful only insofar as they helped identify potential localities for excavation; their mixture of components of various ages made them less useful for detailed chronological purposes. Excavation was oriented toward the vertical rather than toward the horizontal since the acquisition of stratigraphic information meant observable time. Intrasite variability was largely ignored. Interunit and intersite variability was important because it informed on the essential sequence within the site and the temporal relatedness of different sites.

The preoccupation with time was manifest analytically in a narrow perception of what constituted a meaningful artifact type or assemblage. Archaeological systematics and the development of local and regional chronologies were based on highly prepared, dominantly stylistic artifacts (Dunnell 1986a:173). Little-modified objects, such as plain body sherds, amorphous tools, unutilized flakes, and fire-cracked rock, were rarely collected or if collected were not always reported or saved. This was true of contemporary French Paleolithic archaeology as well, which prompted Sackett to suggest that "one of the sadder if more informative exercises in the history of archaeology would be to excavate the spoil heaps of our predecessors in order to discover the amount and kind of artifactual material so many of them discarded" (1981:91).

The criteria by which one determined whether a type was meaningful was whether it had historical significance. For those, like Krieger (1944:272) and Ford (1954:391), the "only useful types were those that allowed assemblages to be described in terms that permitted chronological ordering" (Dunnell 1986a:172). Diagnostic types were used, not unlike paleontological type fossils, to identify space-time units. Similarities and differences between assemblages were measured using diagnostic trait lists, which, in turn, allowed the development of higher level classes such as phases and periods (Willey and Phillips 1958).

These higher level units were defined by one or a few diagnostic features (Paleo-Indian equalled primarily fluted points, but secondarily big game). They represented a series of discrete, internally homogeneous, qualitative entities, not unlike the synchronic units dealt with by social anthropologists. This was a "specific kind of history—a history of material culture—developed which at best described the succession of the preserved archaeological assemblages in each culture province" (Griffin 1974:xiii).

The result of this preoccupation with time was "to restrain, and even to a considerable extent, predetermine, what a prehistorian would see" (Sackett 1981:91). These traditional approaches were not bad or wrong in some absolute sense, clearly they were not anymore so than is true today, but the field methods were strictly tied to the prevailing theoretical program or paradigm.

The embeddedness of collection techniques in beliefs concerning the nature of the record, or questions concerning that record, are revealed through careful historical studies that focused on the sometimes-hidden assumptions, on basic definitions of what constituted an artifact or a feature, and on what kinds of information were recorded.

This understanding has immediate practical application to research in archaeology, as we come to lean more heavily on data and museum collections recovered in previous years. Studying the historical context of data collection can illuminate the conditions or biases under which data were collected and the constraints on that data set for contemporary analysis. Do these collections constitute a meaningful sample? What are they missing? How much? Do they provide a basis for making valid statements about a particular site, region, or period of occupation? Unfortunately, one can derive an "endless list of ways in which systematic [and other] biases can be introduced into collections" (Kintigh 1981:472). It may never be possible to correct for these kinds of biases, but it is possible to understand them.

Understanding why the past looks the way it does is but the first step in using the insight gained from the history of archaeology for the larger purpose of developing an archaeological theory (Binford and Sabloff 1982:150; Sackett 1981:89). The development of any scientific theory is a process of confronting inadequacies in received wisdom and inventing new theories to understand the world of experience; the confrontational experience involves past theories and the products of one's predecessors. Binford articulates this position well when he argues:

> A productive researcher needs a wellfounded set of ideas regarding the state of the art both past and present to understand why past workers chose to invest their time as they did. He or she needs to make judgements as to what is in fact worth seeking through research effort at the present time. If we gain such a perspective on how the state of the art changes, then the past deeds that we criticize need not be seen so much as misdeed relative to our contemporary frame of reference but as important contributions necessary to the genesis of the point of view from which our criticism derives [1981:4].

Knowledge changes, but many of the problems and controversies of the past are still viable. Historical study enables us to look to the past and to see that some things are correct, just as others are clearly wrong. By examining how earlier concepts were worked out, by learning the earlier wrong assumptions that had to be refuted one by one, and by learning from past mistakes, one can contribute materially to a conceptual clarification that makes solutions possible (Mayr 1982:17). Understanding history is the first step for those who wish to transcend it (Sackett 1981:89).

A Methodological Caveat

I have addressed the issue of relevance in very narrow terms—the history of archaeology is relevant if contemporary archaeologists can extract something of value from it. Such a narrow approach raises some critical methodological questions, for the past in the service of the present may be seen to entail a limited, internal approach that treads perilously close to presentism. Yet, to a certain extent, internal, presentist approaches are justified. Science, or at least mature science, differs from politics, economics, art, or literature insofar as it is largely insulated from its social environment (Kuhn 1977:118–119, 148). In biology, for example, Mayr argues that "it appears that the influence of social factors on the development of specific biological advances has been negligible" (1982:6). Although such would seem to be less true of the sciences dealing with human beings, since more people have an active stake in the product, the point is well taken. External factors are less important, except perhaps when a new scientific discipline is emerging (e.g., Rudwick 1985) or when a new technology (e.g., computers) or a significant change in attitude toward science occurs (Kuhn 1977:118–120).

Much of the history of science, as a result, tends to emphasize concepts and theories internal to the science, conceiving of it as largely self-contained and independent of its environment (Hinsley 1986:230). Such internal history is predominantly concerned with the development of scientific ideas by practitioners; understanding how participants made sense of their science; determining the catalysts for change as they occurred within the field; and understanding how those changes were integrated into the discipline (Kuhn 1979:122). This, of course, contrasts with external history, which concentrates on the interface between the sciences as a whole and the society in which they were practiced as well as on the social, economic, industrial, or governmental forces that promoted or inhibited the growth of particular sorts of scientific enterprise in particular countries at particular times (Kuhn 1979:123).

The dichotomy between internal and external history, while primarily methodological, frequently divides along disciplinary lines. Internal accounts are generally written by practicing or trained scientists; external accounts by historians or sociologists (Knight 1987:7; Kuhn 1977:152). The reason is obvious enough: the practicing scientists' interests and training are in the concepts and theories relevant to modern science. The historian, generally untrained in modern science, is less inclined to examine theory and more inclined to examine the social, political, and historical contexts of the field. Historians are not archaeologists: they have different motivations, arenas of study, intellectual tools, and goals (Hinsley 1986:230). Even though they appreciate that "one of the most important goals of investigation is to contribute to our understanding of the historical contexts and processes out of which present-day anthropology has emerged" (Stocking 1968:108), they sometimes fail to see the nuances and traps of the discipline that may limit the quality of their analysis.

Archaeologists are better qualified to write the history of the problems and concepts of archaeology than historians, but by the same argument, historians are far better equipped to write the biographical or the social history of archaeology. Given a history of archaeology that is being written for the sake of the present, the appropriate direction and practitioner are clear.

But in taking this internal approach, by asking what the study of the history of archaeology can do for archaeology today, such studies can slip into "Whiggish history" (Butterfield 1931), thinly disguised attempts to "legitimize a present point of view," leading to anachronism, distortion, misinterpretation, oversimplification, misleading analogy, and neglect of context (Stocking 1968:8; see also Kuhn 1977:107; Mayr 1982:12). Some "whiggishness" can be effective in moderation (Hull 1979; Stocking 1968:9), again because the history of science is not like the history of other aspects of the human endeavor. Science has that epistemic thread, spun from its empirical core, that runs from present to past. Truth in scientific matters is not altogether relative. We can measure knowledge; we know more than we used to. In science, we are addressing many of the same fundamental issues and ideas that scientists addressed one hundred years ago and using the same scale, the empirical realm. We are also using the same tools. We can identify the ideas that worked, and the ones that did not, and get a sense of why they may or may not have worked.

By critically evaluating the past—how others understood problems, attempted solutions, and got those solutions wrong—we gain a deeper understanding not only of previous modes of thought but also of our own. For errors in science, or at least nontrivial ones, reveal much of the context of the science in which they were embedded. We learn and understand science by acknowledging and exploring mistakes (Mayr 1982:20). For this reason, perhaps, histories should even be polemical. "Such histories will arouse contradiction and they will challenge the reader to come up with a refutation. By a dialectial process this will speed up a synthesis of perspective. The unambiguous adoption of a definitive viewpoint should not be confounded with subjectivity" (Mayr 1982:9).

Conclusions

Hinsley has remarked that the history of anthropology should not be left to anthropologists (1981:10), nor the history of archaeology to archaeologists (1986:217). I agree, but not just because of his conviction, exemplified rather than argued, that a nonanthropologist or a nonarchaeologist can bring important insight to such studies. Rather, I agree with Hinsley because were the history of archaeology left to archaeologists, it would scarcely be written. And what would be written would likely have little conceptual relevance to contemporary archaeology.

That the history of archaeology by historians would have little relevance to contemporary archaeology is not itself troubling. What is troubling is the vision of the history of archaeology becoming only the province of historians, leaving archaeologists without the full understanding of the field that comes with an appreciation of history.

This concern is what has prompted me to define relevance as I did. To the degree that we lack an active knowledge of the history of the field, we limit our efforts to transcend that history. Much of what we do as archaeologists we do because of what we inherited. The nature of the inheritance is sometimes quite subtle; other times not. The history of archaeology unveils that inheritance, which is why we as archaeologists *need* to study the history of archaeology.

Let me close the circle, however, by arguing that a history of archaeology written only by archaeologists would be very narrow indeed. Granted one can justify an internal, presentist approach, at least when the desired end is a better understanding of contemporary archaeology. But that approach fails to recognize that science is not comprehensible on purely internal grounds. Interpretations are subtly influenced by social and personal preconceptions of reality (as remarkably well illustrated in Rudwick 1985), which is disregarded when one concentrates only on the internal element. Although such influences may be weaker in the traditional "hard" sciences, in the truly difficult sciences, like archaeology, the "interpretation of human affairs is itself a socially conditioned phenomenon" (Trigger 1984 : 292)—a point elegantly documented by Trigger, who has shown how American archaeology has been shaped, though not completely determined, by middle-class Euroamerican values (1980, 1986).

Thus, the dichotomy between internal and external history, so far as it is valid (see chapter 7), presents a dilemma: just as the historian might miss the subtleties of scientific debate, so might the scientist fail to grasp the full historical context. Internal and external approaches are not so much mutually exclusive as they are complementary concerns (Kuhn 1977 : 120, 1979 : 123). Together they can expose historical myth and reveal why the past looks the way it does.

My ending plea, then, is this: let's not leave the history of archaeology to historians or even to archaeologists. Let the historians write the history of the field from their larger, more dispassionate, less proprietary perspective. Let the archaeologists write the history of the problems and of the concepts of archaeology but be at liberty to use the history for the primary business at hand, understanding archaeology and the past. After all, archaeologists have a higher stake in the outcome.

Acknowledgments

I would like to thank Andrew L. Christenson for soliciting the paper that led to this chapter and for sharing his thoughts on the relevance of the history of archaeology. Donald K. Grayson, Bruce G. Trigger, David J. Weber, and David R. Wilcox have my special thanks for much-appreciated critical comments on a draft of the paper presented at the conference.

2

"Social Archaeology" in the Nineteenth Century: Is It Right to Look for Modern Ideas in Old Places?

Christopher Chippindale

A study that is to be published elsewhere (Chippindale 1987) is the starting point of this chapter. Only a summary is given here. The original study looks at intellectual issues from a well-documented period and uses public sources, largely the major books of the new prehistory during its founding decades and especially the years between 1865 and 1870. I have not depended on unpublished sources or letters, believing that the studies as printed in their various editions are more likely to represent the considered opinions of their authors than are correspondence or ephemeral statements. Furthermore, those published texts—considered or not—were primary influences on other workers in the field. The present chapter concerns itself with a basic question of method in writing the history of archaeology that arose while I was working on the substantive issue. Rather to my surprise, I have not found any explicit answers to the question in the literature, which may be because the Daniels and Willeys of the business, wiser and older than I, know better than to mess with it.

Intellectual History as the Story of Who Was Right

History, in a famous phrase, is the story as written by the winners, and this is at least as true of intellectual history as of any other. It is not a democratic business in which orthodox contemporary opinion is the mainstream story. The people who matter are those who were right, the persecuted Galileos and the unnoticed Mendels, as well as the Newtons and Darwins whose stature was recognized in their own time.

For many stories in the history of archaeology, it is clear enough who was right in the end. The invention of the idea of prehistory (Daniel and

Renfrew 1987) is a case in point. The standard books are right to notice a few words that the authors quote without much regard for their exact intellectual context, for example, John Aubrey's writing in about 1685 of British stone rings, "These Antiquities are so exceeding old that no Bookes doe reach them" (Aubrey 1685, noticed in Chippindale 1983:68), or John Frere's referring Suffolk handaxes in 1797 "to a very remote period indeed, even beyond that of the present world" (Frere 1800, noticed in Daniel 1981c:38—40). Aubrey and Frere lived in intellectual worlds entirely different from ours, but because they grasped fundamentals we now know to be enduring and essential to the growth of the discipline, it is reasonable to concentrate on that lasting insight. This is why John Lubbock's *Pre-historic Times* (1865) is important and why Samuel Lysons' *Our British Ancestors: Who and What Were They?* (1865), an equally substantial book, is left to rot on the library shelves.

There is still much work to be done in these well-tilled fields. The basic facts about the invention of words for prehistory are not clear (Chippindale 1988). Likewise, a Chinese hypothesis of a three-age system (Olsen 1987), plainly set out centuries before the proposal of Lucretius that marks the start of Western ideas on the subject, is another reminder that the point is less that C. J. Thomsen proposed a three-age system for organizing the objects of ancient Denmark during the 1820s and 1830s and more that this formulation, among many sketches and proposals over many centuries, made an intellectual foundation for a new academic discipline (see chapter 7).

Balance in Judging Who Was Right in the Past: Looking Too Hard for Past Allies

A handful of archaeologists are trying to work with formal geometrical analyses of artifacts, using the generative formalisms of shape and design grammars. We have accomplished a couple of conference symposia, a paper or two (Chippindale 1986; Hassan 1988), and a book proposal (Boast et al. 1987). The chances are that our brave new vision of archaeological grammars will have no great influence—the fate of 95% or more of these things. Meanwhile, we maintain our morale by remembering what John Aubrey said of our kind of archaeology exactly three centuries ago: "there is no way to retrieve them [the ancient monuments] but by comparative antiquitie, which I have writt upon the spott, from the Monuments themselves . . . By comparative Arguments to work-out and restore after a kind of Algebraical method, by comparing them that I have seen, one with another, and reducing them to a kind of Aequation" (1685). Here is a splendid motto and blessing for our group, words that come directly from the founding father of British field archaeology, commending our faith in algebra, equations, and mathematics.

We are, of course, doing what most groups do while trying to establish themselves intellectually. By appealing to the ancestors, we demonstrate that our approach represents an authentic spirit that informed the past masters; at the same time we can present it as a new idea, fresh and aggressively up-to-date, by noting its links with rule-based systems, artificial intelligence, and other fashionable ideas.

This approach is a dangerous business because a trawl through the tonnage of old literature will, in the end, produce some idea or statement or quotation that, treated out of context, can be presented as a precursor of one's own partisan line. The balance has to be struck between finding a partisan justification for one's own view and a proper notice of the real intellectual context of previous work. I do not think our design grammars are exactly what John Aubrey had in mind. But the heart of this business is in the right place, I think, because it is the intellectual equivalent of re-examining the old collections in the light of fresh methods of analysis. By looking at the past experience of methods and ideas that are of a class with one's own—even though they were not at the time perceived that way— valuable guidance may be gathered about the strengths and weaknesses of the "new" approach.

Balance in Judging Who Was Right in the Past: Looking Too Hard for Past Errors

Searching for sympathetic ancestors is a dangerous business requiring a good sense of balance. So is the opposite tack—of searching too hard for past error—and here I believe there is real cause for concern in how we choose to view the work of not so long ago. A knowing superiority from hindsight is the easiest and most pernicious attitude to fall into.

A case in point is V. Gordon Childe's diffusionist framework for European prehistory, as worked out, for example, in *The Dawn of European Civilisation* (1925) and in his lifework within the same intellectual framework of a barbarian Europe being slowly educated by influence from the higher cultures of the "Most Ancient East." In due time, the calibrated radiocarbon chronology showed that the expectation on which Childe worked was wrong. The megalithic monuments of Malta and northwestern Europe are older than their supposed Eastern parents: "The whole diffusionist framework collapses, and with it the assumptions which sustained prehistoric archaeology for nearly a century" (Renfrew 1973:85). It has become customary now to deprecate Childe's diffusion, and an equally doctrinaire principle, autonomous explanations in European prehistory, has seemed near. But Childe knew, and plainly stated (1939:10), that his explanatory framework was based on axioms that were given rather than supported by empirical evidence.

The point is not that Childe was wrong, which he clearly was. Rather, it is that in the complete absence of any other secure basis for chronology in Europe, reaching to the eastern Mediterranean was a sensible strategy. When Childe related gray ceramics from Vinča, the tell in the Danube basin of what is now central Yugoslavia, to gray ceramics from Troy, on the Asiatic shores of the Bosporus, he was connecting the only stratigraphic sequences available to him. The entire intervening area of the Balkans was, in these matters, a blank on the map. The pattern of diffusion from a civilized eastern Mediterranean to a barbarian north seemed clear in early history and the protohistoric period and was most obviously exemplified by the transfer of domestic animals and plants. It was a most reasonable expectation for the general pattern of European prehistory, and, as Renfrew (1973:36–37) recognizes, it is hard to see what else could have been and should have been done when only the Near East offered a historical chronology. Diffusionist explanations may have been in error, but they may also have been necessary, an inescapable stage in the progress of the discipline that enabled it to advance from the 1920s to the 1950s and 1960s when independent chronologies at last liberated European prehistory from dependence on an axiom that had been untested because it had been untestable. Although we casually say that Childe was quite wrong, in the ersatz summary that students are fed, no advice has yet been offered for what else Childe could have done.

Two specific points are worth noticing. First, Childe was perhaps the first person to realize that his own diffusionist framework was crumbling under the impact of radiocarbon dating, and his well-based fear that his lifework had been based on error seems to have been a factor in his suicide in 1958 (Green 1983). These events were nearly ten years before the classic articles that pulled down the old order (e.g., Renfrew 1967, 1968). Second, Renfrew's demolition of the diffusionist framework (1973) was accompanied by a manifesto of processual archaeology and autonomous explanation as the necessary intellectual alternative. But other responses were possible. French prehistorians, such as P.-R. Giot (1971), were equally quick to understand the consequences of the new chronology but had no regard for the new American archaeology, to which current French thinking in these matters owes virtually nothing (e.g., Joussaume 1985).

Most researchers, even the great theorists, are unoriginal, work in received paradigms, and creep but slowly forward. Masterpieces are often not, when examined carefully, so very different from the forgotten, routine literature of their time, which is why Darwin's theory of evolution had so many precursors and, in archaeology, why the new prehistory of the 1860s depended on so much that had been in place for decades (Chippindale

1987). It is only afterwards that any fool can see that the great men were wrong.

Who Is Right at the Moment?

Umberto Eco, one of the sharper thinkers in the very sharp discipline of semiotics, is prepared to work indifferently with many high and low arts. Monumental architecture, fashion, graffitti, punk lifestyles, pulp romantic fiction, soap operas, soft pornography are all equal objects for study. An intellectual rationale for his indifference is our inability to forecast which of these aspects of our culture will seem, two and three centuries hence, important, enduring, in some sense "right."

The antiquity of mankind has been established for more than a century. It seems simple to see who was right in the debates of over a century ago, but when it comes to more recent and more contentious issues, it is not yet clear who is right. A recent review article (Earle and Preucel 1987) identifies the major theoretical debate in archaeology as between "processual archaeology" and its "radical critique." Perhaps it is—in the United States—but only in the particular intellectual position of American archaeology. Perhaps the real theoretical advance is actually somewhere else, in the application of artificial-intelligence techniques within the French tradition of artifact classification (Gardin et al. 1987). Perhaps self-conscious theory in all its variants is a passing fashion, and the major long-term trends are of a different character. Perhaps what matters is neither fashions of theory nor styles of practice in what archaeologists *think* they are doing but, as an economic determinist would argue, the shift in the balance of the discipline out of research-oriented university departments and into salvage work under commercial contracts.

Three approaches can be identified in judging who is right on these issues at the present time. A first is Earle and Preucel's critical attempt to assess the merits of the approaches in terms of their contemporary aims and current successes.

A second approach is Sabloff's (see chapter 3) historical view. Different contemporary approaches can be seen as conscious or unconscious reformulations and developments of older approaches, so their value can also be assessed in terms of the past successes, failures, and natural limitations of their intellectual parents. If a new mode has the essential characteristics of a past tradition of work, then its future intellectual trajectory is likely to parallel that of its predecessor.

A third approach, offered by Embree, is ethnographic (chapter 6). The field is directed by its influential members, both by their ideas and by their patronage and control of resources. The state of the art resides in what those people are doing and what they perceive themselves as doing, without necessarily having primary regard for what is "correct" in any absolute or external sense.

Tracing a Precarious Modern Concept into the Far Past

So far, so good. When discussing closed issues in the history of the discipline, it is fair to tell the story of who is right. When it comes to current debate in the field, it is a matter of judging where the best bets are being laid in a race that is not yet finished. Trouble starts when these two interests are combined, when one is asked, as I was, to trace the intellectual history of a rather new idea whose staying power is quite unclear and whose long-term importance we do not yet know.

For the history of archaeology element in the International Union of Prehistoric and Protohistoric Sciences Congress planned for 1986, Sabloff and Renfrew invited papers about the origins and development of social and economic archaeology. In response to the invitation, I searched for the origins of a social archaeology in the new prehistory of the 1860s, specifically in the work of Sir John Lubbock.

But did social archaeology exist 120 years ago? The phrase in its current British usage was coined by Renfrew, who calls it "the reconstruction of past social systems and relations" (1982:10; 1984:3). Like Sabloff (1985:71), I am unconvinced that it is either necessary or worthwhile to define social archaeology as a distinct subfield within the modern discipline. Insofar as archaeology always works from the physical evidence of objects toward inferences about past human societies, all archaeology is social archaeology of a kind. Redman et al., who also used the phrase, reflect this unwittingly when they say the essential aspects of a "social archaeology" are "the combination of increasing methodological rigor and sophistication with a concern for addressing meaningful cultural questions" (1978:xiii)—a definition that equally describes what any thinking archaeologist of any period or of any theoretical persuasion tries to do.

Social archaeology, then, is an odd creature to try to track back to its nineteenth-century lair in Europe. Either it is just another name for good archaeology in general, or it is the creation within the last 15 years of one of the symposium's organizers to define his offshore variant of North American processual archaeology. (The other symposium organizer denies its independent existence as a distinct approach.) Unless I wanted, as a kindness to a senior colleague, to discover a founding father for him, as our group pretends John Aubrey is to design grammars, it seemed a most unpromising way to approach Victorian states of mind.

A further consideration discourages the enterprise. The founding of prehistory in the crucial years from 1859 to 1865 and the bringing into general use the word *prehistory* in the European languages after 1865 (Chippindale 1988) precedes by a decade the recognition of sociology and of social history. The first major books in sociology are by Spencer (1873; 1876). For a British book of social history to make a famous impact, one has to wait until Trevelyan's *English Social History* (1944). So nowhere was there a developed concept of a historical or even a contemporary study concerning the social as a force in human action to complement, in the new prehistory of the 1860s, the understanding of technology and chronology that was offered by the three-age system and by the new geology and new biology with their chronological ordering and evolutionary thought.

Here, then, is good cause to expect nothing by way of a social archaeology 120 years ago. Even if social archaeology were to be the major force of good in the subject today, there seems no basis in the Victorian context to expect its genesis there in anything properly resembling its modern form.

The Social in Archaeology, Then and Now

How then to proceed? In the decade from 1860 to 1870, the Victorians of that critical period for the invention of prehistory had no sociology and no social history because these approaches to the world had not yet been invented. In fact, and against the expectations that these historical facts encourage, the phrase *social archaeology* turns out not to be a new invention of our own era, but to have been used by the philologist A. H. Sayce. In 1875, Sayce, who deciphered cuneiform and discovered the history of the Hittites, remarked: "Before society there is no language properly so called, because there is no conscious thought, no intercourse between man and man; consequently our linguistic researches will be bounded by the limits of social science and social archaeology" (1875:239).

Scholars of the period certainly had a lively interest in the social. It was there—in a different form, the form appropriate to its historical context. Instead of a neutral social science, it was ethics, morals, and the history of morals that offered themselves as the framework for treating the social dimensions. And the moral questions were inescapably about virtue and vice, "the distinction between right and wrong, or good and evil, in relation to the actions, volitions or character of responsible human beings" (*Oxford English Dictionary*, s.v. *moral*).

A chronological aspect of ethics, and therefore of the social, was provided by the long tradition of thinking within a framework defined by the idea of progress, of historical change such as plotting the development and improvement of morals and virtue—an intellectual style of working with the long-term patterns of human society that long precedes the Darwinian concept of evolutionary biology. Another tradition of thinking and working was arguing contemporary issues in ethics and philosophy by reference to sup-

posed historical authority—establishing the primacy of a view by its antiquity and therefore by its corresponding "natural" authority.

John Lubbock and the Archaeology of the Social

The best way to explore these issues is to study Sir John Lubbock, the
key figure in Victorian British archaeology, an intimate of Darwin, Huxley,
Spencer, and Tylor, a ubiquitous president of scientific societies, and a
champion of an integrated ethnology in which the lengthy time perspective
of prehistory would have a crucial role. As a Liberal politician and social
reformer, he had a lively interest in practical matters of the social, as well
as the intellectual. His *Pre-historic Times, as Illustrated by Ancient Remains,
and the Manners and Customs of Modern Savages* (1865) is the major
(though not the first) text of the new prehistory. Its intellectual parentage is
clear enough and well known: the combination of the Nordic antiquaries'
system of ages of stone, bronze, and iron—a scheme that did not demand
any great antiquity for mankind (Chippindale 1988)—and the evidence of
very ancient occupation from the caves and gravels of France and Britain
and the application of a four-stage prehistory: Paleolithic, Neolithic, Bronze
Age, and Iron Age and a long chronology to the archaeology of Europe as a
whole. The combination process is the subject of two-thirds of *Pre-historic
Times*, corresponding to the first part of its subtitle, "as Illustrated by Ancient
Remains." It deals with chronology, with technology, and with the antiquity
of humans and finds in these matters the evidence for an evolutionary progression. No serious obstacle is found to the notion that technological skill
rises consistently and progressively with time once the surprisingly accomplished carved art from French Paleolithic caves is discounted.

In a second part, corresponding to the second part of the subtitle,
"the Manners and Customs of Modern Savages," Lubbock deals with the
social. Two chapters describe contemporary savage societies while a third
attempts a comparative analysis of their degrees of savagery. Occasionally,
savages have ordered themselves by evolutionary expectations, and the
Tierra del Fuegians are sufficiently and uniformly savage in every respect.
More often a savage tribe declines to be wholly backward or wholly advanced and presents instead a disconcerting mixture of progressive and ret-
rogressive traits. When looking at the Fijians, for example, "the mind is
struck with wonder and awe at the mixture of a complicated and carefully
conducted political system, highly finished manners, and ceremonious po-
liteness, with a ferocity and practice of savage vices, which is unparalleled
in any other part of the world" (Erskine, quoted in Lubbock 1865 : 364).

A final chapter notes the broader implications. Despite the inconsis-
tencies of savage virtue and vice, Lubbock sees a pattern of progress from
savages—slaves to their wants, neither noble nor free—to civilized persons
whose lives are spent, thanks to printing, in communion with the greatest

minds, with the thoughts of Shakespeare and Tennyson, and the discoveries of Newton and Darwin. Ever the rational optimist, Lubbock ends with a peek at the future and sees how mankind always progresses towards less pain and more happiness as science abolishes the evil that comes from ignorance and sin: "Utopia, which we have long looked upon as synonymous with an evident impossibility . . . turns out . . . to be the necessary consequences of natural laws" (1865:492).

Lubbock's succeeding book, *The Origin of Civilisation and the Primitive Condition of Man* (1870), further explores the social. It deals almost exclusively with contemporary societies, their arts and ornaments, marriage and relationships, religion, character and morals, and language. The origin of civilization and of the primitive condition of mankind is not, in Lubbock's scheme, to be taken as an archaeologial question or, even, as a question to which prehistory can make a contribution. Yet Lubbock's attitude, his view of the social, on the face of it astonishing for the leading new prehistorian, can clearly be traced to its intellectual roots. The thesis of the *Origin* is a social, moral, and cognitive progression of savages that must advance steadily from the beginning in just the same manner as technology develops. But no relevant *evidence* is offered. Instead there is a circular argument, by the doctrine of survivals, in which backward traits are taken as old and civilized traits as new and in which a general grading of savages is made by their relative state of nastiness and immorality on the unilinear ladder of progress. Without evidence of real chronology, of the kind that archaeology may hope to provide, the evidence of survivals can and does tell nothing about what is old and enduring. The story of morality becomes a dogma of advancement—technological, biological, social, moral—from a creature rather resembling an ape to one, it must be said, with the more upright virtues of a Victorian gentleman.

One hundred twenty years later, we can see where the difficulty lies—in the belief that evolutionary change must necessarily follow a single and certain path upwards to progress. We know of other routes to social complexity than agriculture; we recognize that the possibility of complex civilization does not depend on the technological advances of bronze working and wheeled vehicles; we see that health, life expectancy, and perhaps the "quality of life"—as we try to imagine such a thing for the remote past—may even have dropped rather than advanced during the Paleolithic-Neolithic transition. A disillusion with some consequences of the path our society has taken in the last century, and to which the world seems irreversibly committed, has given us a different perception of change itself. We no longer automatically equate increasing social complexity with evolution and evolution with progress, nor do technological, social, and economic change seem to match exactly human happiness. Utopia appears to recede at least as fast as we approach it. The Australian aborigines, most backward to Lubbock for their failure to change, advance, and progress, can be seen in a new light, their long-term stability indicative of an excellent adaptation to their environment. If aboriginal societies had not changed at all for many thousands of years, they can now be considered evolutionary successes rather than evolutionary failures.

Change, Evolution, and Progress in Lubbock's Archaeology

Studying Lubbock's archaeology with the social in mind brought me to a realization that his new prehistory was not, as I had thought, a clean and clear application of the new biology, the new geology, the new evolutionary order to the human past. It is much more complex. Even today, perhaps the hardest part of Darwinian evolution to grasp is its aimlessness (Dawkins 1986). Australopithecines did not wish to turn into humans, any more than feudal societies consciously decided to become industrial. So the new evolution—a style of change that has no dream of advance, no aims or planned direction—was conflated with the old and comfortable idea of progress—a manner of change with a necessary direction and a fundamental commitment to moral improvement.

Archaeological evidence documented change running along with progress in the sphere of technology, and Lubbock followed its course. The evidence for the social did not, but it was made to follow the idea of progress against the balance of the evidence, for modern savages simply did not provide a consistent combination of uniform advancement, stage by stage. Seen in this light, Lubbock's prehistory is more of its time and less a modern thing than it had previously seemed to me or, I think, to historians of archaeology. This has been noted elsewhere; Peter Riviere, introducing a reprint of *The Origin of Civilisation*, plainly says it is nothing of the sort: "one hundred and eight years after its first appearance *The Origin of Civilisation* is generally unknown and unread. Those ignorant of it might defend their neglect of it on the grounds that its contents are so hopelessly wrong that there can be no justification in drawing a student's attention to them" (1978:xiv). These harsh words may be fair, but if they are, they equally apply to Tylor's *Researches into the Early History of Mankind and the Development of Civilization* (1865), Maine's *Ancient Law* (1861), Morgan's *Ancient Society* (1877), and the other well-regarded classics of evolutionary anthropology, for they all depend on some version of the doctrine of survivals.

Here, then is an explanation of the two aspects of Lubbock's new prehistory. The three- and four-age chronology, and the new ways of evolutionary thinking, provided a new paradigm for technological studies within archaeology and showed a pattern of growth and progress. There was no equivalent break to make a social prehistory imaginable. Instead, the remoteness of the physical evidence from long-standing philosophical and ethical concerns—law, marriage, abstract religious faith, morality—encouraged the honorable habit of philosophical fantasy-history, a perfectly valid frame for debating moral issues but one that had no point of contact with the empirical evidence from the earth.

An Alternative Social Framework: Wilson's *Prehistoric Man*

A surer approach, less dependent on moral virtue and on a dogma of progress, more "correct" in the sense of more closely prefiguring the pattern of the discipline's later development, can be found in a less well known scholar's work. Daniel Wilson (Trigger 1981:69–74), is remembered now mostly for his first use of the word *prehistoric* (1851; see Chippindale 1988). Wilson's *Prehistoric Man: Researches into the Origin of Civilisation in the Old and the New World* of 1865—the same year as Lubbock's *Pre-historic times*—has a similar ambition as that of Lubbock's book, to present a general account of prehistory and the origin of civilization within the new framework. Many of the subjects are the same and so is much of the intellectual apparatus, but it marks a major advance over Lubbock's work in four separate ways.

Firstly, there is neither a dogma of universal progress nor a dogma of necessary decay, but the recognition that modern human groups, however simply savage they might appear, had a long and perhaps complex history. "The Indian of the American wilds is no more primeval than his forests. Beneath the roots of their oldest giants lie chronicled memorials of an older native civilisation; and the American ethnologist and naturalist . . . have been studying only the temporary supplanters of nations strange to us as the extinct life of older geological periods" (Wilson 1865:8).

Secondly, Wilson set aside the "illogical association of the concomitants of modern intellectual and social progress with the indispensable requisites of man's primary condition as created in the Divine image, a being of intellectual and moral purity" (1865:3). Mankind's prehistory will not be a moral fable, either a fall from grace in the biblical manner or an advance from savagery to civilization after the habit of reforming liberalism.

Thirdly, Wilson saw the significance of those signs of really substantial development among ancient and modern primitives that so disconcerted Lubbock's evolutionary schemes—the accomplished art of the Dordogne Paleolithic caves, the sophistication and complexity of some savage languages (1865:51). Though clearly uncertain about what to do with these facts, Wilson at least recognized that the tidy equation of the simple, the amoral, the immoral, the backward, and the savage would not do.

Finally, Wilson—who had himself emigrated from Scotland to Canada—saw the value of comparative methods, especially between the Old and the New Worlds, in exploring the varied possibilities of change and evolutionary development. He compared, for example, the discovery of metallurgy in North America and in Europe. He drew from the North American example the correct proposal that there could be found in Europe evidence of a Copper Age intermediate in technical skill and in chronology between the recognized ages of polished stone and of bronze (1865: 178–180).

Discussion

The pursuit of the social, though not of "social archaeology" specifically, into the 1860s has been a valuable experience. To my knowledge, no previous scholar has looked at the new prehistory in relation to the idea of progress, and it has been a great surprise to find that Lubbock's novel science was the older doctrine in new clothes. It has changed, in my judgment, the relative standing of Lubbock's and Wilson's contributions, and it has drawn my attention to the relationship of the new prehistory to wider ethical issues. It was a surprise, for example, to discover that Charles Kingsley's *Water-Babies* (1863), one of the classics of Victorian literature, was written as a conscious contribution to the debate on evolution and specifically—as Kingsley's surviving correspondence with Lubbock shows—as an illustration of the view that evolution may go either way, that water-babies may change into land-babies and land-babies into water-babies. Who are the professors to say that one is better than the other? It was instructive to see how strong the pattern was in nineteenth-century thought that societies freely evolving will necessarily take the same predictable and predetermined course. For example, in Marx's dogma, across the political spectrum from Lubbock's liberalism, societies inevitably follow a course from feudalism through capitalism to socialism to communism—a theme in nineteenth-century social and intellectual theorizing, touched upon by many historians and commentators, that deserves a more central place. It emphasizes that the radical element in Darwin, for example, is less the idea of evolutionary change, for this was glimpsed by many others in previous decades, than it is evolution's lack of planned direction.

This study also illuminates modern issues, such as the confusion that still continues when change is equated with evolution and evolution with progress. It has helped recognize the recurrence of the doctrine of survivals as a substitute for real chronological information. It has pointed out the persistence of arguing contemporary issues using the belief that what is ancient must be natural. An excellent contemporary case is a recent feminist writing on the true and natural role of women in society (e.g., French 1985).

None of this would have been possible if I had not pursued the idea of the social into the archaeology of the 1860s, that is, if I had not taken a modern starting point for the study. None of it would have been possible if I had pursued the idea without respect for the context, that is, if I had not tried to respect the real circumstances, the intellectual and ethical environment in which those concepts existed and the social world the human beings who had these thoughts inhabited.

Most history of archaeology is written by archaeologists. But a twin qualification is required. The archaeologist provides the intellectual geography of the subject, the recognition of what has been valuable and lasting within the discipline, the rationale for choosing the key insights from a mass of ancient scholarship. The historian provides not just the technical expertise in dealing with documents (which may be overemphasized as a skill) but a wider understanding of the intellectual ecology of the subject, the means by which we understand the shape of the ancient discipline within a wider world (see chapter 1).

I subtitled this chapter with a question, "Is it right to look for modern ideas in old places?," and now I have an answer. It is fruitless and worthless to look in old places for specific modern forms. It is correct and valuable to look in old places for modern concerns, for the gestations and births of modern issues, with due regard for the date and place of conception. The history of archaeology is the history of the ideas that have prevailed, the ideas that have been right in the long term, and it is proper to see the past from the present. The necessary qualification is some real understanding of context, some real respect for the potentials and possibilities that were available, and a decent humility about our ancestors' accomplishments. I do not expect that my own work will—a century and a quarter from now—look as good as Lubbock's, whose grotesque limits and whose period character are so patently obvious to us today.

Acknowledgments

I am grateful to Lester Embree for conversations that may have improved my understanding of these matters.

3

Analyzing Recent Trends in American Archaeology from a Historical Perspective

Jeremy A. Sabloff

The organizer of the conference that has resulted in this volume asked me to discuss factors that influenced the changes from the original edition of *A History of American Archaeology* (Willey and Sabloff 1974) to the second edition (1980). Therefore, what follows is a personal account of the intellectual influences on my thinking between 1970–1971, when the first edition was written, and 1978, when the second edition was formulated. I should emphasize that the comments in this paper are my own and do not necessarily reflect the view of Gordon R. Willey, the senior author of the volume.

It was felt that, because there are relatively few histories of archaeology and only a very few that have undergone revision, future historians of the discipline might be interested in a commentary on the writing of the second edition. While it certainly is complimentary enough to be told that a book of which one is coauthor is worthy of discussion at a conference, it is even more flattering to hear that an analysis of the background to the writing of the book would be of value. I am sufficiently modest, however, to wonder if such an exercise is really worthwhile. Nevertheless, I have decided to accede to the organizer's wishes because they fit in nicely with one of my own hobby horses and allow me to attempt to further a personal agenda, to wit, that more histories of American archaeology should be written.

Gordon Willey and I named our book *A History of American Archaeology* rather than *The History* because we fervently hoped that it would be the first of many on the subject and that it would exercise scholars sufficiently to goad them into writing other histories. We did not envision it becoming the standard text; we just hoped to get our "licks" in first. Instead, surprisingly and inexplicably, it has become the lone book-length, scholarly treatment of the subject that has been published since 1974 (but see Fagan [1977] for a popular treatment of the subject). So, in the hope of stimulating more attempts in this area, I will discuss the intellectual background of my thinking during the writing of the second edition of *A History of American Archaeology.*

Before turning to a consideration of the writing of the second edition, however, let me digress for a moment so that I can provide a justification for my concern with the need for more histories of American archaeology, especially for the recent history of the subject, the past 25 years in particular.

The Importance of Historical Analyses

Henry Ford contended that "history is more or less bunk," but as an originator of the assembly line manufacture of automobiles, he was clearly a believer in efficiency, too. To a scholar trying to understand recent trends in archaeological thought, however, the two beliefs are obviously incompatible. To toss aside the history of archaeology is to promote inefficiency because the apparent ignorance of the historical roots of many current intellectual positions in archaeology seems to be leading to dead ends and to the inefficient repetition of past mistakes. To archaeologists committed to an efficient, productive development of the discipline, history and historical analyses cannot be bunk. They are essential.

Ignorance of the historical background of modern methodological and theoretical arguments is not bliss. It is stupidity. Just because it has not been the normal practice of historians of science to grapple with very recent developments in various disciplines does not mean that critical historical analyses of the past 25 years of American archaeology would not be quite fruitful. Although it may be difficult to obtain a historical perspective on such a recent past, it is far from impossible and definitely worth the effort. Moreover, the rejoinder that the revolutionary nature of modern archaeological thought has resulted in discontinuities with the discipline's past and therefore has rendered historical analyses irrelevant or purely esoteric is palpably false. As Willey and I argued (1980:248), contrary to the stated views of many writers (e.g., Martin 1971; Schiffer 1976), there has been no revolution in archaeology at least in Thomas Kuhn's (1962) terms. Developments in the past few years have reaffirmed rather than weakened this position (see also Binford and Sabloff 1982). At best, archaeology today is in a "crisis" stage, to use Kuhn's terminology. The complete "rethinking" of the materials of archaeology has yet to happen (see Hacking 1981:2). No powerful new, problem-solving theory has emerged in the field. What we see instead is a bewildering variety of polemical views about just what archaeologists should do, while much of the discipline continues to do what it has been doing for years, albeit with much greater technical sophistication and lip service to wider theoretical goals.

The great success of the "new archaeology" of the 1960s was its clarification of the goals of archaeology. A similar success in the realm of methodology, however, did not emerge (see Sabloff et al. 1987). Only in the past few years has the methodological crisis in archaeology clearly been recognized and come to the fore in the archaeological literature, in some cases as a direct outgrowth of the research of the 1960s and in others as a reaction to a "failure" of new archaeology to produce revolutionary results (Binford 1977, 1981, 1983a, 1983b, 1986; Binford and Sabloff 1982; Dunnell 1986b; Gould 1980; Hodder 1984, 1986; Leone 1986; Meltzer et al. 1986; Watson 1986; etc.). To begin to appreciate the myriad intellectual positions that have emerged in recent years, a historical perspective can be quite useful because many of the most visible positions have clear historical roots. Additionally, knowledge of the problems that these positions have faced can help students avoid past mistakes and evaluate which positions are potentially productive ones (see chapter 2). As I have contended, if archaeologists cannot learn lessons from the past, who can?

Let me mention a few brief examples of the potential utility of a historical perspective on current polemical positions in archaeology. For example, in examining the intellectual underpinnings of the "postprocessual" school of thought, especially in its "symbolic" guise (see Hodder 1986 and Leone 1986 for good overviews), one can see a return to aspects of cultural relativism, idealism, and the whole Boasian tradition in North America. Clearly, archaeologists need to carefully evaluate the blueprint of the postprocessualist plan in light of the historical development of the Boasian tradition (cf. Harris 1968; Stocking 1968, 1974) and particularly the growth of American archaeology in that tradition (Willey and Sabloff 1980: chapter 4), if many of the dead ends of the past are to be avoided. The recent presentation of Hodder's (1986) "contextual" approach also needs to be viewed in light of the successes and failures over the past 40 years of Taylor's (1948) "conjunctive" approach.

Calls by some scholars (see particularly Moore and Keene 1983) for "theory now" and an end to what are perceived as the shackles of the "methodological tyranny" of the past two decades also need to be viewed in light of the agendas of the 1960s that similarly called for immediate theoretical development (e.g., Binford and Binford 1968). Moreover, the nonexplicit, often-unexamined development of methodology in American archaeology in this century can provide some useful perspectives on this position, too.

Obviously, the whole phenomenon of the new archaeology of the 1960s and 1970s also can be better understood through historical analyses of its component parts, as Willey and I tried to show in the first edition of our book. Analyses of the growth of materialist thought and the environmental perspective have much to offer to an understanding of the current scene, as does an examination of the development of ethnoarchaeology. In addition, the history of the various social sciences in recent decades (the "new geography," the "new sociology," the "new psychology," etc.) can illuminate and provide perspectives on the modern debates in American archaeology. The same can be said for the history of the philosophy of science. In the latter regard, the tie between the new archaeology of the 1960s and logical positivism (e.g., Fritz and Plog 1970) could be productively and non-polemically appraised in light of the changes in Hempel's thinking from the 1940s to the 1960s (Hempel 1965).

In sum, there appears to be great confusion in the literature and among students about where the field is or should be heading, and there have been relatively few attempts to analyze critically the field as a whole and to evaluate the alternative intellectual approaches that are current to-day. Given that there has yet to be a revolution in American archaeology, it can be argued that the current approaches should have strong intellectual continuities to past thinking. If all the current polemical positions have good historical roots, then critical historical analyses of these positions should be quite edifying. The conclusion is clear: we need more histories of American archaeology that focus on recent trends in the field.

Writing the Second Edition of *A History of American Archaeology*

The second edition of *A History of American Archaeology* was writ-ten in 1978 and published in 1980. In many ways, writing the second edi-tion was as difficult as writing the first. As before, we had to be incredibly selective in what we commented on, and we had to work very hard to main-tain a historical stance. This selectivity and care was true for chapter 7, where the emphasis was mainly substantive, and for chapter 8, where the emphasis was methodological and theoretical. I would like to pay particular attention here to chapter 8, which we entitled "The Explanatory Period: Continuing Methodological and Theoretical Innovations (the 1970s)." The quote by a favorite writer of mine, Brian Aldiss, from a book that he wrote on the history of science fiction—"this is the way of histories; that as they come closer to the present and future, the errors of proportion become greater; so does the writer's subjectivity" (1973:261)—accurately reflects some of our qualms about attempting to analyze a recent period historically. Yet, at the same time, we were not making any claims for objectivity. The earlier chapters had hardly been objective, although we tried to maintain a certain distance between the subject matter and ourselves and were not overtly polemical (in the sense that Harris's [1968] history of anthropology was). Certainly, we argued our point of view, and the final chapter was no different. Nevertheless, we were concerned about our relative lack of per-spective on the period, and because most scholars were more familiar with the literature of the period than with earlier writings and had been partici-pants in the intellectual events of the 1970s, we knew that we would be open to more criticism then ever before. Despite all the potential pitfalls, however, we strongly felt that the attempt was worthwhile and that it was an exercise that could be useful to the field even as a simple lightning rod for argument.

Our techniques were the same as before: a careful reading of as much of the available literature as possible and discussions of our ideas with a number of archaeologists. In my case, my colleagues Lewis Binford and Linda Cordell were particularly helpful in providing critical comments on my views of the implications of the archaeological literature and research of the 1970s. In our writing, the one advantage we had over other American archaeologists—for certainly when writing about the immediate past the view that everyone is a historian might receive some support—was the explicit historical perspective and background we had gleaned from our research for the first edition. The ability to see potential continuities from the 1960s and earlier that this perspective engendered was clearly of much value to us.

The views that I expressed in chapter 8 were influenced by a series of factors and events that had occurred since the writing of the first edition in 1970–1971. I clearly was quite impressed by the methodological problems facing the field, and through time I began to perceive some of these problems as an "operational" crisis. This perception, which became the guiding and organizing force of my research and my writing of chapter 8 arose through a concatenation of circumstances. Most importantly, I became editor-elect of *American Antiquity* in 1977 while I was teaching at the University of Utah. When I began to receive manuscripts, I was struck by the disjunction in many papers between what was promised in the opening paragraphs and what was delivered in the bodies of the works. In fact, the pattern was so noticeable that my assistant editor, Lynne Sebastian, and I came to recognize what might be termed the litany with which many manuscripts began. The author would note his or her "systemic" point of view and holistic conception of culture, cite Binford (1962) and Flannery (1968) among others, talk about the problem-oriented goals of his or her research, and perhaps mention the hypothesis he or she would be examining (or testing) in the paper. Unfortunately, in many cases, the rest of the paper never referred back to this opening boilerplate.

In teaching a course at that time on the new archaeology, I also was distressed to see that despite the growing lip service to the need for understanding cultural processes, little headway seemed to be taking place. A good example, which I later discussed in the second edition, was Fred Plog's stimulating *Study of Prehistoric Change* (1974). Although Plog developed a sophisticated, promising model of cultural change, he was forced to admit that the data at hand in the Hay Hollow Valley were insufficient to test it. Many other similar examples appeared, though few authors were as explicit about the problems as Plog. Clearly, good ideas were not enough. I came to feel that the links between ideas and data were too weakly developed to allow much progress in the field.

I had also seen this disjunction firsthand while doing field research on the island of Cozumel with William L. Rathje in 1972–1973. Both Rathje and I saw the project in what would now be labeled "middle range" or "bridging" terms. Many Maya scholars were interested in trade, but when it came to characterizing trading centers in material and behavioral terms, there was a visible gap. We hoped to fill this gap by delineating the nature of a trading center "on the ground" and had many ideas about it that we hoped to examine (Rathje and Sabloff 1973; Sabloff and Rathje 1975). Unfortunately, as aware as we were of the issues, the fieldwork brought home to me how unprepared we were to actually forge behavioral-material links before going to the field. We were saved, in part, by the ethnohistorical record with which we were able to work during the subsequent analyses (Freidel and Sabloff 1984).

Another important influence on my thinking was my involvement with computer simulation. In particular, my collaboration with Dorothy Hosler and the late Dale Runge on a simulation of the "collapse" of Classic Maya civilization (Hosler et al. 1977) was highly stimulating and revealed the incredible difficulties that Hosler and Runge faced in converting verbal statements to mathematical ones. Moreover, it was obvious that much of the problem lay in the dearth of good, unambiguous means to monitor ancient behavior. This view was reinforced by my association with the members of the 1978 School of American Research Advanced Seminar on "The Use of Systems Models and Computer Simulations in Archaeological Research" and the provocative discussions that took place during the seminar sessions (Sabloff 1981).

Other influences at this time included: (1) my growing awareness of the nature of cultural resource management research—I was principal investigator of part of the Central Utah Project archaeological fieldwork while at the University of Utah—and the need to link large-scale data collection with current method and theory; (2) my new interest in historical archaeology, which was stimulated by a reading of Stanley South's (1977) volume, raised the possibility that historical archaeology plays a critical role in the linking of data and theory; and (3) my first introduction to the burgeoning practice of ethnoarchaeology and its vast potential.

Most importantly, all these impressions were consolidated by my move to the University of New Mexico at the end of 1977 and by my association there with Lewis Binford. Innumerable conversations with Binford, which later led to our joint teaching of the introductory graduate seminar in archaeology at the University of New Mexico (examining the development of archaeology in historical perspective and then looking at future directions in the field) and the writing of two articles (deriving from our seminar lectures) on the nature of the current intellectual scene in archaeology (Binford and Sabloff 1982; Sabloff et al. 1987), helped crystallize my ideas about the methodological and theoretical problems facing archaeology today. Although we did not always agree, my discussions with Binford were thought provoking, especially because our differing perspectives from hunter-gatherer and complex society research gave us fresh, contrasting viewpoints on a variety of topics. His arguments for the necessity of bridging theory helped organize my somewhat disparate thinking in this area and were crucial to forming the principal focus of chapter 8.

These influences were solidified while writing the second edition because Gordon Willey has a predilection for concrete examples, and he frequently challenged to me to come up with clear, data-based examples of the ideas I brought forward for inclusion in both chapters 7 and 8. This insistence forced me to grapple with the linkages between ideas about cultural behavior and the archaeological record. Such challenges not only affected the writing of the new edition but also influenced my views on the current directions in Maya archaeology (Sabloff 1982, 1983, 1986; Sabloff et al. 1984; Sabloff and Tourtellot 1987).

Conclusions

Although the current intellectual scene in American archaeology is rife with excitement, it is also fraught with potential disaster. The challenge for teachers—to sort out the competing polemical positions and offer students the means to evaluate successfully the productive potential of these positions—is daunting but critical. Historical analyses of the arguments are important; they provide a context for the arguments and indicate what arguments have had positive, negative, or neutral effects in the past. I hope that my brief remarks in this chapter will stimulate others to examine their own thinking and to use such formulations as bases for discussions of the development of archaeology over the past quarter century.

4

The History of Archaeology and the Archaeological History of Chaco Canyon, New Mexico

Jonathan E. Reyman

American archaeology is slightly more than a century old; its history is short. Like many other disciplines, American archaeology has not followed a unilineal development, but has had separate local, regional, and areal developments, each with its own evolutionary sequence. Similarly, the major historical syntheses of American archaeology (e.g., Taylor 1948; Willey and Phillips 1958; Willey and Sabloff 1980) rest on the foundations of more localized histories such as Caldwell (1958), Griffin (1952), Kidder (1924), and Roberts (1936).

There are also internal links that unify the evolutionary sequences and histories among areas within the Americas. Theoretical and methodological schemes first developed and applied in one area are often used later in other areas. As these applications are reported, subsequent histories reflect these similarities or parallels. The Midwestern Taxonomic System (McKern 1939), the area co-tradition (Bennett 1948), settlement pattern analysis (Willey 1953), and the interaction sphere (Caldwell 1964) were all applied in areas other than those for which they were first developed (e.g., Strong 1935 [Midwestern Taxonomic System]; Martin and Rinaldo 1951 [co-tradition]; Marshall et al. 1979, Willey 1956 [settlement patterns]; Reyman 1970b, 1971b, and Frisbie 1972 [interaction sphere]).

Published Reports: A Limiting Factor

A characteristic of histories of American archaeology is that they necessarily are based on published materials. Some scholars approach their task specifically "with reference to the published writings of particular archeologists" (Taylor 1948:45). Others are less explicit about this approach but are no less dependent upon published works as perusal of their bibliographies indicates (e.g., McGregor 1965; Willey and Phillips 1958). All recognize that reliance on published reports is a limiting factor, often severely so. Taylor (1948:47) notes: "Kidder, however, unlike most other Americanists, has provided a resolution for this anthropology-history ambivalence. This way out is neither clearly marked nor a point of frequent reference in his writings; in fact, its only explicit statement is pretty well hidden from the general archeological public, being found in an obscure typewritten progress-report filed in the library of the Peabody Museum of Harvard."

Published reports, in turn, are often limited by external factors such as costs and space limitations imposed on the writers by the publishers. Taylor states: "It is realized that many times the archeologist may wish to include in his reports certain data . . . but is prevented from doing so because of publication or other restrictions. In such cases, the vision and intention of the archeologist may not be criticized. . . ." (1948:45). For example, a comparison of Frank H. H. Roberts, Jr.'s published Bureau of American Ethnology (BAE) reports with his original field notes indicates that significant data were omitted (Taylor 1948:71–72), notably for small artifacts and certain exotic finds such as elaborate turkey burials (Reyman 1971b:181–182). Cost restrictions prevented Roberts from publishing full site reports, so he chose to publish the architectural data that he believed were more useful to other southwestern archaeologists (Reyman 1970a, 1971b). Thus, some of Taylor's criticism of Roberts is unwarranted for Taylor's own reasons.

There is a dilemma here, perhaps unavoidable. Prior to World War I, American archaeology was a relatively small field; it was easier to keep abreast of developments. The *BAE Annual Reports* contained summaries of each year's work and publications; similar reports from other institutions had the same. Eventually, some reports lagged behind events (e.g., the *BAE 13th Annual Report for 1891–1892* was not published until 1896). Nevertheless, through personal contacts and correspondence, scholars generally knew what others were doing, Frank Cushing visited Adolph Bandelier at Zuñi in 1893 and read to him his latest paper (Lange and Riley 1970:44), and George Pepper corresponded widely, often exchanging unpublished primary data (Reyman 1982a). The growth of archaeology since World War II has meant that few archaeologists know what more than a small number of their colleagues are doing. The need for information grows, yet so does the gap between work done and work reported. Attempts to narrow this gap have not been successful.

Owing to the limitations of the published literature, there is a demonstrable need for a thorough examination of unpublished materials. As discussed in this chapter, these materials are significant for the history of archaeology and the archaeological history of Chaco Canyon and are essential for correcting errors of fact and interpretation.

Chaco Canyon in Southwestern and American Archaeology

Chaco Canyon, New Mexico, after more than a century of archaeological fieldwork, is one of the better-studied regions in the American Southwest. Described and sketched by Simpson (1850) and Jackson (1878), more thoroughly studied by Mindeleff (1891), and excavated beginning in 1896 under the aegis of the Hyde Exploring Expedition (Pepper 1920), the Chaco ruins are second only to those at Mesa Verde in the public's awareness.

Chaco Canyon was the locus of three major methodological developments: dendrochronology (Douglass 1929, 1935); geological and climatological studies (Bryan 1925, 1941, 1954); and cross-dating of sites using dendrochronology, masonry, and ceramics (Hawley 1934). The study of Chaco materials furthered research done on other problems: Mexican-Southwestern interaction (Ferdon 1955; Frisbie 1972; Hewett 1936; Reyman 1970b, 1971b, 1978, 1985); archaeoastronomy (Reyman 1971a, 1971b, 1976a, 1976b, 1982a; Williamson 1981); settlement patterns (Marshall et al. 1979; Powers et al. 1983); and architecture (Hewett 1936; Judd 1964; Lekson 1983; Lekson et al. 1984; Mindeleff 1891; Pepper 1920; Reyman 1971b, 1982c, 1985; Vivian and Reiter 1960). And, some of the earliest regional studies (Holsinger 1901), site reports (Pepper 1920), and multidisciplinary research (Kluckhohn and Reiter 1939) were based on Chaco materials. Thus, Chaco Canyon has been the setting for important archaeological research, much of which has had applicability and significance elsewhere.

Unpublished Materials: The Overlooked Record for Chaco Canyon

The published record of Chaco Canyon archaeology is important, but the unpublished record may be of equal significance, especially for specific problems. The history of archaeology and the archaeological history of Chaco Canyon are incomplete and inaccurate because there is a general lack of knowledge about the unpublished record, a shortcoming that this and other works in preparation should help rectify (Reyman 1987b, 1987c, 1987d; Reyman and Nickels 1987). I am not referring to recently excavated materials and the normal lag between fieldwork and publication. Rather, most of the data discussed below were collected between 1896 and 1905; other data I recently rediscovered while reading unpublished materials from 40 years ago and then while studying aerial photographs from the 1970s. In some cases, the apparent reluctance of archaeologists to consider seriously these earlier materials led them to overlook supporting evidence for observations reported therein and to overlook evidence clearly visible in the later aerial photographs. Space limitations prohibit a full presentation of these data, so a sample is provided of the problems, their importance, and the unpublished data available to resolve them.

Why have these unpublished records remained hidden? First, they are scattered among a dozen institutions and several individuals with no comprehensive catalog available (see chapter 17 for a discussion of this problem). For example, Pepper worked at four museums; each retains part of his materials. His personal collections and papers were dispersed after his death in 1924, and it now takes time, money, and persistence to locate them. Unfortunately, some materials have been destroyed, either deliberately or because of poor preservation conditions. The loss has been considerable.

Second, materials are misfiled, mislabeled, or uncataloged, so one must often search through stacks, boxes, and cabinets to find them. The sheer volume of material makes the task exhausting. For example, the photographs I discuss below were found by examining more than 8,000. Richard Wetherill's field notes, in one case, were included among some of Pepper's materials, but there was no indication of their existence in the museum's catalog. Often I found important data in files already examined by others who either had not recognized their significance (Reyman 1982a) or, more often, had not examined the contents of a file or box, item by item.

Third, scholars too often accept what they read as true (Reyman 1987a). In his foreword to Pepper's *Pueblo Bonito,* Wissler states:

> The author [Pepper] long delayed the preparation of this report in the hope that further work could be taken up at the ruin and that a more exhaustive study . . . could be prosecuted; but as neither of these desirable extensions of the work now seems possible, he has decided to issue his notes in their present form as a record of what he has done.
>
> Finally, . . . what is published here are his field notes supplemented by descriptive data for the most important specimens. The author is to be commended for . . . placing before us *his field record in full* [1920 : 2; emphasis added].

Many archaeologists accepted this statement as true. I never did; no archaeologist publishes all the data. My skepticism was rewarded when I discovered a letter from Wissler to Pepper (18 December 1918, American Museum of Natural History) in which Wissler notes that the Pueblo Bonito manuscript is only part of the total record for the site. Why Wissler did not mention this in his foreword is an interesting but unresolved question.

Fourth, publication is expensive. There are more than 10,000 pages of Pepper's and Wetherill's notes and other materials and thousands of photographs. Some of these primary data significantly alter our understanding of the archaeological history and the history of archaeology at Chaco Canyon. Full publication of this material has been delayed owing to lack of funds. Given the amount of unpublished material from other early workers, the task is enormous. The value of much of the material is great, and its often-deteriorating condition requires quick action. A possible solution is to encourage students to place increased emphasis on library and museum theses and dissertations.

There are five problems for which the unpublished Chaco data have significance: (1) a recently discovered site at Chaco; (2) the beginning of stratigraphic excavation in the Americas; (3) Casa Rinconada; (4) the Pueblo Bonito-Chetro Ketl wall; and (5) Chacoan burials.

The "Ohmygod" Site

In 1981 archaeologists surveying near the east side of Pueblo Bonito discovered wood, daub, and other debris. Their surprise at finding a site in a planned roadway gave the site its name. They first thought the debris was backdirt from Chetro Ketl; later, other possibilities were considered, such as a small prehistoric or historic structure (C. Randall Morrison, personal communication 1983–1984).

In 1984, I examined a collection of photographs at the Maxwell Museum of Anthropology at the University of New Mexico. Jeannette Cameron, Pepper's daughter, donated the photographs to the university in the 1930s (Dorothy Keur, personal communication 1982). Among them is photograph 4.368, "Wetherill House and Store, Looking West." The two buildings were probably erected between the spring of 1897 and July 1898, when Wetherill built his last house on the west side of Pueblo Bonito (McNitt 1966:175). Aside from this photograph, there is no other record of the structures. Their location in the photograph and the construction materials correspond to the location of and debris at the "Ohymygod" site. This site is apparently the remains of Wetherill's second house and store that, until now, have not been mentioned in the published literature; they were an unrecorded, unremembered part of Wetherill's Chaco Canyon settlement.

Stratigraphy

Nels Nelson and Manuel Gamio are usually credited with the first stratigraphic excavations in North America (Willey and Sabloff 1980: 84–91), although some note that "Richard Wetherill [Wetherill 1894] . . . was the first to make use of natural stratigraphy as applied to archaeological problems in the Southwest" (McGregor 1965:41; see also Kidder 1924; Prudden 1897). Nevertheless, Nelson's work in New Mexico's Galisteo Basin (Nelson 1914, 1916) is usually cited as the earliest systematic excavation in the United States.

In fact, Pepper's 1896–1899 excavation notes and other records (Figures 4-1 and 4-2) make it clear that he conducted stratigraphic excavations 15 years before Nelson. In excavating Chacoan burial mounds, Pepper (1896a, 1897, 1920:341) laid out a grid system and then dug following natural stratigraphy. Stratigraphic layers were also recognized and often fol-

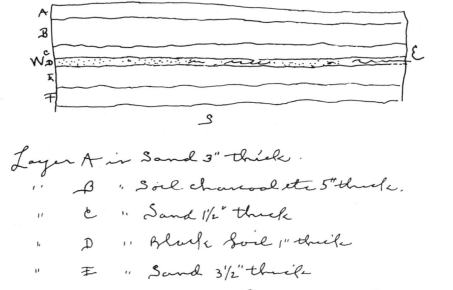

Layer A is Sand 3" thick.
"   B " Soil charcoal etc 5" thick.
"   C " Sand 1½" thick
"   D " Black Soil 1" thick
"   E " Sand 3½" thick
"   F " Soil which was below the
door level. These measurement were
taken about a foot West of the southern door and 3" North of the S wall
the inflow has been from the East
because the Sand layers increase
in thickness as the Eastern fort of
the room is mand.

Figure 4-1. Tracing of George H. Pepper's original stratigraphic profile and notes for room 32, Pueblo Bonito, 1896. Department of Anthropology Archives, American Museum of Natural History.

lowed in room excavations at Pueblo Bonito (Pepper 1896b, 1897, 1898, 1899, 1920:137, passim). The following statement is typical:

> Stratigraphical excavations in connection with the old ceramics are producing evidence for comparative study, and this with the occurrence of similar ceramic forms in nearby culture areas will help to

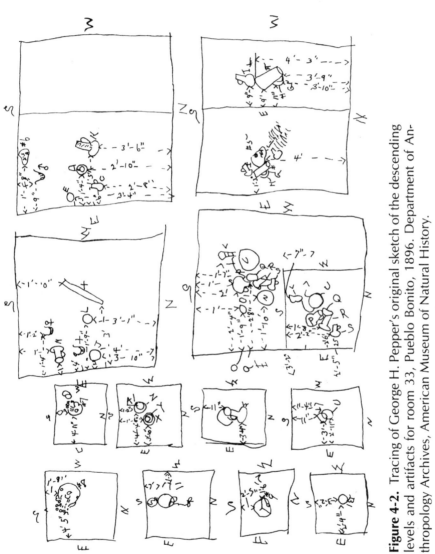

Figure 4-2. Tracing of George H. Pepper's original sketch of the descending levels and artifacts for room 33, Pueblo Bonito, 1896. Department of Anthropology Archives, American Museum of Natural History.

solve the problem of clan migrations and the length of time that the towns were occupied, as with it comes a general knowledge of time periods in connection with the evolution of architectural and cultural refinements [Pepper n.d.:7; reprinted with permission of the Latin American Library].

Two points are worth noting. First, for some reason, most of Pepper's discussions of stratigraphy and all his drawings were omitted from *Pueblo Bonito* (room 32 is an exception; the discussion is included [Pepper 1920:137; see also Pepper 1909], but the drawing [Figure 4-1] is not). Lister and Lister state: "Stratigraphy, he [Pepper] thought, would be a good technique for unraveling the history of the settlement, and his records indicate that such investigations, never before applied to a Southwestern site, had been planned for Pueblo Bonito" (1981:30). They are referring to the statement that "a general study of the underlying strata [was] planned as part of the extension of the work, but owing to circumstances beyond the control of those in charge, this most desirable phase of the investigations was impossible" (Pepper 1920:375). These "underlying strata" were those below the pueblo. Pepper had already dug rooms using both natural and cultural strata, so only the underlying strata remained to be examined.

Second, Nelson (1920) contributed notes at the end of Pepper's monograph based on a two-week field session at Pueblo Bonito in 1916. Nelson had access to Pepper's field notes and knew of Pepper's stratigraphic work. Thus, Nelson's lack of comment on Pepper's work is puzzling.

Casa Rinconada

The largest, most complex, and best known of the Chacoan Great Sanctuaries (Great Kivas), Casa Rinconada was dug in 1931, restored in 1933, and further stabilized in 1955 (Vivan and Reiter 1960). It is the subject of much speculation.

Morgan (1977) argues that the arrangement of 34 wall niches provided the Chacoans with a "computational center" to calculate important calendrical dates and to mark directly the solstice sunrises. He posits similar functions for other Chacoan Great Sanctuaries such as Chetro Ketl I–II. Williamson (1981:72–74), in a more carefully done and cautious study, also concludes that Casa Rinconada has an alignment to the summer solstice sunrise. The northeast "window" and niche 7 provide a line-of-sight alignment to this event. But there is an incorrect assumption in both studies, namely, that Casa Rinconada, *as it now exists,* closely resembles the site as it originally existed or even as it existed when first excavated. Morgan makes the same erroneous assumption in conjunction with Chetro Ketl I–II.

A recently discovered, unnumbered Pepper photograph taken in 1896 or 1897 and Holsinger's (1901) photograph 35 show that the so-called window did not exist except for a small part of its westernmost inside edge (Reyman 1982b:907). Its present size and shape are the result of the archaeologists' construction. The same is true for several niches, including niche 7. Furthermore, the roof support beam in the northwest seating pit would have blocked the line of sight to the summer solstice sunrise.

At Chetro Ketl I–II, Morgan assumes that all 29 niches were open and contemporaneous. The published reports (Hewett 1936; Vivan and Reiter 1960) show that this was not the case. Morgan's methodology is flawed, his conclusions are incorrect, and his hypotheses are unnecessarily complicated. The Chacoans could have obtained the same astronomical information from simple observations and counts similar to those made by the historic Pueblos (Reyman 1971b, 1976a, 1976b, 1980).

The Pueblo Bonito–Chetro Ketl Wall

Marietta Wetherill, Richard's widow, discussed the Pueblo Bonito–Chetro Ketl wall with Gordon Vivian. "She brought up the story of the wall between Bonito and Chettro Kettle. According to her it was about 4 feet high and extended all the way between the two pueblos. When I asked her what became of it she said that Dick wouldn't let the Navajo use stone from the ruin so when they built some of the post and residence the Navajo went out and hauled in this wall and it's now in the buildings" (Vivian 1948:3).

Archaeologists with whom I spoke tended to doubt that the wall existed. I did not. Assuming her observation was accurate, I checked aerial photographs for evidence of the wall; it is clearly visible on some of them. A brief field check in 1983 provided evidence of a masonry wall. A test excavation is now planned.

The implication is significant. This wall, when considered with the Northeast Foundation Complex at Pueblo Bonito, the Hillside Ruin, and Talus Unit 1 behind Chetro Ketl (Judd 1964:143–153; Lekson et al. 1984), suggests that the Chacoans planned to join Pueblo Bonito and Chetro Ketl; the resulting site would have been almost 1,200 m long. Planning for a site this size presumed or anticipated the need for more living and storage space. This, in turn, suggests that the Chacoans had or expected to have a much larger resident population than some have assumed.

Chaco Canyon Burials

The apparent paucity of Chaco Canyon burials has confounded scholars: "One of the more intriguing mysteries of Chaco Canyon is the relative absence of burials associated with Bonito Phase houses" (Hayes 1981:61; see also Akins 1986; Hewett 1936; Judd 1954:325–342; McNitt 1966; Windes 1984). Explanations for this are limited only by one's imagination.

> One theorist . . . had the dead of Pueblo Bonito floating down Chaco wash, one by one, on log rafts. Here . . . we have a single explanation that accounts both for our depleted forests and the absence of a communal burial graveyard. . . . These individual rafts floated westward down the Chaco and into the San Juan; thence, into the Colo-

rado and Gulf of California. The alluvial fan at the mouth of the Rio
Colorado is . . . one place I never thought to look for Bonitian burials
[Judd 1954:342].

The number of burials recovered from Chaco Canyon varies from one
source to another. McNitt (1966:334) gives the number as 302 using published and unpublished reports. Akins' (1986) careful review of unpublished
and published materials puts the number at 600 to 700. Prehistoric population estimates for Chaco also vary, partly because of the burial problem.
Judd (1954:340) estimates 5,000 burials for Pueblo Bonito; Pierson (1949)
puts the total canyon population at 4,400; and Hayes (1981:51) calculates
the peak population at 5,600. More recently, the apparent paucity of burials
and hearths at town sites such as Pueblo Bonito has led some workers to
revise sharply downward their estimates of the maximum population. For
example, Judge (1984) argues that Chaco Canyon was essentially a ceremonial center with a resident population below 2,000; the total population
swelled and then ebbed with the onset and conclusion of ceremonies.
Windes (1984:83–84) and some others concur (see Reyman 1987a).
      Lister and Lister state: "After four seasons, Pepper ended his associ-
ation with Pueblo Bonito as puzzled over the paucity of human burials
within the town or its trash heap as he had been at the conclusion of the first
sterile month. A few burials had been found in several so-called burial
rooms. . . . But the grave sites of the bulk of the populace must, in Pepper's
opinion, lie concealed beneath thick deposits of sand and mud to the west
or east of the structure" (1981:36–37). Pepper (1920:376) was puzzled
about the location of the Pueblo Bonito burials, but he found no general
paucity of burials. Neither did Wetherill who, with others (Akins 1986:12)
and Pepper, unearthed hundreds of burials, few of which are reported in the
published literature. Pepper (1920:339–351) states that some burials came
from mounds. Most later archaeologists have assumed that Pepper and
Wetherill dug small house sites (Hosta Butte phase) and their adjacent trash
heaps not burial mounds (Akins 1986:13).
      Although Wetherill (1896:44) labels one small house site on the
south side of the arroyo "Burial Mound #5," he also notes that it is a house
site. Elsewhere in their unpublished notes, Wetherill and Pepper make it
clear that they are digging burial mounds, not house sites or trash heaps.
The lack of architecture confirms that these are not house sites; the general
absence of trash in the fill suggests that neither are these trash heaps. Pepper
states: "As this mound was in reality the talus slope of the mesa the soil was
full of stones which made the process of uncovering extremely difficult . . .
almost all skeletons found in this mound had charcoal about the bodies and
some of them had flat stones over the places of interment, but no stone
graves were found. We photographed the ruin on the hill nearby [probaby
Casa Rinconada], of which this was no doubt the grave yard" (1896a).
      In one mound, Wetherill (1896:19) recovered at least 10 burials

from a 1 by 3 m trench; elsewhere, Pepper and Wetherill found so many skeletons but so few unusual pots and grave goods that they lost interest and abandoned the work. One mound was so large that a grid of 64 squares, each 8 by 8 ft, did not cover its entirety! From this mound they recovered about 40 skeletons from a single trench, most in poor condition. Unfortunately, none of the skeletons and few of the grave goods are extant. The former existence of these mounds is further confirmed by recently discovered photographs taken by Pepper and Wetherill (Reyman and Nickels 1987).

The mounds may have contained burials from Pueblo Bonito and other towns, and Pepper's and Wetherill's failure to recognize their source may have come from an assumption that most Great Pueblo burials would be as elaborate as those found in rooms 32 and 33 at Pueblo Bonito (Pepper 1909). In fact, these intramural burials may constitute an elite group (Reyman 1978; cf. Akins and Schelberg 1984).

The possibility that most Pueblo Bonito burials are still at Chaco cannot be overlooked. Pepper (1920:376) notes that they may lie east or west of the site. Cemeteries adjacent to Pueblo Pintado, Peñasco Blanco, and Kin Bineola are described, and all were partly excavated (Holsinger 1901; Pepper 1896a, 1897, 1899, 1920). There should be a cemetery near Pueblo Bonito, about which Marietta Wetherill makes a pertinent comment in reference to an old photograph: "This is the burial mound near Pueblo Bonito. There are a lot of these mounds and most . . . are about 20 feet high. The wind has blown the sand and ashes off the bones and there are bones and skulls and pottery all over the mounds. Some of these are very large and are *acres* in extent" (Vivian 1948:3; emphasis in original).

Judd (1954:340–342) tested various locations but found nothing. He concluded that if a cemetery existed for Pueblo Bonito, it was more than a quarter mile from the site. However, given the depth of the silt west of the site, more than 6 m deep in some places (C. Randall Morrison, personal communication 1987), it would be worthwhile to dig several deep trenches to check there for a cemetery. Marietta Wetherill was a good observer, and there is no reason to reject outright her statement about the Pueblo Bonito cemetery. Indeed, one might look in the area of the Wetherills' graves. It is a raised location (though perhaps due only to talus debris) and might have been chosen as Richard Wetherill's burial site to inter him with the very people he studied.

The lack of hearths at Pueblo Bonito is another example of what was reported rather than what was found. As noted, Pepper's *Pueblo Bonito* is incomplete. The unpublished data include some unusual finds, such as six dessicated rabbits in rooms 1 and 2 and a fragment of a painted stone tablet in room 6 (Pepper 1896c). More hearths were found than reported in the published literature, and when these are added to those cited by Pepper (1920) and Judd (1954, 1964), few archaeologists are likely to conclude that there is a paucity.

In summary, the lowered population estimates seem unwarranted. The "deserted ceremonial center" hypothesis was unfounded for the Maya, and there is little reason to accept it for Chaco. The unpublished record makes it clear that the apparent paucity of burials and hearths is just that, apparent, not real. The wall and planned intersite construction between Pueblo Bonito and Chetro Ketl suggest a growing population with a need for more space. Looking only at the published record and disregarding the unpublished data badly skew conclusions about the archaeological history of Chaco Canyon.

Conclusions

I began by stating that the published record is a limiting factor for writing both the history of American archaeology and of archaeological (cultural) history. Ignorance of and failure to use unpublished materials eliminate important data from consideration. Resultant histories are often inaccurate, as shown for Chaco Canyon. The same is probably true for other areas of the Americas.

In some cases, poor storage conditions have damaged and continue to damage these materials. Students should be encouraged to undertake more museum and library studies and to publish their findings. These materials are a treasure house of information that must be made available.

While not everything is worth publishing and evaluations must be made, it is better to publish too much than too little. As in the case of Chaco Canyon, publication will add significantly to our knowledge and often has implications for other areas. It would benefit all scholars if this were done soon.

Acknowledgments

This research was funded by grants from the National Science Foundation (GS–2829, GS–40410, BNS77–08070), the Wenner-Gren Foundation (Grant-in-Aid #4012), Illinois State University, and the Andrew W. Mellon Foundation and Roger Thayer Stone Center for Latin American Studies at Tulane University. The assistance and cooperation of Donald Brand, James Cameron, and Dorothy Keur; Anibal Rodriguez of the American Museum of Natural History; C. Randall Morrison of the Bureau of Indian Affairs; William Grewe-Mullins and Janet Miller of the Field Museum of Natural History; Thomas Niehaus and Ruth Olivera of the Latin American Library at Tulane; Jerry Brody and Marian Rodee of the Maxwell Museum of Anthropology; E. Wyllys Andrews V of the Middle American Research Institute at Tulane; Nancy Henry and Brenda Holland of the Museum of the American Indian-Heye Foundation; James Glenn of the National Anthropological Archives; Rosemary Joyce of the Peabody Museum at Harvard; Frederick Matson and Sharon Yorke of the Pennsylvania State University; Dwight Drager and James Ebert, formerly of the Remote Sensing Center at the University of New Mexico; Donald Ortner of the Smithsonian Institution; and Gloria Fenner and Susan Harris of the Western Archaeological Research Center are gratefully acknowledged. The reproductions of Pepper's drawings were made by Bonnie Lauber-Westover. Any errors of fact or interpretation are the sole responsibility of the author.

5

The History of Archaeology and the Liberal Arts Curriculum

Susan J. Bender

My purpose here is to review the role of the history of archaeology in the liberal arts curriculum. I approach this task by first assessing the place of archaeology in the disciplinary hierarchy of a typical liberal arts college. Archaeology—when it is represented at all in the liberal arts curriculum—is generally viewed as marginal to the major social sciences. Furthermore, when archaeologists are represented on the liberal arts faculty, they are used as Jacks-and-Janes-of-many-trades and have little opportunity to teach courses in their discipline's history. However, by sharing my own experience of integrating the history of archaeology into a core, interdisciplinary liberal arts curriculum, I hope to demonstrate that a broad perspective on our discipline's history can yield exciting and innovative scholarly experiences for professor and student alike. Moreover, such a perspective moves the history of archaeology from a minor upper-level course to the center of a required curriculum.

In the typical liberal arts college, archaeology is a small component in the overall educational scheme; it is but one of anthropology's three major subdisciplines, while anthropology programs are frequently embedded in two- or three-discipline departments. In a survey of anthropology programs at liberal arts colleges listed in the 1986–1987 American Anthropological Association *Guide to Departments,* I found that 27 of 45 anthropology programs, or 60%, are located in combined departments, typically departments of sociology and anthropology. Clearly the disciplinary commonalities in such departments favors the presence of cultural anthropologists over archaeologists, and in fact I found that, although the number of anthropologists within these departments ranges as high as nine, in no instance does the number of archaeologists exceed two. Similarly, the number of anthropologists within these combined departments averages between three and four, yet the majority of these departments (60%) have no archaeologists at all on their faculty. Only four, or 15%, of the departments include the maximum of two archaeologists.

In independent departments of anthropology, archaeology is represented more evenly but still on a very small scale: 72% (or 13) of the departments include one archaeologist, while 23% still have no clear archaeological component. The remainder of the departments have two archaeologists on their faculty. These numbers bear witness to the small role that archaeology plays in the typical liberal arts curriculum. Trained archaeologists are rare birds in these settings, and typically they are required to offer a wide range of courses, including overlapping areas of bioanthropology, such as human evolution or human osteology.

At the risk of being somewhat parochial, I offer my own educational experiences as an example of what one might encounter archaeologically in a liberal arts setting. I received my undergraduate education at a small, eastern women's college. Here I encountered but one anthropologist, who was interested in occult phenomena. Because I was not, our paths never crossed, and my education in anthropology was confined to my experiences as a special returning student and later to formalized graduate studies. After receiving my Ph.D., I returned to the liberal arts educational setting as an assistant professor at Skidmore College. Here I am responsible for offering nine different courses, including three that are decidedly bioanthropological. Although I have had an abiding interest in the history of archaeology since first reading Glyn Daniel's *Idea of Prehistory* (1962) in graduate school, it seemed then that there would be little opportunity to bring that interest into my scholarly career.

My personal experience and the data gleaned from my brief survey beg the question: where can the history of archaeology—traditionally a minor area of inquiry within archaeology—fit into a curriculum that is so narrowly proscribed by faculty size and teaching load? The answer, I believe, lies in developing a perspective on the history of archaeology that ranges outside the confines of our own disciplinary perspective. As professional archaeologists, we are interested in the history of archaeology as it provides us with an understanding of our intellectual roots. Historical inquiry supplies a necessary perspective on the contextual development of methodological and theoretical positions that impinge directly on our research (see chapters 1–3). Such an endeavor has intrinsic merit to the trained professional, but it is certainly not at the core of the teaching needs of a liberal arts institution. With the introduction of core curricula, however, liberal arts colleges are increasingly defining educational goals that can clearly include components of the history of archaeology.

Typically such curricula proceed from an interdisciplinary perspective and are meant to address broad epistemological concerns while encouraging critical thought. Among the big questions asked by these curricula: How are intellectual traditions established and how do they change? How do these traditions shape what we consider to be the "truth" about the world? The emphasis is on the process of the acquisition of knowledge, rather than on the content of any one specific discipline. Abstracted from its specific content, the history of archaeology addresses just such epistemological questions. Archaeology is a means of knowing about the past; its methods and theories provide us with specific pathways to knowledge about past human activity. In fact, as Grayson (1986) points out, archaeologists have a long history of considering the all-important epistemological question, Do we actually know what we think we know? The radical changes in our thought about the human past over the past 150 years provide an elegant example of the process of scientific revolution (Kuhn 1962), in which intellectual traditions are shaped and reshaped and the truth, in our case about the human past, can be seen as a somewhat elusive commodity.

Skidmore College's own particular version of a core curriculum encourages faculty to focus courses on an area of inquiry and to bring the understandings of a number of different disciplines to bear on the relevant questions. The purpose is to bring different ways of knowing to the same subject. The truth about any one topic may not lie within the methodological or theoretical confines of a single discipline; rather the various disciplines offer us sometimes-competing and sometimes-complementary perspectives on knowledge. This particular perspective is one that has an air of eerie familiarity for anthropologists, who find themselves consistently confronted with competing modes for interpreting human variation. Humanism and science, past and present—each has a place within our discipline, while the discipline continues to wrestle with the problem of maintaining our seemingly evermore-elusive strands of commonality. Thus, it seems that my disciplinary training suited me well for participation in the core curriculum.

The four major sections of Skidmore's core curriculum are defined around various areas of inquiry. One section, "Science, Society and Human Values," seems ideal for considering the lessons of archaeology's past. Courses in this section of the curriculum are charged to "examine the interaction between scientific inquiry and the society in which such inquiry occurs, exploring ways in which the two are mutually determinative and are constitutive of human values. While the emphasis should be upon theoretical developments in the sciences, relevant technological advances may also be considered as they shape and are shaped by theoretical inquiry" (Skidmore Liberal Studies Committee 1984:5). What subject can better reflect the interplay between larger sociocultural values and scientific inquiry than archaeology's history? Inquiry into the human past has always trod on sensitive sociocultural ground. Such inquiry necessarily carries with it assumptions about the nature of humans, their cultural activities, and their relationships to the natural world. As Fowler has so aptly noted, "Interpretations, or uses of the past are seldom value neutral" (1987:241).

Other guidelines for courses in the "Sciences, Society and Human Values" section of Skidmore's core curriculum seem also to define the experience of archaeology's history. These courses are further asked to "begin from a specific concept, idea or theory within the natural sciences or mathematics. They then should develop the impact of science on society and/or the ways in which cultural assumptions and social institutions shape the questions asked by scientists and the answers that are perceived or permitted. Courses may relate changes to a sweep of historical changes in a cultural tradition" (Skidmore Liberal Studies Committee 1984:5). Once again, archaeology's history, the history of the idea and understanding of prehistory, seems particularly well suited to this framework for inquiry. Our current understanding of the past is built upon radical changes in the concept of what it means to be human, engendered in the intellectual and social revolutions of the Victorian era. Notions of the mutability of the human form and culture were hard won intellectual revelations. The concern uttered by one oft-quoted Victorian lady, "Those awful monkeys! My dear, let us hope that it is not true, but if it is, let us pray that it will not become generally known" (Campbell 1985:18), is no longer at the core of research into the human past, although it was once a pressing issue that had to be met head-on by nineteenth-century scholars. That our understanding of the human past has moved from the realm of biblical interpretation to scientific pursuit has everything to do with changes in the Western intellectual tradition, where empirical research wedded to technology has become our primary means of knowing.

Finally, that our inquiry into the human past has been and is a fundamentally interdisciplinary enterprise is amply attested to in the literature. Grayson (1983) has pointed out that establishment of the fact of human antiquity is the result of the work of natural historians, while interdisciplinary research continues to set the standard for data acquisition and analysis in archaeology today. Convinced then of the close fit between the nature of archaeology's history and the fundamental goals of Skidmore's core, interdisciplinary curriculum, I seized upon the opportunity to construct a course about the discovery of the human past that would be at the heart of my college's educational goals.

The result of my endeavors is the course "Discovery of the Human Past," which is structured not only to teach archaeology's history but to create an understanding of that history in a wider sociocultural context. I want students to understand that the history of archaeology is driven by internal and external developments. Hence I begin the course from a comparative perspective in which we consider how a culture's worldview can dictate what is possible to learn about the human past.

The particular examples that I settled upon are drawn from Aztec (Fagan 1984a), ancient Greek (Wace 1949), and eighteenth-century European cultures (Goguet 1761). The concepts of time and of the past are markedly different in each of the three examples, yet all share in a worldview that essentially mitigates against reconstruction of the human past through archaeological activity.

These perspectives on the past are then contrasted with that expressed in Carl Sagan's *Dragons of Eden* (1977:15–17). This model, of course, presents the prehistory of the earth and its human inhabitants as scientifically datable, knowable, and almost incomprehensibly ancient. At the same time, I try to get students to articulate their own expectations of the human past. Here we find that, although their views are somewhat more anthropocentric than those expressed by Sagan, they share with him the wider conviction of the length and accessibility of the human past. Finally, we consider links between Goguet's (1761) eighteenth-century concept of the past and our own. Here I direct students toward an understanding of the linear, developmental concept of the past that is very much a part of our intellectual tradition. While students typically begin with the statement "Yes, but there are no other ways of looking at the past," they end by being able to articulate other perspectives on time and the past. They, of course, retain their conviction of the rightness of their own perspective—how could we come up with anything better? For many students, this portion of the course is the most illuminating. Comments on course evaluations reflect that they have never before entertained notions of the mutability of our ideas about the past. The Aztecs—as always—catch their imagination and make them entertain new perspectives.

Having established that, in our own intellectual tradition, study of the human past lies squarely within the province of science, I next move students toward an understanding that specific scientific traditions incorporate and propagate particular worldviews. Kuhn's observation that in science "what a man sees depends upon what he looks at and also upon what his previous visual-conceptual experience has taught him to see" (1962:113) is at the heart of our concern. This perspective considers differences in archaeological and antiquarian approaches to the past (after Daniel 1981c). Such considerations pursue differing sources of information, models of interpretation, and results of study. In other words, the two types of "normal science" are compared, if antiquarianism can indeed be termed a science. Students are then poised to consider the nature and content of the scientific revolution that led to the archaeological paradigm for study of the human past. Although I anticipated some degree of difficulty in the use of Thomas Kuhn's work, I have found that students are able to extract useful and instructive heuristic principles from it as they examine the content of the nineteenth-century scientific revolution in the study of human antiquity. If I have erred in this section of the course, it is in assigning too little of Kuhn's work—emphasizing the role of revolutionary over normal science. In course evaluations, a surprising number of students comment upon the usefulness of their exposure to Kuhn's ideas.

The next section of the course studies how and why our Western intellectual tradition generated the model of human antiquity that permeates our thought today. Donald Grayson's book *The Establishment of Human Antiquity* (1983) forms the core reading for this section, and I have found it to be a superb instructional tool, despite my initial reservations about the level of its erudition for an undergraduate course. What is most remarkable about this book is the sense of drama that it creates in following the outlines of a building scientific revolution. Students actually become offended at the resistance of established French scientists to publishing, let alone debating, challenges to Cuvier's geology. As evidence mounts, and resistance to the claims of Boucher de Perthes begins to crumble, there is a palpable sense of triumph in the classroom. In this text, students are led through a scientific revolution, seeing how anomalies or challenges to normal science are initially dispatched, yet continual observation and accumulation of anomalous evidence requires an eventual reshaping of the interpretive paradigm. The fact of human antiquity is established.

The remainder of the course centers upon the impact of this new perspective on the human past, the archaeological pursuit. We initially consider why natural historians, and not archaeologists' predecessors, the antiquarians, discovered human antiquity. Students come to see that there was nothing in the inventory of antiquarian field and analytical methods that would ever lift the "thick fog" over human antiquity bemoaned by Rasmus Nyerup in 1806 (Daniel 1981c:56). Hence the founding of true archaeological research depended heavily upon techniques borrowed from uniformitarian geology and upon structuring concepts borrowed from the emergent field of evolutionary biology (Kennedy 1985). Clearly with such influences, the primary structuring questions under the new paradigm of the past would have to be concerned with chronology—a chronology that at first appeared more geological than prehistorical as human prehistory was ordered into "epochs" under the influence of Gabriel de Mortillet (Daniel 1981c:103).

We then study the ways in which early archaeologists began to "own" their own territory by developing dating and field techniques and principles of interpretation that were specific to their own data base, archaeological remains, while retaining the imprint of natural science. In this section of the course, I use Glyn Daniel's *Short History of Archaeology* (1981c) as a primary text with mixed success. While the interpretive sections of this volume contain some important and illuminating heuristic themes, they are not as deeply developed as I would like, and Daniel's discussion of the historical development of inquiry in particular culture areas does not fit my purposes well. What does work in this section of the course are biographies and primary sources reprinted in Heizer (1969). Through these texts students are able to identify changing questions, concerns, and methods of investigation while they become aware of many of the interesting personages of early archaeological research. Figures like Schliemann and Arthur Evans are not only enormously engaging, but they also illustrate well developments in archaeological research. Selections from Fagan (1978) and Daniel (1967) add much to our discussions in this section of the course as well. Imagine the consternation of my female students as they read of the English scholars' debates during the early twentieth century about whether women could or should participate in fieldwork (Daniel 1967:222–224,

237–238). Here again they are confronted with the social dimensions of scholarly inquiry.

I then take students through parallel and related developments in paleoanthroplogy. We look at the prerevolution and postrevolution interpretations of human fossil remains and at the impact of developing chronologies on our interpretations of the origin of humanity. I use this section to drive home the point that technological innovation—in chronometric dating techniques particularly—has everything to do with our current understanding of the human past. At this point I bring students back to Carl Sagan's model of the human past, emphasizing now the genesis of those exact knowable dates and events he so confidently places before us. Using a popular journal article (Judson 1984), I also attempt to get students to articulate the paradigm for inquiry under which we now operate, the paradigm that produced Sagan's model. I want them to recognize that we now trust that the truth about the human past can be learned through rational empirical science, illuminated in particular by sophisticated technological applications.

Finally then, we consider the question, Is our scientifically based understanding of the human past free of bias? One way to approach the question is to discuss articles by Kehoe (1985) on creationism and Fagan (1978) on Chinese archaeology, both of which deal with culturally based sources of bias in current interpretations of the human past. A second way to approach the question is to analyze a student-conducted survey of popular knowledge about the past. In both cases we center our discussion on the social context of knowledge, considering the interplay between the scientific pursuit and the "truths" we believe. Fowler's (1987) article on uses of the past will become required reading for this section of the course in future offerings. Hence we end the course in the modern era with a model of the human past in which we place much confidence, yet we recognize that that model of the past is far from reified.

The course I have described represents a first iteration in a continuing process. As always, certain areas of the course still require improvement. Foremost among my concerns is that the course in its present state has a decidely Eurocentric perspective. In it I deal only minimally with developments in American archaeology—a shortcoming that is largely in response to the appropriate and available texts. For example, one of my chief concerns is the use of primary texts for sources of information. Heizer's *Man's Discovery of His Past* (1969) provides an accessible and pertinent set of readings, but these readings center on developments in Old World archaeology. Finding no equivalent source for primary texts in American archaeology, I have allowed the course to focus on European developments. In the next version of the course, I do want to integrate archaeological developments in the New World more effectively, although I have not yet settled upon the appropriate means for doing so.

The course would also benefit from a more in-depth discussion of current developments in archaeology, emphasizing a move from cultural-historical to processual models of interpretation. Once again, the difficulty in finding suitable readings that concisely articulate recent trends in the discipline have constrained this element of the course. Much of the available literature is simply too specialized to be read and understood by beginning undergraduates. The change in interpretive model is, however, an important consideration for a course such as this because it clearly reflects the process of the conduct of science, which is after all the core consideration of the course.

I must confess that, despite such shortcomings, I review this course with some satisfaction. That processes of critical thought have been encouraged is attested to by some of the more exemplary written work that I have received. While learning a great deal about the history of archaeology, students must also come to grips with the process of the acquisition of scientific knowledge, including its glories and its pitfalls. In addition, I credit this course with success on another level; through its development, I have been able to teach a course in the history of archaeology as a part of Skidmore's core curriculum. The history of our discipline became the vehicle for entertaining critical epistemological questions, while moving the subject matter from a marginal to a central element in a liberal arts curriculum.

6

Contacting the
Theoretical Archaeologists

Lester Embree

Since 1978 I have been reflecting upon a tradition in contemporary science that I call American theoretical archaeology. This is part of a more general project in the phenomenological philosophy of the human sciences. Enough has been accomplished that a brief reflection on the goals and methods of the research is possible. Such a reflection will facilitate further efforts within the project and may be of interest to those who reflect on archaeology for other purposes.

Human Scientific Research on a Human Science

In 1978 I decided·to research empirically a tradition in American archaeology. The philosophical rationale for this decision and some autobiographical remarks are offered here. A member of a humanities discipline, I was originally inclined to look down from my library window at people who seem to like manual labor in the hot sun, but vicarious participation in my former wife's doctoral training led me to a profound respect for archaeology's attempt to use nonverbal remains as a basis for knowledge of how human life works. Who would have thought a philosopher would consider attending an archaeological field school like Grasshopper Pueblo?

What Is American Theoretical Archaeology?

Once intrigued by archaeology, I was attracted to a vociferous activity that called itself the "new archaeology." This development was especially interesting for a history-oriented philosopher of human science who, like everyone else at that time, was fascinated with Thomas Kuhn's (1962) approach to natural science. The new archaeologists of the 1960s published manifestos and polemics, looked to other disciplines—philosophy of science included—for ideas, and soon thought they had made a revolution. Moreover, these were contemporaries who could be contacted in person, over the telephone, or by mail.

I sought contact with what is best called a *scientific tradition*. Calling it a tradition rather than a community or even an "invisible college," appropriately emphasizes the diachronic aspect. My interest is not in what was happening at any given time, but in how aims, ideas, and methods stayed the same or changed. Initially it seemed that there might be two or three dozen new archaeologists, chiefly Lewis Binford and his friends, and a few hundred publications from a period of about 15 years; but gradually it became clear that there were at least 150 people actively so oriented in the early 1980s and thousands of publications from a period of about 35 years. The size of the developed tradition was not unanticipated because it has been suggested that natural science communities contain about 100 people (Kuhn 1977:297; cf. Price 1986:64, 119–134). Still the task was like identifying a dialect within a language. Some definitely belonged, others definitely did not, but many were somewhere in between. In order to identify members of this group, I first used so-called snowball sampling. By this technique, people who surely belong to the group are asked who else does; those who accept "nomination" are added to the list and the process is repeated. By this means, I developed a list of 48 members. A large proportion of the names on my list were labeled in the *Guide to Departments of Anthropology* of the American Anthropological Association (which includes Canadians) as specializing in "theory," "methods," or "method and theory." The last label has been especially important for members of the tradition. In 1985 I made another list of those persons who were thus labeled in the 1984–1985 *Guide*. I sent a questionnaire to these 428 archaeologists that included a list of all the other recipients.

Despite prodding, the response rate was disappointing: 46 questionnaires were returned and some were incomplete. The effort was not abandoned, however, because those who did respond represented all major doctoral programs, all generations (including most of the "elders" of the tradition), and most of the prominent archaeologists. The collective advice, as it were, was accepted from the respondents by subtracting the number of assertions that a person was not in method and theory from the combined number of other responses to whether a person worked (1) more in method, (2) more in theory, or (3) in both. When the 428 entries were ranked there was no sharp cutoff, but practically everybody that I had any reason to suspect belonged to the tradition was in the top 25%. Just to be sure, the top 33% of the list was retained, yielding 142 archaeologists.

Subsequently, this list was sent back to the 142 archaeologists along with a fulsome discussion of the present state of the research. None have complained of the company in which they have been placed, many have responded who had not done so before, and membership for two additional people has been argued for persuasively. Probably a few, nevertheless, do not belong on this list, but there are also probably a few that have been overlooked. To avoid a false sense of exactness, it is best to speak in estimative terms of about 150 active people. In addition, there may be as many as 450 more in North America who sympathize with the general orientation of theoretical archaeology but are not particularly active in research and publication. If so, there may be as many as 600 American theoretical archaeologists. Yet that would be but a fraction of a discipline that claims perhaps 5,000 members in the early 1980s. There is some reason to believe that this is the leading tradition within the discipline.

A tradition needs a name as well as a membership. Because the expression *new archaeology* has always been regarded ambivalently from within as well as without, an alternative expression, *theoretical archaeology,* has been suggested and seems to be finding some acceptance. The new archaeology is usually considered to have begun in 1962 with Lewis Binford's "Archaeology as Anthropology," but if one lists theoretical archaeologists by the year they obtained their doctoral degree, then it is quickly apparent that the beginning of theoretical archaeology needs to be taken back at least another decade to about 1950. The eight "elders" of the tradition are Paul Martin (Chicago 1929), Irving Rouse (Yale 1938), Gordon Willey (Columbia 1942), Robert Braidwood (Chicago 1942), Walter Taylor (Harvard 1943), Albert Spaulding (Columbia 1948), Richard MacNeish (Chicago 1949), and Betty Meggers (Columbia 1952).

In addition to the 8 elders mentioned, 5 more theoretical archaeologists on the list received their degrees in the late 1950s, 40 in the 1960s, and 70 in the 1970s; estimates for the early 1980s are less definite because it takes time for an individual to be recognized. Table 6-1 lists the theoretical archaeologists who received their Ph.D.'s between 1956 and 1980 by year and by university.

The universities from which the American theoretical archaeologists have most frequently come are, in the order in which they became productive, the University of Chicago, Harvard University, the University of Michigan, Yale University, the University of Arizona, and the University of California at Los Angeles (UCLA). Most of these remain strong programs for the general orientation, and now there are also concentrations of theoretical archaeologists at Arizona State University, the State University of New York at Binghamton, Southern Illinois University at Carbondale, the University of Massachusetts at Amherst, Northwestern University, the University of California at Santa Barbara (UCSB), and Southern Methodist University (SMU).

Theoretical archaeology is not a monolith. Not only have there been controversies within it but individual differences in interest and emphasis have naturally changed over the years. It is likely that there are subgroupings or subtraditions that further research would be able to identify. Archaeologists can be sorted according to the programs from which they received graduate training, the area of the world in which they do field work, and the theoretical problems on which they work; but whether these principles will make the inner dynamics of the tradition intelligible remains to be seen.

All theoretical archaeologists seem to share (1) the goal of explaining how collective human life works and how changes occur through time and (2) the strong tendency to separate discussions of theories from discussions of data that might support or undermine them. This tradition shares with archaeologists of other traditions the hope that knowledge will be gained through observation of remains found in or on the earth.

Studying American Theoretical Archaeology

Because practically all members of the tradition under consideration are alive, it is possible to use methods of data collection that are not available to researchers of the past who are limited to reading texts and interpreting pictures. Nevertheless, my chief method remains textual interpretation of publications. There seems nothing remarkable about the technique employed here, although if one is accustomed to working with a single author, one must struggle to follow what interrelating participants in a tradition are thinking over the course of time.

I have secured the curriculum vitae of each theoretical archaeologist, and on this basis, I am developing a chronological-alphabetical bibliography that will contain well over 2,000 entries. When complete, this mode of arrangement will help clarify just what happened before, along with, or after what. Also from this source, charts and lists can be constructed that disclose patterns of Ph.D. production, institutional affiliations, areas of specialization, funding patterns, preferred publication outlets, and so on. Containing as it does a disciplined selection of relevant information, the curriculum vitae is a very interesting document. Having studied hundreds of them, I urge historians to reconstruct curricula vitae for people from whom they cannot be obtained directly.

Furthermore, I have sent out several questionnaires. The questions were in part solicited from and drafts "test marketed" on selected informants, and the results were fed back to the people approached either directly or through publications—the reactions to results sometimes being more valuable than the original responses.

In addition, I have begun formal interviewing of some informants and I hope to contact eventually about 20% of the group. Leaders have proven quite cooperative, as have more junior people. These interviews cover the individual's careers, usually guided by their curricula vitae and include the question of what they would like to research if there were no problems with funding (i.e., their dream project). One of the goals of interviewing is to establish enough social relationship with the informant that follow-up contacts over the telephone are fruitful.

Finally, I have visited some archaeologists in the field, at their institutions, at conferences, and in classes—always an interesting "ethnographic" experience because I am an outsider who in these situations does not enjoy the status I hold in my own discipline. Informants sometimes have difficulty relating to a philosopher who asks odd questions and who sometimes seems insightful but more often seems terribly ignorant.

TABLE 6-1. Theoretical Archaeologists: Who Came from Which University When?

	Chicago	Harvard	Michigan	Yale	Arizona	UCLA	Other Universities
1956	R.McC. Adams						
1957		Sanders					
1958							
1959	Watson						South (N. Carolina)/ Tolstoy (Columbia)
1960		Chang Deetz					Berger (Illinois)
1961							
1962							Dummond (Oregon)
1963	Longacre	R. E. W. Adams Cowgill					
1964	Flannery		Binford	Trigger			G. Bass (Pennsylvania)
1965	J. Brown J. Hill	Sackett					Gould (UCB)
1966	Klein Whallon		Cleland Parsons	Lipe v.d. Merwe Dunnell			Tringham (Edinburgh)
1967	Wright	Muller			Dean Wilmsen		
1968	Struever	Moseley	Ford		Gumerman Leone		Armelagos (Colorado)/ Benfer (Texas)
1969	F. Plog	Sabloff		Voorhies			Bryant (Texas)/ Issac (Cambridge)/ Price (Columbia)
1970	Gladfelter		Blanton Saxe			D. Read R. Taylor	

Year							
1971	G. Clark Redman	Rathje	Speth Wobst		Zubrow		LeBlanc (Washington U)/ Matson (UCD)/ O'Connell (UCB)/ D. Thomas (UCD)
1972	Buikstra		G. Johnson			Glassow	Ammerman (London)/ Casteel (UCD)/ Cordell (UCSB)/ DeBoer (UCB)/ Hardesty (Oregon)/ Nance (Simon Fraser)/ Washburn (Columbia)
1973			Earle B. Smith	Yoffee	Reid Schiffer	Hietala	Grayson (Oregon)/ Hassan (SMU)/ Madsen (Missouri)
1974	Fritz	A. Gilman/ Kohl/ Marcus/ Yellen		Stark			Bettinger (UCR)/ Bonnichsen (Alberta)/ Gunn (Pittsburgh)/ Marquardt (Washington U)/ Peebles (UCSB)/ Sheets (Pennsylvania)
1975			Drennan Jochim				Tainter (Northwestern)/ Trinkhaus (Pennsylvania)/ Vierra (New Mexico)
1976		Freidel	Brumfiel		Kowalewski Raab		Goldstein (Northwestern)/ Goodyear (Arizona State)/ Hayden (Toronto)/ Perlman (U Mass)/ Reidhead (Indiana)
1977		Odell	Braun S. Plog		Eighmy Wilcox		Aldenderfer (Penn State)/ Gifford-Gonzales (UCB)/ Roosevelt (Columbia)
1978	Conkey						O'Shea (Cambridge)/ Pokotylo (British Columbia)
1979			Carr Keene Kus				Haas (Columbia)/ Upham (Arizona State)
1980			Steponaitis			DeAtley	Feinman (CUNY)/ Kent (Washington State)/ Paynter (U Mass)

Note: UCR, University of California, Riverside; UCB, University of California, Berkeley; UCD, University of California Davis; UCSB, University of California, Santa Barbara; SMU, Southern Methodist University; CUNY, City University of New York.

Such contact with theoretical archaeology is not the same as being trained in archaeology, but it does produce an invaluable background familiarity beyond what the mere reading of publications can bring. One thing that has become quite clear is that archaeologists are trained to focus their attention on current issues and, hence, are disinclined to ponder the development of their own tradition. That attitude probably best serves the goals of science. It also shows a major difference between archaeological research and my research on archaeology.

All groups tell stories about their past and one ignores legend at one's peril. In-house historiography of archaeology is more reliable than folklore, but it is still produced from an archaeological point of view. From a standpoint outside the discipline, things can look somewhat different. These differences are partly due to research interest, but ultimately it is all a question of how adequately the relevant data are collected and analyzed. Not only the prescientific lore but also the archaeological historiography of theoretical archaeology are data for the present philosophically motivated historical research on theoretical archaeology.

One result of my work is a tentative descriptive model (Embree 1988) documented chiefly from questionnaire responses of the structure of cognitive activities that make up the scientific endeavor called American theoretical archaeology. For theoretical archaeologists the "methodologies" for the collection of archaeological data and their analysis in the laboratory and on the computer are determined by the explanatory models or theories that these data would support or undermine. As some say, theory drives method. Observation and analysis of data and the building of explanatory models together make up what I call *substantive research* and are what most theoretical archaeologists are chiefly engaged in.

Theoretical archaeologists sometimes engage, however, in various sorts of reflection upon the archaeological endeavor. Besides the expected reflection on the new methodologies and equipment for data collection and analysis, some have attempted to model archaeological explanation formally, others have written textbooks, still others have engaged in polemics, some have offered programmatic manifestos, and still others have written chronicles and histories. Such reflection upon aspects of substantive research by archaeologists can be called *metaarchaeology*.

In a signification of the term different from that used in theoretical archaeology, a philosopher can consider metaarchaeology "methodology" and find it immediately interesting (Embree 1980). But once the different sorts of research within theoretical archaeology are sorted out, it is clear that substantive research is more important. This is because substantive research can proceed without metaarchaeology (but the contrary is hardly the case) and because if metaarchaeology is done for archaeological purposes, which it seems to be, it is substantive research that reveals whether such secondary reflection has had an impact. Finally, *philosophy of archaeology* is different from archaeology, metaarchaeology included, if only because it is conducted from an outsider's standpoint and for ultimately nonarchaeological purposes. This will be readdressed at the end of the essay.

Some more general comments about the approach of this research may be of interest. While some of the methods, for example, using questionnaires and interviewing, derive from the social sciences and while social relations among the theoretical archaeologists are not ignored, the aim is not merely sociological if only because I seek a *diachronic* account of how theoretical archaeology has worked and changed during some 30 years. It is an account that distinguishes tendencies (or subtraditions), phases, and also relations of influence. The tradition is approached not only from its beginning and working forward but also from a "present" in the early 1980s and working backward. Perhaps "sociohistorical" is a good characterization of the research.

Theoretical archaeology seeks accounts that are nomothetic, and I am in favor of using such accounts in the historical sciences. I am conducting parallel research into a tradition that calls itself "cognitive anthropology," and I plan to look at the so-called new history to see why theoretical archaeologists have not been much interested in it. If I were a historian of science, I might attempt a nomothetical model of postwar American human science in general, its developmental pattern and social condition (e.g., Mullins and Mullins 1973; Murray 1983), but my work on the theoretical archaeologists is *idiographic;* I am interested in one unique scientific tradition.

If a sociology of science focuses on scientists as human beings, the present research is again not sociology because the concern is focused on how scientific activities relate to scientific objects. On the other hand, it is not the history of ideas because it is concerned not only with ideas but also with real objects, such as potsherds, and how they present themselves to scientific groups. In view of this concern with scientific activities as they relate to real as well as ideal objects and with such objects as they present themselves to scientists, the approach can be considered phenomenological (Embree 1981).

Science is approached as something that is done by *groups*. This should already be evident in the above discussion of the scientific tradition as a unit of analysis somewhere between the individual scientist and the entire scientific discipline. No doubt a psychology of the typical theoretical archaeologist could be developed just as biographies could be written. Despite some evident personality influences, the need for such considerations has thus far not emerged. Nevertheless, there is an alternation between researching the contributions of individuals and researching the larger tradition to which they belong.

Finally, the research is chiefly *internalist*. This approach can work when the focus is on intellectual activity and its goals and when intentional analysis has priority over causal analysis—which is not to say that science is an activity not performed by humans or that it goes on without a context.

There is interest in external factors, such as institutional contexts, when they exceptionally facilitate or impede research (e.g., the productivity of archaeologists at the Museum of Anthropology at the University of Michigan is aided by an enviable institutional matrix as well as by a fine mix of talent). Likewise, while much personal information is picked up willy-nilly about personal relations, rivalries, love affairs, and so on, these are also only relevant when they help or hinder research in significant ways.

At times I have been concerned about results of my research influencing theoretical archaeology. Many philosophers of science practice a sort of "missionary approach" that includes preaching to scientists, especially if they are not themselves natural scientists, about how they ought to think. I advocate a more *ethnographic* approach in which scientific traditions are investigated to find out concretely how science is actually done. Nevertheless, I have proposed new expressions (such as theoretical archaeology, metaarchaeology, and substantive research), attempted to identify the tradition's beginning, circulated lists of apparent members, and so on. Ultimately it is for the theoretical archaeologists to decide whether to pay any attention to suggestions from an outsider. Natives have been known to exploit their ethnographers. My responsibility is to philosophy.

In sum, I approach the contemporary scientific tradition called American theoretical archaeology using social-scientific as well as historiographic methods to produce a narrative of how science was done by a group that grew from about 8 to about 150 during some 30 years. The result will be called *The Rise of American Theoretical Archaeology.*

Philosophical Purposes

The preceding exposition shows that various sorts of data and various perspectives on them have been selected to the disregard of others. Especially if one is engaged in research where there are no clear exemplars to emulate, it seems wise to be conscious of such decisions. Furthermore, one can attempt to state the reasons for such decisions. Archaeological history of archaeology seems to have archaeological purposes, that is, to help archaeologists better understand and thereby do what they are doing (see chapters 2–3). My research has philosophical purposes. Some work on the philosophical level is discussed before the rationale of the whole effort is sketched.

Some Philosophical Projects

In terms of the previous discussion of cognitive activities, not only is substantive research more important than metaarchaeology but within substantive research, *observation* is the bottom line. This basis is to be expected in an empirical science and remains the case even if theoretical interests determine which data are gathered and which methods are used to analyze them. Archaeological observation is interesting in more than one way. For one thing, archaeological observation is a mode of historical observation and as such is complex. Four levels of awareness and their objects can be distinguished. Level 4, the awareness of explanatory models, is based upon level 3, the awareness of past lifeways, which is based on level 2, the awareness of past material culture, which itself and all higher awarenesses are based on level 1, the awareness of present remains. In other species of historical awareness, texts and pictures are used in place of physical remains in this scheme.

There seems no difficulty in asserting that the perception of nonverbal remains of level 1 is observation. On the other hand, in level 4, thinking and other sorts of awareness focusing on explanatory models, which are concatenations of concepts or ideas, is not observation. Still, if observation is defined as awareness of particular realities, then the archaeological species of historical awareness as represented by levels 2 and 3 can also be considered observation.

In another essay I attempt to show that the historical awareness of past material culture is learned, in other words, that archaeologists are taught to "see" not only the difference between what are and are not remains but also what the functions of cultural objects in past societies were (Embree 1988). While these processes can be modeled logically, I deny that they are necessarily inferential. Second, I address some problems this process raises for empirical knowledge, in which observation is the bottom line and yet proves to be somewhat historical itself. Perhaps objects can remain the same while presenting themselves differently.

How archaeology relies on the "observation" of remains is even more complex. In a recent paper (Embree 1987b), Gordon Willey's study of settlement patterns in the Virú Valley of Peru was used as a case study for how the observation of remains can not only be performed for a few months in Peru in a direct perceptual way, as well as via aerial photographs, maps, and drawings, but also can be performed from thousands of miles away and for years afterwards at the Smithsonian Institution, using representations of the same sorts. This recourse to indirect awareness is not unlike how astronomers observe stars using mirrors and photographs. And insofar as such archaeological observation is drawn out over considerable periods of time, the stages and aims of its progress may be more easily discerned and understood.

Another and not unrelated project focuses on how scientists can alter their explanatory models during data collection and analysis. This shift would seem especially accessible in archaeology where not only the observation of a single case but also thinking about the explanation of some aspect of human life often go on for years. There may be sufficient documentation for William Sander's work in the Basin of Mexico during the 1960s to use it as a case study in this connection.

Some additional projects of philosophical relevance to the history of theoretical archaeology conceived but not yet developed include the effect of new technology on data collection and analysis, the use of mathematical models and how they have affected the credibility of nomothetic goals and results, the adaptation of theory from other disciplines, the development of subordinate specializations such as ethnoarchaeology and midrange research, and the development of "applied archaeology" that promotes social identity and political aims.

General Philosophical Rationale

The empirical research characterized above is being conducted for philosophical reasons. For most outsiders, philosophy of science is positivist philosophy of the natural sciences or philosophy of the social sciences that at least implicitly advocates that the social sciences ought to imitate the natural sciences and in any case seems chiefly to consist of applied logic. I proceed, however, from a phenomenological position. I consider the human sciences fundamental, and as should be clear, I subscribe to a history-oriented approach. Some explication of these differences is in order, if only to show that there is more than one true approach in the philosophy of science.

A cluster of tendencies now usually called Continental philosophy has been a growing alternative to the prevalent tendencies of Anglo-American philosophy since the 1960s. Phenomenology is the tendency within that cluster that, among other things, did not throw the philosophy of science baby out with the positivistic bath of naturalism and logicism. In the latter respect, Edmund Husserl, the founder of phenomenology, was himself a philosopher of logic and mathematics and also of psychology and physics.

It is not terribly controversial to suggest that philosophy is the pursuit of an integration of epistemological, axiological, and praxiological reason and that epistemology comes first within it because justified valuing and willing are based on justified believing (Cairns 1984). It is not controversial at all to suggest that philosophy of science is the centerpiece of epistemology. The plot thickens when persons contend that the human sciences have a priority over the natural sciences, which are the disciplines that have achieved far more and have been more clearly applicable in changing the world through scientific technology.

The notion that the psychological, social, and historical sciences belong together and can be called the human sciences is within the provenance of Continental philosophy. What human sciences have in common are subject matters that, humans and their groups and institutions included, have *cultural character*. Cultural character includes, most prominently, use or function (Gurwitsch 1974). Thus, for example, the sun is used by all humans to distinguish night and day, morning and afternoon, the seasons, and years; the sun is the original chronometer. If objects are originally encountered with cultural character and if this character must somehow be disregarded in order for a cultural object to become a natural object suitable for natural-scientific investigation and if the order of the sciences derives from the order of their objects, then the human sciences come first.

The difference of the human sciences, phenomenologically considered, has to do with the matters investigated. Human science is scientific in that it is subject to critique and acceptance, modification, or rejection on the basis of publicly accessible data. The difference is not in whether mathematics is or is not used because there are formal and nonformal procedures in both human and natural science. Likewise, both kinds of science can posit in principle unobservable entities. The issues concern instead whether all sciences employ interpretation of texts, whether psychic lives require approaches different from those for physical objects, whether historical observation is significantly different from what physicists do with cloud chambers, but above all whether cultural objects are approached differently than natural objects.

Among the human sciences, the historical sciences seek knowledge of human cultural life that is not merely synchronic but diachronic and that can be nomothetic as well as idiographic. Archaeology differs from the other historical sciences in that it chiefly resorts to data that are neither texts nor pictures but rather physical remains, which gives it access to a larger array of societies and all strata of them, as well as to longer periods of time. These are some of the reasons for beginning with archaeology in the philosophy of science (Embree 1987a).

The emphasis on the history of actual scientific practice more than on the logical reconstruction of idealized scientific results is not, however, peculiarly phenomenological. Since the 1960s and the work of Norwood Russell Hanson and Stephen Toulmin (fueled by an interest in Thomas Kuhn's [1962] approach to the history of the natural sciences), there has been a growing new philosophy of science within the mainstream (Brown 1977). This approach seems not only to want to look beyond form to get at content but especially to look beyond the idealized notions of science found in textbooks to get at how science is actually done, including how it changes. On that basis, philosophers of science better know what they are talking about. For the philosopher of historical human science there is the added benefit in this approach of gaining familiarity with the science being researched through trying one's hand at it.

Philosophical Critique

But is an empirical attempt to know how science is actually done anything more than what historians and sociologists of science seek to do? How is such an effort philosophical? These questions are most easily answered with reference to critique. Already on the level of substantive research, the scientists themselves evaluate research that is projected (e.g., in grant proposals) as well as that being performed. Cases of reports, the bodies of which do not live up to the claims in their introductions, are not unknown. It can also be asked whether the methodology is overengineered or underengineered. In short, *science is inherently normative.*

In the archaeological history of archaeology there is already evaluation in merely the selection of research to be mentioned, and the same goes for other modes of metaarchaeology, including textbook writing. From that point of view, one could ascertain whether an example of research belongs to a scientific tradition, for example theoretical archaeology, and then ask whether the results directly or indirectly relate in an explicit or explicable way to the goal of that tradition, for example describing and explaining how society works and changes over the long run. Yet this would still be archaeological critique.

When the scope is widened beyond the discipline, however, and questions about service to the purposes of human science, science in general, knowledge at large, and, ultimately, wisdom are asked, then the critique is philosophical. Nevertheless, it needs to begin with how science is actually done.

Part II

Contexts of the History of Archaeology

Introduction

There are two aspects of context in the history of archaeology. The first is the sociopolitical context within which archaeology has taken place in the past. The second is the context within which the history of archaeology is written. The first issue has already been touched upon by Chippindale and Bender and the second was mentioned by Sabloff. In this section both of these aspects of context are considered in more detail.

Archaeology, says Hinsley (chapter 7), is narrative—a form of origin myth—and thus the history of archaeology is metanarrative—the story of the storytellers. One aspect of the story is regionalism—distinctive styles of archaeology are produced in different regions, and Hinsley uses the shell-midden work in the eastern United States in the 1860s and 1870s as an example. Another aspect of context is evident at public moments when archaeological finds are first placed before mass audiences. Using examples from *The Illustrated London News*, Hinsley shows how archaeology fits the technological, imperialistic, and male-dominated world of the last half of the nineteenth century. Touching upon an issue raised by several other authors, Hinsley argues that there cannot be distinct internal and external histories of archaeology because there is a constant flow of cause and effect between the internal ideas of the discipline and the society within which it operates.

Kehoe (chapter 8) is also concerned with the contexts of nineteenth-century archaeology, particularly during the 1840s, when European industrial capitalists were trying to legitimize their power. She states that historians of archaeology have generally dated the beginnings of recognizable archaeology to this period, with such persons as J. J. A. Worsaae and E. G. Squier, because this is when ideas such as the three-age system and its notion of progress were first applied by scholars who were members of industrial states. She argues that histories of archaeology have been written by members of the dominant class who see the origin of the discipline in the works of men sharing their own ways of thinking.

Latin American archaeologists have long been interested in the history of the discipline, and they have produced numerous volumes on the topic, most of which are little known. Because archaeology in Latin America often has important political implications and direct meaning to the local inhabitants (Madrid 1986), the influence of sociopolitical factors on archaeology and archaeological interpretation can be clearly seen (a similar situation holds in many other areas of the world, including southern Africa [e.g., Garlake 1982]). Schávelzon (chapter 9) provides a bibliographic overview of historical writings about mesoamerican archaeology from the 1870s to the present. He discusses the goals and approaches of historical studies and how they have shifted from mere compilations of previous work, to judgmental histories that attacked ideas no longer in favor, to more critical but sympathetic histories inclined to judge previous work in its own context. Schávelzon argues that the trend in historical studies must be toward better understanding of and accounting for the important social, political, and economic contexts within which archaeology is done in Mesoamerica.

McVicker (chapter 10) examines the careers of two American archaeologists, Marshall Saville and Frederick Starr, who worked in Mexico at the turn of the century. At that time, the region was considered ideal for collecting antiquities for American museums, and both Saville and Starr avidly-pursued artifacts even as the tide of anthropology was changing. Neither made a lasting impression on the discipline because new trends set by Emil Boas and his students predominated. McVicker shows, however, that Saville's and Starr's archaeological works can be understood by looking at their personal agendas and their institutional contexts, and he suggests that their contributions today rest on the artifacts and the notes they left in museums.

Classical archaeology is the oldest organized subdiscipline of archaeology in the United States, and Dyson (chapter 11) discusses his research on the ideological and institutional factors that have led to what he calls the "intellectual ossification" of the field. He argues that success in classical archaeology is tied to conservative graduate training controlled by a small number of individuals at a few eastern colleges and guided by an ideology that has changed little in the last century. He contrasts this with American prehistoric archaeology, which has been less tightly controlled institutionally and more open to new ideas. Finally, he suggests some fruitful lines of research to study trends in classical archaeology.

One issue touched on briefly by Hinsley and Kehoe is gender and the history of archaeology. I had hoped this topic would be discussed in detail at the conference, but I did not receive a paper on the subject. Only a little has been written about women in archaeology from a historical or a biographical perspective (e.g., Williams 1981), although some recent work may begin to fill this void (e.g., Desmond 1988; Irwin-Williams n.d.).

The presence of women in what Kehoe calls consensus histories of archaeology is small—of 562 individuals whose gender I could determine in the index of Willey and Sabloff (1980), 31 (6%) were female and of 405 individuals in Daniel's (1981c) index, only 12 (3%) were female. These data do not necessarily indicate any gender bias in these volumes because we do not know the actual gender ratio of archaeologists for the times and locations covered. The current proportion of women in archaeology, however, is much higher. According to the 1983–1984 and the 1985–1986 American Anthropological Association *Guide to Departments of Anthropology,* of the recent Ph.D.'s awarded with specialization in archaeology in the United States and Canada about 65% went to men and 35% went to women. Archaeology graduate programs in Europe have a similar or a higher proportion of women (Damm 1986:215). Detailed studies of women in archaeology's past and in the written histories of the discipline are necessary before any bias in the presentation of women can be determined.

Another gender question is who writes the history of archaeology. Here the issue of gender bias is more defined—of 131 articles and books on the history of archaeology listed in the first 10 years (1977–1986) of the *History of Anthropology Newsletter,* only 19 (14%) were written by women (multiple publications by the same author are included in this count). Of the 19 papers presented at the conference from which this volume came, only 2 (11%) were by women. It could be argued that for some reason women are less interested in history than are men, but of the dissertations completed or in progress in 1984 in history departments, 64% were by men, 36% by women—the same gender ratio as for archaeology dissertations. For some reason women in archaeology have chosen not to write about the history of archaeology.

These data do nothing more than raise the issue of who writes and who is included in histories of archaeology. The two issues are related, but I cannot begin to suggest how the presentation of the history of archaeology would change if more women conducted research on the topic.

7

Revising and Revisioning the History of Archaeology: Reflections on Region and Context

C. M. Hinsley

It is impossible to visit the middle Mississippi Valley—near the lands of the village farmers of ancient Cahokia, the historical meanderings of Sieur de Lasalle, and the riparian childhood of Mark Twain and Huck Finn—without being struck by a sense of continuity, process, and flow. In a number of ways during this decade, Americans have attempted a regional return to the middle of America, to the long-term values and longed-for stability associated with F. Scott Fitzgerald's "dark fields of the Republic rolling on under the night." Calvin Trillin, who came from Kansas City, Missouri, once said that many nonnatives thought of the Midwest as that "big space between the coasts." And at a recent conference on regionalism in Chicago, Wilbur Zelinsky, a geographer at Pennsylvania State University, described the Midwest as a region that "starts around Pittsburgh and gets obvious in Ohio."

However partial or whimsical the definitions, it is clear that following the Irish Boston of Kennedy, the hardscrabble southwest Texas of Johnson, the hard-eyed southern California of Nixon, and the odd blend of technocracy and Georgia populism of Carter, we arrived seven years ago back in the midwestern memories of Reagan—hard work, struggle, and lifesaving in the ever-flowing river. As a young summertime lifeguard, Garry Wills tells us in *Reagan's America: Innocents at Home*, the future president saved seventy-seven lives and lost none: perfect, no-loss seasons on the river. By contrast, Samuel Clemens's world of historical, flowing change was anything but a no-loss world. Indeed, American life on the Mississippi to the author of *Innocents Abroad* was marked by darkness, tragedy, and stupidity (Wills 1987).

Regionalism is a slippery concept but an important business, for geographical locus has always been a critical factor in archaeology, and it is equally so in writing the history of archaeology. Archaeology is best understood as narrative, a particular and powerful form of origin myth that began in nineteenth-century Euro-American societies to take on increasing importance as a vehicle of validation for social groups engaged (or enmeshed) in industrial growth, capital accumulation, and colonial expansion (see chapter 8). The social and political primacy of this particular narrative myth is evidenced by the frequency and the public nature of the narration. Beginning with the Paris Anthropological Exposition of 1867 and extending past the First World War, virtually every one of the dozens of industrial and scientific expositions in Europe and the United States displayed the story of human social evolution through archaeological and ethnological artifacts and accompanying text. For the millions who experienced them, these exhibitions functioned ritually as personal exhortations and public palliatives; they were intended as milestones of assurance, marking regional, national, and global progress (Rydell 1984).

The broad narrative myth of archaeology, however, is not and never has been univocal; elaborations and challenges constantly arise, and at times the clamor among professionals and amateurs alike can be deafening. Consequently, the history of archaeology emerges as metanarrative. It is the story of the storytellers, seen in the variety of time, place, method, motive, and both institutional and personal power. In relating the metanarrative of archaeology's history, the conditioning elements surrounding the actors are all-important, for they often determine the variant forms of the story.

Few current histories of archaeology trace the narrative making in such terms. Instead, most still look inward for a logic of progress in data gathering and in theoretical modeling. However one modifies such history—introducing notions of paradigmatic structures, admitting occasional wrong turns or even the exclusive nature of the scientific community under conditions of "normal science"—it still remains essentially Whig history, an Enlightenment legacy that assumes what it purports to illustrate: an upward trajectory toward more accurate, cumulative knowledge. As such it celebrates the generative powers of theory and data, a dialectical process of testing and changing that is presumed to be largely autonomous and self-regulatory.

The result of such a historical approach is characteristically a set of straightforward markers of development: the first uses of "real" stratigraphic method, the first Pecos conference, the discovery of dendrochronology, the application of carbon-14 dating. It also produces periodization schemes that may be intellectual, institutional, or both. In other instances, organic metaphors emerge, and the story of archaeology reads as the biography of a collective organism. Thus, for instance, Glyn Daniel's popular treatment, *A Short History of Archaeology* (1981c), begins with "The Birth of Archaeology" and proceeds through antiquarians, excavators, and explorers to the stage in which "Archaeology Comes of Age (1914–1939)." Just as in certain models of human development the healthy individual grows to maturity defined in terms of autonomous judgment, so the science of archaeology is in this view gradually weaned from various dependencies through growing pains into robust adulthood: reliance on outside disciplinary authorities diminishes, and undisciplined imagination and idiosyncratic methods gradually disappear. Archaeology "is now a respectable and understood branch of historical science (or learning)," Daniel concludes (1981c:195; see Daniel 1967 for a similar metaphor).

Various efforts to "contextualize" archaeology have appeared in reaction to the shortcomings of this historical approach. But here, too, lie dangers. In a recent article "The Last Sixty Years: Toward a Social History of Americanist Archeology in the United States," Thomas Patterson, drawing on the analytical categories of Antonio Gramsci and Nicos Poulantzos, argues that a fracture occurred after 1890 within the politically dominant class in the United States (Patterson 1986). One fraction, dominated by international monopoly and finance capital, he calls the Eastern Establishment; the other, dominated by "national capitalists," is identified as the Core Culture. Patterson reviews the political and economic dynamics of twentieth-century U.S. history, through the New Deal to the post-Vietnam era and attempts to correlate changes in archaeological focus, method, and theory with these elements of the dominant class and the institutions, such as the Carnegie Institution of Washington, the Smithsonian Institution, and the Institute of Andean Research, which served as their agents.

It is a suggestive thesis. "The milieu of archaeologists is neither sanitized nor isolated," Patterson tells us. "Archaeologists participate in the world around them, and, at one level, their participation has little to do with motivation, intention, or will" (Patterson 1986:20). One can hardly disagree: as much is true of most people, including humanists and scientists. The difficulty lies in locating the "level," the region of flow between internal and external, the estuary where outside influences and considerations shape or color the process of archaeology and its results, and occasionally vice versa.

The patterns and attitudes that Patterson attributes to the interests of the twentieth-century Eastern Establishment and Core Culture in actuality have deep and winding roots in American history. Here he describes the Carnegie Institution's work in Central America under Sylvanus Morley and Alfred Kidder:

> The Carnegie archaeological program was not value free and neutral, for it carried a subtle political message to the revolutionary government of Mexico and to the peoples of Central America. By focusing on the Maya, "the most brilliant culture of the pre-Columbian world," the archaeologists were implicitly questioning the unity of the Mexican state and the cultural attainments of the ancient societies of central and northern Mexico—the regions that controlled the modern state. . . . The Carnegie's search separated the modern residents of Central America from their past. The archaeologists saw the

Maya past as a period of brilliance—an era of exotic societies characterized by great achievements [1986:12–13].

It may be that Morley displayed such an attitude toward the Mayan and Mexican cultures, and the Carnegie people may have "separated the modern residents of Central America from their past," thereby creating at least the psychological conditions for further domination and exploitation. But this process was neither new nor peculiar to Central America. John Lloyd Stephens displayed precisely this attitude toward the past and present residents of Central America as early as 1840. Throughout *Incidents of Travel in Central America*, Stephens expressed his dismay that such a lovely country should rest in the hands of incompetent, disorganized, fallen people.

> The city of Copán was buried in forest and entirely hidden from sight. Imagination peopled the quarry with workmen, and laid bare the city to their view. Here, as the sculptor worked, he turned to the theatre of his glory, as the Greek did to the Acropolis at Athens, and dreamed of immortal fame. Little did he imagine that the time would come when his works would perish, his race be extinct, his city a desolation and abode for reptiles, for strangers to gaze and wonder by what race it had once been inhabited [1841:1:146].

Stephens's words illustrate that the ruins of Central America presented an empty stage for the fertile mind of the North American explorer to fill with actors and scenarios. When he wrote of the positive "moral effect" of the monuments, he clearly meant that they were matters worthy of the artistic and imaginative capacities of civilized men, beyond the feeble powers of the poor, degraded peasants. Furthermore, the detachment of the ruins from the current population of the region was prelude to another set of attitudes of considerable import: the observer's own romantic attachment to the archaeological sites and artifacts and the desire to acquire them through purchase, perhaps even ultimately to remove them entirely to a North American or European metropolis.

Describing the House of the Governor at Uxmal, Stephens rhapsodized: "If it stood at this day on its grand artificial terrace in Hyde Park or the Garden of the Tuileries, it would form a new order, I do not say equalling, but not unworthy to stand side by side with the remains of Egyptian, Grecian, and Roman art" [1841:II:429–430]. Stephens expressed here an opinion that had become orthodoxy by the end of the nineteenth century and that had a clear parallel in North American archaeology until the mounds survey by Cyrus Thomas in the 1880s; that is, that "these degraded peoples could not possibly have created such wonders. There must have been a previous, superior race." The belief was central to the cant of imaginative and actual conquest. If it often took the form of acquisitiveness—Stephens did in fact try to buy Copán, Uxmal, and Palenque and thought of moving them to New York—it had nothing to do with monopoly capital.

The Carnegie people had inherited, it seems, a set of assumptions with its own peculiar history: a mixture of romantic imagination, ethnocentrism, and proprietary stewardship.

Jeffries Wyman and New England Regionalism

Where, then, does the historian look for context in archaeology? The multiple social and political contexts of archaeology's history are to be traced within the narrative structures themselves. As amateur enterprise or as professional discipline, archaeology has gone forward in numerous microenvironments of time and place, each producing distinctive inflection and style. This progress is particularly true in the multiregional United States. Because the preeminent geopolitical, economic, and psychological fact of U.S. history has been constant areal expansion of borders and demographic movement, North American archaeology has been especially subject to variation in regional-temporal style. In addition to the fact that North American work, for complex historical reasons, has deep local and regional roots, different parts of the country have come to archaeological attention or prominence at successive stages of national political-economic growth and of professional growth of archaeology. One has only to recall the early attention to the Ohio River valley under conditions of questionable land tenure, national self-definition, and political insecurity, all of which colored interpretations of the Mound Builders; or the boosterism of the Charles Lummis and Edgar Lee Hewett Southwest between 1900 and 1920, which laced the archaeology of the region with anti-Eastern antagonism and simultaneously linked it with commercial exploitation (Hinsley 1986); or the (re-)discovery of the prehistory of the Mississippi River valley, along with Civilian Conservation Corps-style fieldcamps, in the New Deal archaeology of the 1930s. The result, in each case, was an archaeology with distinctive flavor and flourish that is inseparable from, indeed written into, the scientific results themselves.

Consider, for example, Jeffries Wyman, professor of anatomy at Harvard University and curator of the Peabody Museum from its founding in 1866 until his death in 1874. Wyman was an exemplar of the tradition of genteel natural science. There was an apparent randomness, even whimsicality to his work; early promise was followed by wandering. A significant contribution to comparative anatomy appeared in 1847, when Wyman first described the gorilla and offered osteological comparisons between apes and humans. Then, during the 1850s, Wyman seemed to lose focus and scatter his energies over a range of fascinating but seemingly unrelated topics. In 1853, for instance, he offered a paper on the nervous system of frogs; six years later he was examining "some unusual modes of gestation" among Surinam toads. But beneath the random appearance was a consistent set of concerns, a method, and a style. Wyman's natural history was metaphorical and microcosmic, a blend of morality and science. Unconcerned with grand taxonomies or sweeping statements, he resembled most closely a sketch artist, anxious to reproduce the local world faithfully.

The founding of the Peabody Museum coincided with a new trans-atlantic awareness and a renewed emphasis on strict empiricism in American archaeology. Immediate results were limited. Charles Rau (later curator of antiquities at the Smithsonian Institution) regretted that Wyman and others by 1868 had still found no evidence of "high antiquity" in America. "The subject, however, is far from being exhausted, and different results may yet be obtained," he added hopefully, as he encouraged the aging Wyman to look in caves as well as in shell heaps (Rau to Wyman, 11 November 1868, Jeffries Wyman Papers [JWP], Harvard Medical School). The position of the shell-heap archaeologist was indeed uncomfortable, for while some parties hoped for rude antiquity, others longed for signs of lost high civilizations. "The art relics which I found and those which you describe," Daniel Brinton admitted to Wyman, "alike disappoint me in character. The oldest accounts seem to describe tribes of a much higher grade of culture than existing monuments indicate. In the light of modern researches the old chroniclers seem to have colored their pictures rather too highly" (25 October 1868, JWP).

The American enthusiasm for shell heaps after the Civil War now appears to have been the peculiar product of a specific cultural moment (Christenson 1986). It was an innocent yet serious combination of science and picnic, of mundane backyard scrabbling and high aspirations. "Such investigations cannot fail in time to have most important results," Brinton predicted. "American archaeology will in time rank equal with that of Egypt and the Orient" (Brinton to Wyman, 6 April 1868, JWP). "They delight me, these *Chiffonier* [rag-picking] expeditions among the shell heaps of nations almost as it would to dredge the Tiber," Oliver Wendell Holmes wrote with characteristic excess to Wyman (21 October 1868, JWP). More familiarly, the young George Peabody began a letter to Wyman: "My uncle tells me you have been pitching into some clam heaps at Salisbury" (27 May 1867, JWP). S. Weir Mitchell left an engaging image of Wyman in the kitchen middens that captures the spirit of this playful science:

> I had once a like pleasure in raking over an Indian shell-heap with Wyman. The quiet, amused amazement of the native who plied the spade for us was an odd contrast to Wyman's mood of deep interest and serious occupation. He had a boy's pleasure in the quest, and again displayed for me the most ready learning as to everything involved in the search. Bits of bones were named as I would name the letters of the alphabet: bone needles, fragments of pottery and odds and ends of nameless use went with a laugh or some ingenious com-

ment into his little basket. In truth, a walk with Wyman at Mount Desert [Maine] was something to remember [1875 : 356].

Shell-heap archaeology offered an effortless transition from natural history to human prehistory, for the observational skills necessary for analysis, identification, and enumeration of shells and bones of animals, birds, and fish were easily transferred to stone implements or potsherds. Wyman's work in Florida has become classic today for a number of reasons. Wyman paid some attention to stratigraphy. He was a pioneer in distributional analysis of pottery types, noting that the absence of pottery may be as significant as its presence. He subdivided sherds according to paste and surface features and noted their distribution among the various sites. On the basis of repeated visits, Wyman became the first to positively establish the American shell heaps as artificial accretions, and he estimated a minimum age (1,000 years), partly on the basis of dendrochronology, for his St. John's mounds. Furthermore, he surmised that most, if not all, had been completed prior to white contact. While he doubted that the historic Floridian tribes or their direct ancestors had built the shell heaps, he did not claim a great antiquity for the people who did (Wyman 1875).

Wyman established a pattern in his reports that became standard practice. He began with description of natural features, flora, fauna, precipitation patterns, and so forth, then moved to description of sites and the mode of his investigation itself. But to see him only as a precursor of modern archaeological method misses the totality of his science. Wyman does not simply set the ecological stage to introduce his investigation and findings; he invites us to participate in the experience as travelling companions and fellow explorers. The setting is an integral part of this experience. The opening sections of *Fresh-Water Shell Mounds* read as much like a travel book as an archaeological report.

The scenery of the St. John's presents striking contrasts. The first objects which attract the eye of the traveller as he enters its mouth are the waters breaking roughly over the shoals and sand bars; these passed, there opens a dreary view of drifting sands. As he ascends he is impressed with its magnitude, but the low flat pine-clad shores are extremely monotonous. In the upper and narrower portions, especially above Lake George, the scene changes.

Wyman then describes the wildlife of the St. John's, past and present, including

the loathsome buzzard circling at times gracefully among nobler birds, or oftener, and truer to its nature, quarrelling with its kind as it gluts itself over disgusting food; the snake bird of strange make and habits, the fish hawk whose massive nest of sticks and moss crown many a dead and shattered cypress . . . the alligator lazily drifting with the current, or lying in his muddy wallow in the sun, all as they were in the days of the early explorers [1875:5–7].

These passages, written in 1874, represent nineteenth-century nature poetry in flowering. Here Wyman is painting, in graceful phrases, a dynamic and exotic landscape, bidding us to join him in filling in the human details that he has discovered in the shell heaps. "I sometimes think," Wyman confided to Robert C. Winthrop in 1874, ". . . that we should stand in the presence of the more attractive scenes of nature as well as works of art, give our whole souls to them and pass on" (19 February 1874, Peabody Musuem Archives, Harvard University). For Wyman the scientific and artistic landscapes were indistinguishable. The final product was a reconstruction—half art, half science—of prehistoric human ecology. All that is missing from the opening picture is the hand of humanity.

What are we to make of this blend of archaeology and poetry? How are we to evaluate Wyman's artful science?

Wyman was a figure of midcentury New England. What was happening in the middle decades of the nineteenth century—deeply felt in Wyman's New England—was a massive shift of balance in American society, hastened by the machinery of civil war and economic forces suddenly unleashed—a transition to new, more powerful forms of obtaining and utilizing knowledge. The institutionalization of science and the modernization of the American university that took place after the Civil War were analogous to and proceeded in tandem with the development of new corporate forms of American business and finance: the large corporation, the impersonal factory production units, the interlocking directorships, the labor unions, and so forth.

This ambitious, rapid growth of commercial America, however, threatened cherished values, the very ones that Wyman embodied: modesty, quiet virtue, the religious awe of the poet who took nature as he found it, not to exploit but simply to behold. The service of Wyman to American culture, within and beyond archaeology, was to ease the transition from poetry to science, from the tradition of New England natural theology—which had always emphasized attention to detail for moral improvement—to more powerful, secular methods of scientific understanding and control over nature and humanity.

Archaeology in the Public Eye

The popular apprehension of archaeology in the previous century occurred most dramatically at public moments—those points when the archaeologist sought or encountered a public audience. These moments, too, provide critical insight into both self-image and public image. In the nineteenth century these points of communication were, not surprisingly, frequently visual encounters. Arbiters and arousers of public opinion in the second half of the century discovered the communicative power of mass-produced visual images—illustrations, cartoons, photographs—among the classes of industrial society. The new technologies that revolutionized the printing industry in the final decades of the century only augmented this impact.

Historian Warren Susman noted (1984) that between the Civil War and the First World War Americans created what he called (borrowing from Vachel Lindsay) a "hieroglyphic civilization"—a culture that understands itself and others chiefly in terms of visual symbols. The turn to the eye as the primary source of knowledge had been a part of European consciousness for several centuries; from Newton's *Opticks* to Darwin's *Origin of Species* the human eye was celebrated as the most perfect gift of God or product of Nature. Nineteenth-century theorists of social evolution drew a clear distinction between literate and preliterate peoples, for it seemed a major and unquestionable advance to have moved from information passed by mouth and ear to knowledge that was written down, visually retrievable, and available for literary exegesis. Humans had indeed progressed, it appeared, from ear to eye. The emergence of the museum, a clear expression of Western bourgeois values that reached its apogee in the period, confirmed the triumph of the eye: it was a visual feast. George Brown Goode, who organized and directed the United States National Museum after 1881, reminded an audience in 1889: "There is an Oriental saying that the distance between ear and eye is small, but the difference between hearing and seeing is very great." A major cognitive shift had occurred: "To see is to know" (quoted in Rydell 1984:44). The museum, Goode thought, should be a "house full of living ideas" displayed to the public eye (1889:262).

Austen Henry Layard, the midcentury English explorer who established the model of the archaeologist as an intrepid agent of civilization, was always aware of the importance of visual transmition to the public back home. Sir Stratford Canning, the British ambassador to Constantinople who financed his first excavations at Nimrud, bluntly observed to Layard that the public are like picture-loving children. Layard's aunt and uncle encouraged him to work up a book with some good biblical connections for the Scripture-hungry publics of England and America. The young archaeologist listened carefully. *Nineveh and Its Remains* (1849) took the public by storm and became a best-seller at 8,000 copies; ultimately Layard wrote two pairs of books about his Middle East excavations, each consisting of a written account and a volume of illustrations. *The Illustrated London News* followed the course of Layard's work with text and drawings, rejoicing in the spread of imperial civilization to the benighted periphery. "It is gratifying that England has not only rendered herself the first of the nations by those sterling qualities which so strongly characterize her natives—that she uses these means to extend and disseminate the wealth, and comfort, and advantages produced by the arts of civilization, at the same time that she

Figure 7-1. Shipping the Great Bull from Nimroud, 1850.

administers happiness and contentment by inculcating the tenets of pure religion . . ." (Baron 1976:24). Curiously, this text of 27 July 1850 accompanied an illustration, "Shipping the Great Bull from Nimroud" (Figure 7-1), that portrayed not the export of English values but the process of removing the 100-ton sculpture from its site to a ship for transit to London. The central contrast in the illustration lies between the passive, onlooking native population and the technological feat and its constitutive elements: ship, cables, winch and pulley. While the local flagpole stands flagless, the Union Jack frames the right side of the picture—a quiet statement of relative political power.

Upon its arrival in the British Museum six months later, the "Human-headed and Eagle-winged Bull from Nimroud" (Figure 7-2) became a public spectacle, symbolic of "the union of intellectual power with physical strength" (*The Illustrated London News*, 26 October 1850) that so aroused Victorian admiration. Removed from its resting place, the winged bull towers over the Victorian couple; as the husband gestures to point out features to his wife, she peers forward in awe at the stony, bearded virility. The subtle act here is binary: he presents, she accepts appreciatively. According to this early imaging, the archaeological enterprise as a whole involved notions of colonial power and appropriation, technological prowess, and male presentation of treasures to metropolitan females.

The arrival of the remains of the Tomb of Mausolus at the British Mu-

Figure 7-2. Human-headed and eagle-winged bull from Nimroud, 1850.

seum in 1859 (Figure 7-3) again focused on the transfer of artifacts from the periphery to the metropolis. The museum does not merely provide setting or background in the illustration, though; it is itself the subject. Massive columns and porticoes dwarf both workers unloading the treasures and passersby. Again the heavy work is watched by men and women, the former in conversation, the latter at various respectful distances. Behind the stone walls of the museum the project goes forward: retrieving and storing "culture," bringing back—as Stephens had envisioned at Uxmal—the monuments of human history to the appropriate locus of study and appreciation.

As portrayed in nineteenth-century visual art, the entire process of archaeological retrieval was divisible into three loci and stages of process that together formed a mental geography of the archaeological enterprise: the site of discovery and excavation; the site and means of transport, usually an oceangoing vessel; and the final resting place in the metropolis—the public square, museum, or university. Each of the three "sites" in this mental geography possesses distinctive characteristics. The excavation site is generally presented as a landscape of destruction and lost grandeur, a silent and awesome vista with slowly moving or reclining figures. It is a reflective and relaxing scene for the cosmopolitan eye, inviting meditation on the fate of empires and the vagaries of history. The process of shipping features machinery and technological ingenuity in the face of physical challenges, as

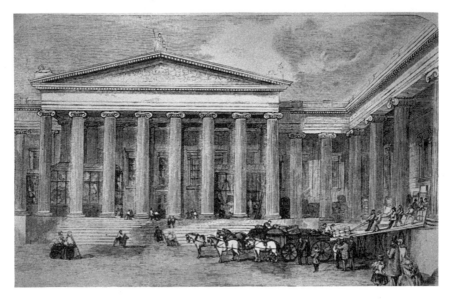

Figure 7-3. Arrival of the remains of the tomb of Mausolus at the British Museum, 1869.

well as brute strength. The site of the metropole, as we have seen, usually appears as an act of observation, education, and appreciation, especially by civilized females.

An illustration entitled "Proposed Method for the Removal of Cleopatra's Needle from Alexandria" (Figure 7-4), which appeared in *The Illustrated London News* on 10 March 1877, encompasses all three stages of this process of cultural transfer. In the upper left corner, the obelisk appears *in situ* with camels and natives. The bottom left and upper right drawings portray the technologies of removal, while the center picture shows the specially designed ship in transit through the rough waters of the Bay of Biscay. The final resting spot—"as it may be" at Westminster—appears in the bottom right. The obelisk has moved from the world of camels to the world of steamboats; the process is collapsed from time to the single page, both descriptive and predictive. The focus, and the lesson, is industrial achievement in the face of challenge and struggle.

If Layard established for the English-speaking world the model of the archaeologist as hero, it was Heinrich Schliemann, an untrained but wealthy and determined German amateur, whose exploits at Mycenae and Troy in the 1870s and 1880s were the most widely reported and carefully followed archaeological adventures of the century. A. T. White wrote in *Lost Worlds: Adventures in Archaeology* (1947) that "every person of culture and education lived through the drama of discovering Troy" (quoted in Daniel

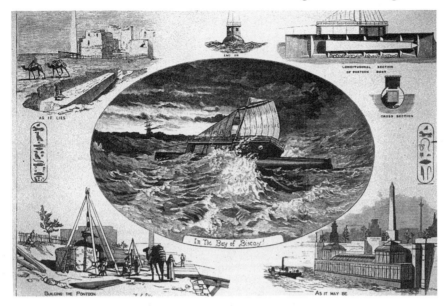

Figure 7-4. Proposed method for the removal of Cleopatra's Needle from Alexandria, 1877.

1950:138). "All over, in houses and on the streets, in mail coaches and on railroads, Troy was being discussed" (Deuel 1977:7). While Cleopatra's Needle was being lost and recovered in the Bay of Biscay in 1877, Schliemann's activities at Mycenae were already being reported in French, German, and English publications on monthly, weekly, and even daily bases. The *London Daily Telegraph* as well as *The Illustrated London News* sent artists and reporters to his camps. Understandably, then, it was one of the high points of the social and scientific season of London when, in March 1877, Schliemann announced his most recent discoveries to the Society of Antiquaries (Figure 7-5). The environment was all-male, clubby, serious. The arched backs, furrowed brows, and bewhiskered, earnest countenances of men straining to comprehend the import of the latest archaeological reports all betokened a serious, scientific, all-male enterprise.

By the 1890s, when Schliemann was in his final seasons and Sir Flinders Petrie's Egypt Explorations Fund had been in operation for some years, this symbolic world of archaeology was fully articulated. Thus, Jacque de Morgan's discovery of the tomb of Queen Khnemit at Dahshûr, outside Cairo, in 1894 appeared in *The Illustrated London News* (7 March 1896) fully encoded (Figure 7-6). Here, in a moment of supreme archaeological triumph, Monsieur de Morgan lifts above his head a crown from the mummy of the queen. All the critical actors are on stage for an act that is biblical in

Figure 7-5. Heinrich Schliemann giving an account of his discoveries at Mycenae before the Society of Antiquaries, 1877.

Figure 7-6. J. de Morgan lifting a golden crown from the mummy of Queen Khnemit at Dahshûr, 1896.

its wonder: the reporter-illustrator taking notes preparatory to telegraphing the good news back to the metropolis; the surrounding, gesticulating natives and site workers, half understanding the miracle before their eyes; most prominently, the two European women excited and enchanted by the discoverer and his ancient treasure, leaning forward in anticipation of archaeological resurrection.

Even thus partially decoded, archaeology as a cultural enterprise in the years between 1850 and 1900 is revealed as an exercise in recovery of the human legacy, whether gold treasure or pottery sherds. But it was a process operating in accord with larger cultural instructions. As we have seen, it occurred in a series of stages and generalized places, strongly mediated by industry and technology, celebrating both the lone male and the machinery of civilization. And, almost exclusively, it was a male exercise. Female gender roles were as clearly prescribed as women's positions in the illustrations: to observe, receive, admire. To the extent that women participated in archaeology it was as audience, helpmates, or preservators; curatorial roles—preparing and preserving the objects hunted and gathered by the males—seemed forecast. It should hardly be surprising that museums of archaeology today are staffed and curated largely by women.

The symbolic coherence of this nineteenth-century enterprise is clear enough, and its images conform to and confirm the accepted economic, political, racial, and gender categories of the age. Additionally, however, there is a remarkable element that can appropriately be called biblical in the portrayal of the excavation sites, whether in Greece, Egypt, or the American Southwest. It consists of a generalized desert landscape with certain stock characters: the woman with either a water jug or a basket on her head, and the reclining figure, sometimes a young man or child (Figure 7-7). Heat and slow movement, quiescence and stasis: it is a scene of repeated pattern, removed from the flow of history. Sometimes portrayed as well through the juxtapositon of drawings with photographs, as in Figure 7-7, it presents a contrast between industrial civilization and "the other." The visual and psychological result is a generalized alternative to civilization. From this perspective, archaeology functions not simply or even primarily as an extension of political-economic hegemony or colonial exploitation. Rather, it presents a subtle dialogue of contrasts, a dialogue about energy and history, social progress and social cohesion, industrial sickness and preindustrial health. It provides the forum for a vital, sublimated cultural debate (Lears 1981).

The tired distinction between internal and external histories of science needs a long rest. Because of its apparently inherent popularity, as well as its political utility in an age of constructing state and national identities, archaeology has been and is today implicated in central cultural concerns. The flow of influences in and out of the discipline has been unceasing; whether theory, funding, or institutional power, nothing in archaeology can be considered strictly internal. A historical method that recognizes archaeo-

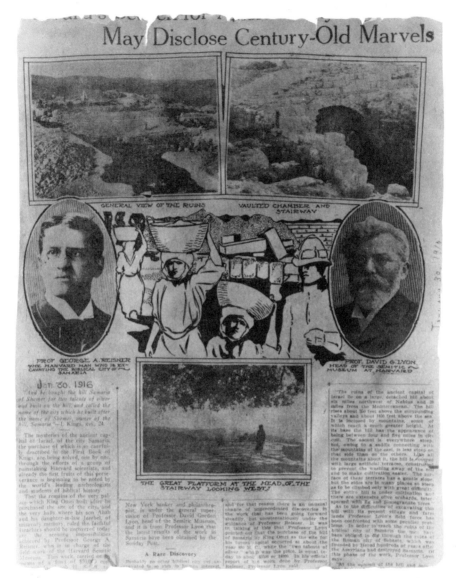

Figure 7-7. Portion of a newspaper article about the excavation at Samaria by George Reisner, 1916. Copyright © President and Fellows of Harvard College, 1989. All rights reserved. Photograph by Hillel Burger.

logical interpretations as variant and vital narrative with powerful cultural categories and messages not only holds the promise of telling us much about the social, political, and regional contexts of the enterprise but may also reveal something about the ways in which hegemonic cohesion is maintained under postmodern, industrial conditions. To this end, visual and textual analysis undertaken with appropriately serious playfulness beckons as an attractive road to follow.

Acknowledgments

Thanks to Barbara A. Babcock for important conversations; to Warren Wheller of Colgate University for excellent photographic work; and to the Colgate University Research Council for generous financial support.

8

Contextualizing Archaeology

Alice B. Kehoe

Bronislaw Malinowski found that "every historical change creates its mythology . . . a constant by-product . . . of sociological status, which demands precedent; of moral rule, which requires sanction" (1954:146). The 1840s was a decade of great historical change, the decade in which the economy of industrial capitalism and the political philosophy of bourgeois liberal democracy rose to dominate Europe and the United States. The social scientist would expect to find associated with these linked economic and political changes a legitimating mythology offering precedent and sanction. Archaeology appeared in the crucial decade to provide the needed mythology.

Standard histories of archaeology (Daniel 1967, 1981b; Willey and Sabloff 1974) agree that archaeology as a discipline and a profession began in the 1840s on each side of the Atlantic. Typical of consensus historians (Reinitz 1978), the authors who cite the 1840s as the birth of archaeology seem unperturbed by the coincidence of this event in several nations and complacent in dismissing work before the 1840s that resembles what after that decade is termed archaeology. So unproblematic a history as archaeology has been given carries a Whiggish flavor. What does the history of archaeology look like if one searches out its context?

History and Myth

Malinowski's insight has been drawn out in this era of deconstructionist critiques most impressively by Hayden White (1973). Where Aristotle had seen history as a deficient and inferior form of discourse, limited to relations of contiguity (i.e., syntagmatic), White argues that history ranks with poetics, is indeed a branch of poetics, embodying, as poetics does, unifying paradigmatic visions (Gossman 1978:8–10). White presents the classical modes and tropes that he recognizes in a selection of great works of history, inferring from the presence of such rhetoric the poetic visions that informed the writers' selections and emphasis from the raw data of events. More recent and radical pursuers of the deconstructionist attack (e.g.,

Cohen 1986) push history almost wholly into the realm of mythology, echoing Malinowski although without citing his pathbreaking essay.

Archaeologists are more familiar with quite a different conception of the proper nature of history: the claim by Carl Hempel (1942) that history is science or it is nothing. Hempel believed that historians must sift through the raw facts of history seeking "covering laws" that "explain an event by showing that, in view of certain particular circumstances and general laws, its occurrence was to be expected (in a purely logical sense), either with deductive certainty or with inductive probability" (1974:92). Malinowski may be said to have provided a "covering law" prompting us to look for a new mythology sanctioning the historical changes in the West during the 1840s. Ironically, Malinowski's "covering law" renders questionable any claim to the discovery of scientific truth in the data of history, for the "law" premises mythology in the guise of history. From Malinowski's point of view, histories are likely to be mere reflections of sociological reality, or the sociological construction of reality, as Berger and Luckmann put it (1966). "Events" represent a selection from the flux of praxis: their singling out, and that of persons represented as historically significant, must be examined for use as precedent and sanction. Their "occurrence," so far as we know it, comes through the historian as agent. As Malinowski noted: "Immediate history, semi-historic legend, and unmixed myth flow into one another, form a continuous sequence, and fulfill really the same sociological function" (1954:126). That function must be sought, the agenda, as it were, to understand histories.

The Agenda of the 1840s

During the 1840s, Western societies realized the passing of economic orders dominated by external mercantile enterprises and internal land-based production (Hobsbawn 1962, 1975). The new order was built on centralization of production in factories paced by machines tended by a proletariat. Ownership of the factories was vested in a middle class asserting its power against the traditional aristocracy based on landed estates. Because the power of this bourgeoisie came from entrepreneurial management of capital, the class stressed the merit of self-determination, the individual's freedom to act according to his own rational choices (Mosse 1974). *Rational* is a key word, for persons considered incapable of rational thinking—uneducated men and all women—were held unsuited for liberty, needful of control.

The bourgeoisie demanded liberal democracy, meaning extension of the franchise to all men possessing property sufficient to use as capital, enfranchisement of the bourgeoisie, whose numbers in the mid-nineteenth century would then give their class majority representation in governing bodies. England and the United States shifted into the new order bloodlessly with the Reform Bill and Jacksonian democracy in the 1830s; continental Europe struggled to the year of revolutions, 1848. By midcentury, a class led by captains of industry drove Western societies, and as we would expect from Malinowski's "law," mythology was created to claim precedent and sanction for their rule (see Fowler 1987). Jacques Derrida calls it "white mythology": "The white man takes his own mythology, Indo-European mythology, his own *logos*, that is, the *mythos* of his idiom, for the universal form of that he must still wish to call Reason. . . . White mythology. . . . inscribed in white ink, an invisible design covered over in the palimpsest" (1982:213). Or one might prefer to term it "ideology. . . . a myth written in the language of philosophy and science," as Feuer (1975:17) does.

From the seventeenth century, Western societies privileged the analytico-referential mode of discourse (Reiss 1982), dichotomizing experience into self and object and making possible the liberal concept of right government as a social contract between reasoning men. Francis Bacon asserted that truth and prosperity will be the offspring of a scientist (in the sense of a man of knowledge) directly conjoining himself with the things of the objective world, creating authority legitimatized through the regular testing of propositions against these objects (Reiss 1982:198–225). Bacon became the patron saint of nineteenth-century science, particularly of the commonsense realism philosophy of science that supported nineteenth-century industrial research and development (Bozeman 1977; Laudan 1981:86–110). Following Bacon, John Locke attempted a political science that would similarly place authority in the reasoning autonomous man analyzing experience. Locke has been termed precociously bourgeois (Wood 1983:178), not surprising in light of his work leading his government's Board of Trade, and his writings became central to liberal democracy as practiced in capitalist nations. The principal tenet was that men educated to reason, to engage in rational (i.e., analytico-referential) discourse, were thereby fit to exercise power, and they alone should exercise it, through the social contract. "White mythology" averred that this historically circumscribed mode of discourse is not a cultural particular but a universal good, a God-given method for discovering truth and achieving material wealth (Wood 1983).

The triumph of bourgeois liberal democracy and its economic foundation in capitalism—mercantile and especially industrial—in the mid-nineteenth century called for demonstration of its right to power. Because Western societies lie in the Judaic cultural tradition conceptualizing time as a linear dimension in which God manifests himself, a legitimatization of bourgeois power needed to be located in linear time conformable with Judeo-Christian revelation. This temporal structure for legitimatization of Western power had been constructed during the eighteenth century (the mercantilist phase of capitalist domination) as purportedly scientific universal histories.

Meek (1976) describes this enterprise of dissecting contemporary formations into a logical cumulative progression necessarily ending with late eighteenth-century Western European states. This predicated endpoint was termed the Age of Commerce. To arrive at it, the philosophes of the English-tenment looked to known history and to the Bible to find that a stage of (subsistence) agriculture had preceded the evolution of market-dominated political economies and that a pastoral stage, exemplified by Abraham and his tribe, had apparently preceded agriculture. (That Canaan is described in the Bible as agricultural when Abraham migrated to it was not remarked.) Logically and biblically, a nonproductive stage of simple gathering repre-sented the initial human condition in Eden. Caught in the analytico-refer-ential mode of discourse, the philosophes retrieve objective examples of each stage of their history from explorers' accounts as well as from classical authors, which was Baconian testing of propositions, deductive confirma-tion by published observations. It was, at the same time, ideology, part of what Agassi (1981 : 386) terms the Enlightenment myth, for the ethnographic instances were selected for their concordance with the *scala naturae* en-throning European man at the top.

Americanists will understand the primacy of ideological position over empirical observation through this passage, popular with the philo-sophes, supposedly summing up the American Indians:

> *America* may with much Propriety be called the youngest Brother and meanest of Mankind; no Civil Government, no Religion, no Let-ters; the *French* call them *Les Hommes des Bois*, or Men-Brutes of the Forrest: They do not cultivate the Earth by planting or grazing: Excepting a very inconsiderable Quantity of *Mays* or *Indian Corn*, and of *Kidney-Beans* (in *New England* they are called *Indian Beans*) which some of their *Squaas* or Women plant; they do not provide for To-Morrow, their Hunting is their necessary Subsistence not Diver-sion; when they have good Luck in Hunting, they eat and sleep until all is consumed and then go a Hunting again [William Douglass 1755, quoted in Meek 1976 : 137].

The real source of this flagrant racism is John Locke, who articulated Britain's policy of pronouncing lands desired for colonization to be *vacuum domicilium* on the grounds that the resident indigenes did not exchange money for private title to land (Wood 1984 : 51–62). Britain was said to wage just war, properly killing or enslaving the indigenes, when it had to fight to take over "unimproved" lands, for had not God ordered humans to "replenish the earth, and subdue it; and have dominion over. . . . every living thing" (Gen. 1 : 28)? *Vacuum domicilium* status for American lands had been argued as early as 1629 by Governor John Winthrop of Massachu-setts Bay Colony (Jennings 1976 : 82, chapter 8), but more strictly on the issue of "replenish" and "subdue," an argument that would protect the In-dians' cultivated fields from which they supplied the Puritan colonists with seed corn. Later in the century, after discovering the Indians' lack of clear private title—cultivated lands were held more or less communally, similar to practices in medieval European villages—and lack of metal currency, and by raising these as grounds for designating "waste," Locke brought colonialist policies in line with contemporary internal policies for enclosure and allowed appropriation of broad territories. Privately held capital is the essential underpinning of liberty as it is the means to the exercise of power in bourgeois society.

The seventeenth century's great instauration, to use Bacon's word, of an ideology instituting a confrontational relationship between men, each premised in the strive to increase his capital and with it his power, particularly his power to act in his own interest, created a wonderfully occluding metaphor. Where formations organized to expand capital, in fact to dehumanize workers, to eliminate exercise of consciousness beyond mechanical adjustment actions, and to operate as if animate components were inanimate (reaching its climax in Taylor's "scientific management" [Beniger 1986:294–299; Braverman 1974]), capitalism's dominance was accompanied by pervasive organic images (Barnes and Shapin 1979). John Locke's compatriot William Petty shared Locke's ambition to extend Bacon's science to societal relations and made direct analogy between a "Body Natural" and the "Body Politick" foundational to his 1691 *Political Arithmetick*. A century later, with the Industrial Revolution, organicism engrossed discourse. Cuvier's comparative methodology developed from biological studies became the model of science (Foucault 1973:131–135). From Saint-Simon and Comte, through Spencer and Morgan, to the superorganic of A. L. Kroeber and Julian Huxley, human history was presented as the life of an organic entity growing through an animal experience into the eventual superior but still vitalistic *üebermensch*. Human populations were conceptualized as inherently bounded in the manner of organisms, discrete entities like men, men striving for unfettered autonomy to manage their capital. Bodies politic naturally had heads, hearts, and limbs interdependent in a hierarchically organized system, healthy only as long as each part exercised its normal function. Such functioning was premised to be comparable to the operation of machines, especially automata, thus subordinating and incorporating mechanistic explanations into an encompassing organic metaphor.

Archaeology as a discipline and as a profession has been intimately linked to the phase of Western culture history dominated by industrial capitalism and bourgeois liberal democracy (P. Levine 1986; J. Levine 1987) and linked on a series of levels.

1. Superficially, archaeology became distinguished as a science in the two-century-long creation of a set of distinct sciences out of natural philosophy, and it became a profession through the concomitant creation of the occupation of scientist.

2. Archaeology was used throughout this phase as an instrument for "national moral rearmament" (Kristiansen 1985:26), supporting nationalist and imperialist claims (Fowler 1987).
3. As a science utilizing the methodology of the natural sciences, archaeology can claim to be objective and its conclusions drawn from incontrovertible facts. Participating in the analytico-referential mode of discourse, archaeology has drawn strength from and has itself strengthened the power of this mode of discourse, in its stronger demonstrations of congruence between observation and hypothesis.
4. Archaeology is par excellence the science positioning human beings in the object frame of the discourse. Unlike biological anthropology, archaeology includes the products of human consciousness, apportioning them as well as the human organism itself to object. In archaeology, the scientist, the person of reason, confronts *all* the material objects.

Archaeology has been recognized since the mid-nineteenth century as a weapon in the arsenal of bourgeois nations. "All power of regulating the future comes from a knowledge of the present state of things, gained by a knowledge of the past. . . . The archaeologist . . . is not, therefore, the useless person that is sometimes thoughtlessly portrayed, but a valuable contributor to the world's progress" (*The Antiquarian*, 1871, quoted in Hudson 1981:100). By grounding the status quo in allegedly natural conditions and processes, archaeologists have helped legitimatize modern nations and also that grander ideology of capitalism and liberal democracy adhered to by modern nations.

Archaeology and the Expression of Western Ideology

Writing the history of archaeology requires probing behind the chronicles of consensus historians. Glyn Daniel effuses, "No words are too lavish in trying to estimate Worsaae's contribution" (1967:97). Why such hyperbole? Why Worsaae?

J. J. A. Worsaae was the first state-supported official archaeologist in Denmark (Kristiansen 1981:40); his appointment in 1847 is an event signifying the institution of archaeology as a profession serving national interests, a role it has never lost (a 1986 sample of members of the Society for American Archaeology revealed that 30% are employed as archaeologists by federal, state, or local governments [Acuff 1986:4]). In the same decade as his appointment, Worsaae published an immediately successful book, translated within the decade into English as *The Primeval Antiquities of Denmark* (1849).

When he wrote his book, Worsaae was a very young man, just past twenty—he literally came of age with the politicoeconomic system he was to live within. Of necessity, this very young researcher utilized the substantial materials, both data and theory, available to him from the work of his elders, especially C. J. Thomsen who had been organizing the national collection of antiquities since 1816 under a model of three successive ages of human history: Stone, Bronze, and Iron (Kristiansen 1985:21). This model had been published in Denmark as early as 1776 (Daniel 1967:90). Worsaae's popular 1843 book on *Danmarks Oldtid* was, in a fellow Dane's opinion, "bold and . . . polemical" (Kristiansen 1985:23): "A people with respect for themselves and their independence . . . must . . . look to the past . . . how they became what they are. . . . Only then can they defend their independence with all their might and work with zeal for future progress" (Worsaae 1843, quoted in Kristiansen 1985:26). Worsaae held out a vision of a long fascinating past to be construed as the reflection of an indomitable Denmark, a nation whose being could not be tottered by military defeats or the challenge to monarchy rending the country in the 1840s. Worsaae's book, and indeed his entire career, exemplified a paradigmatic vision that illustrates and supports Hayden White's argument that the great histories are works of poetic discourse.

Danish nationalism impelled Worsaae but cannot explain why *Danmarks Oldtid* was translated into German and English for general reading outside Denmark. Popular appeal lay in the implicit demonstration of human progress, that leitmotiv of the bourgeoisie. The three successive industrial ages, Stone, Bronze, and Iron, readily lent themselves to assimilation into the Enlightenment's universal history of four stages, Savagery, Barbarism, Agriculture, and Commerce, the last outside the domain of archaeology because it denoted the present.

Sven Nilsson, a Swedish zoologist and antiquarian a generation older than Worsaae (although his contemporary in publishing), equated the industrial and cultural stages (Daniel 1967:107–109) in the manner that was to become standard in the 1860s. By then, Spencer's grandiose theory of human cultural evolution on an organic model (Gould 1977b:113) epitomized the extraordinary extension of the organic metaphor in the nineteenth century, to the point where Spencer could claim the universe itself had grown from an embryonic stage, as von Baer had suggested in 1828 (Gould 1977b:114). A "cosmic defense of Victorian society," Gould (1977b:109) describes Spencer's multivolume *opera*, and Worsaae described himself politically as a conservative (Kristiansen 1981:23). Focusing (particularly in the nineteenth century) on implements, prehistorians laid out a development of manufactures demonstrating the popular Spencerian Law of Progress from simple to complex. They correlated the stratigraphically lower, earlier, and simpler implements in Europe and the contemporary artifacts of "savages" in lands colonized by the Western nations. Thereby they led readers to the conclusion that "the history of technology is, in fact, an account of the gradual triumph of Western science and technology over all other forms of human praxis" (Staudenmaier 1985 : 36).

Locke selected the use of iron as the most critical difference between "flourishing and polite Nations" and "the Wants and Ignorance of the ancient savage Americans" (quoted in Wood 1983 : 134). Two centuries later, Lewis Henry Morgan reiterated, "The production of iron was the event of events in human experience, without a parallel, and without an equal, beside which all other inventions and discoveries were inconsiderable" (1877 : 43). Morgan's contemporaries celebrated the magnificence of iron in the Crystal Palace of 1851, with its most visible skeleton of iron and the culminating icon, Eiffel's Tower of naked iron, 1889. Control of iron, its products and uses, was the keystone of national and personal (e.g., Bessemer, Carnegie, J. P. Morgan) fortunes in the nineteenth century, so the history of its triumph was of the same interest as the histories of landed families and dynastic rules had been to earlier eras. The three-age system had the fairy-tale format of Stone, Bronze, Iron, the last the key to happiness ever after.

On a deeper level, nineteenth-century archaeology, focusing on implements and the monuments and ornaments of unknown personages, fit the dehumanization of producers under industrial capitalism. Prehistoric finds were the products of nameless makers whose personal ties, loves, hates, and yearnings had to be irrelevant to archaeologists who were denied the possibility of such knowledge. Proceeding in the analytico-referential mode of discourse, archaeologists successfully studied the manifestations of human lives as so many objects akin to the anonymous objects of the sciences. That humans could be so studied reinforced the industrial order of the world. The history of mankind could be told through the history of objects; by objectifying humanity, scientists could reach through the sentiments of the softheaded to the true nature of humans.

Deeper yet, the organic metaphor mystified the reductionism of dehumanization. As late as 1959, Kenneth Oakley (1959 : 1) could state: "Man is a social animal. . . . Employment of tools appears to be his chief *biological* characteristic" (emphasis added). And in our own decade, a UNESCO museums' group continues the metaphor when it urges the conservation of artifacts because "the cultural heritage is an expression of each people's historical experience and its collective personality" (Makagiansar 1984 : 4). The "peoples," defined in our own time through political negotiations, are metaphorically "people," that is, *persons* with experiences and personalities. They leave a heritage literally rooted in the soil to be discovered through archaeology. Describing the "development" of a "people" as if analogous to the development of an organism, as if artifacts discovered in a region were mementoes of a life, archaeologists have supported political groups' demands to be treated as bounded entities and accorded the autonomy owed them by the tenets of liberalism. Man was defined as "the tool-using animal" (Mumford 1967:5 credits Thomas Carlyle), and Comte declared, in the 1840s, that "all human progress, political, moral, or intellectual, is inseparable from material progression" (quoted in Pollard 1971:120). Conflating the political, moral, and intellectual into the material justified the archaeologists' practice and let that praxis, in turn, blur the differences between tools and biological characteristics, between inanimate objects and humans.

Conclusions

Contextualizing archaeology in its societal milieu raises and, tentatively at least, answers questions lying between the lines in the Whiggish consensus histories of Daniel and Willey and Sabloff. Why are the 1840s said to mark the emergence of archaeology as a discipline and a profession? Why is Worsaae emphasized over Thomsen, and Squier and Davis over Jefferson? Why is the three-age system, which was noted by the Romans (e.g., Lucretius) and a few centuries later by the Chinese historian Yüan K'ang (Chang 1977:2), described as a discovery by Thomsen and Worsaae? Why are only 2% of the persons cited by Willey and Sabloff women, and only 6% of those cited by Daniel women (1967)—the majority of this small number somehow not making it into his book's index? Archaeology has been implicitly constituted as an instrument of domination and reproduction of the bourgeois democracies (Bourdieu 1977:159–197). For the consensus historians of archaeology, the test of significance has been the degree to which person and work confirmed the paradigmatic vision so well articulated by Worsaae in 1843.

Our loss of innocence is not confined to issues of method and theory within archaeology, Clarke's (1973:13) concern. Financed primarily by the state, directly or indirectly, via universities, archaeology cannot pretend to be a pure search for knowledge independent of the state and its governing class. Nor should archaeology pretend to be independent of economic factors arising from the needs of the lower classes, whether those of the nineteenth-century peasants for arable land (Kristiansen 1985:41–46) or those of the contemporary proletariat for expansion of shopping malls. Archaeology exists along the interface between the state's demand for control, manifested in its expropriation of finds of archaeological material, and the private persons' necessary demand for autonomous control of resources, given that they live in a political economy of capitalist private enterprise. Both sides will color interpretation as well as disposal of data, the state framing finds, as pillars of its "people's" history, to be conserved in archives of knowledge, the public framing relics as objects of aesthetic worth to be privately enjoyed. Consensus histories are written by members of the dominant class, and in the case of archaeology, these writers have been absorbed with men of their class (Patterson 1986) and the state's claim.

The critical difference between those who did archaeology in what Willey and Sabloff (1974) term the Speculative Period (up to the 1840s), and those whose work dates after 1840 was not speculation and its absence nor was it a lack of scientific reasoning, but the vision of the modern state. Jefferson's 1784 excavation of a Virginia mound was certainly scientific, but Jefferson worked as a private individual whose conclusions seemed of no consequence to his government. Squier and Davis, in contrast, though lesser scientists than Jefferson, were published by a state institution with a mission to aid in the nation's increasing control over its territories (Hinsley 1981). Similarly, Edward Lhwyd was not the lesser scientist compared to Worsaae but lacked the paradigmatic vision that renders ancient artifacts significant to a bourgeois democratic state structured by industrial capitalism.

The three-age system may be stratigraphically demonstrable, but it was not a result of excavations. Thomsen used a schema widely accepted from classical sources to organize existing museum collections. The three-age system was a variant of a myth in a standard, familiar format, the three offers or tests to which the culture hero must respond. Stone, Bronze, Iron—like the Three Little Pigs, he who persevered in working the least tractable material in the end won out. As Landau (1984) argues for histories of human evolution, archaeological versions of universal histories are built on a narrative form (and logic [Ankersmit 1983]). When the great historical change from landed estates to industrial capitalism and bourgeois democracies had been achieved, the format for a sanctioning myth was already given. Archaeology furnished the hero—mankind—and the substantive details—stone, bronze, iron—to lend versimilitude to the myth. That the story fit white mythology and that it privileged technology while following an organic metaphor made archaeology in the nineteenth century suited as an instrument of ideology. To ignore this context is to miss the forest for the trees.

9

The History of
Mesoamerican Archaeology
at the Crossroads:
Changing Views of the Past

Daniel Schávelzon

Research on the history of archaeology in Mesoamerica has had a long period of development, and interest in the topic is increasing. There are several historiographic stages in this sequence, and they illustrate how the writing and use of the history of archaeology has changed.

The tendency to review and evaluate past archaeological works has been a part of archaeology in Mexico and Middle America almost from the beginning. In the mid-nineteenth century, many contributions bore such titles as "Recent Expedition to . . . ," which described the work of pioneer explorers. Between 1900 and 1950, writings with such titles as "The Present State of Archaeology in . . ." and "Activities Performed during the Year . . ." appeared. All of these works were historic, even if they only revised recent history. The use of previous investigations, however, was not always the same. On the one hand, there were interpretations or criticisms with academic objectives, and on the other hand, there were works with the clear intention of writing history.

In Mexico and Middle America, the first studies of the history of archaeology appeared simultaneously with the positivist philosophy of the late nineteenth century. One pioneering work was "Reseña Histórica del Museo Nacional de México" by Jesús Sánchez (1877); others include Enrique de Olavarría y Ferrari's (1901) *Sociedad Mexicana de Geografía y Estadística;* Manuel F. Alvarez's (1901) work on Mitla; and the continentwide histories of Manuel Larrainzar (1875–1878), Marquis de Nadaillac (1883), and Hubert H. Bancroft (1886). The period ended with the series of still-unpublished volumes by Manuel Martínez Gracida (n.d.a, n.d.b), written between 1885 and 1910, in which he presented all available information on the ruins of Mitla.

By 1911 in Mexico, a new stage in writing about archaeology's past and another way of viewing general anthropology had begun with Ramón

Mena's article (1911), "La Ciencia Arqueológica en México desde la Proclamación de la Independencia Hasta Nuestros Días" and later with the studies of Luis Castillo Ledón (1924) on the first 100 years of the National Museum. Also active at this time were Juan Bautista Iguíñiz (1912), Enrique Juan Palacios (1930–1931), Paul Schelhass (1935), Henri Cordier (1920), René Verneau (1920), and Paul Rivet (1920). These writings were often apologetic, rescuing ideas that supported those of the historian. Others tended to neutralize or attack other lines of thought considered old-fashioned, anachronistic, or simply unscientific. Slowly and by process of selection, history spotlighted some archaeologists and cast others into oblivion. Archaeology underwent profound transformations, leading to major reinterpretations of what had been done in the past. In most cases, historians sustained academic or institutionally derived positions and rejected paradigms that were not their own. An exception to this general approach was that of Samuel Lothrop (1926), a forerunner of the more modern methodology of the following period, who wrote about the first objects from Palenque to arrive in Europe.

The next period, 1945 to 1975, includes Ricardo Castañeda Paganini's (1946) *Las Ruinas de Palenque,* which demonstrates the changes implemented then. With modern, qualified judgment, he thoroughly examined the colonial writings about the site. He paid little attention to inaccuracies written by the first travelers but emphasized their efforts to expose the world to so many discoveries. Although this work was not the first of this type, difficult, systematic research was required to locate the necessary documents, some of which were being published in Spain without the author's knowledge (Angulo Iñíguez 1933–1939).

The bibliography of the history of archaeology increased greatly at this time, the articles of other times were now books, and the lines of work had diversified. One such line highlighted special personalities or groups: examples include Daniel Rubín de la Borbolla and Pedro Rojas's (1956) controversial work on archaeology in Honduras; Hugo Cerezo Dardón (1957) on the discovery of Tikal; discussions of Juan Galindo's work by William Griffin (1960) and Ian Graham (1963); Manuel Ballesteros Gaibrois (1960) on the Palenque discovery; David Pendergast (1967) on the Walker-Caddy expedition to Palenque; Justino Fernández's biography of Father Márquez (Fernandez and Marquez 1972); and Elizabeth Carmichael's (1973) discussions about English archaeologists in Central America. In a series of articles, Ignacio Bernal, the most prolific writer of the time, covered a variety of issues on the history of archaeology in Middle America (Bernal 1952, 1953, 1961, 1962; Schávelzon 1983c). A simultaneous line of research focused on ways of thinking, as in Robert Wauchope's (1962) study of the "lunatic fringe" of mesoamerican archaeology.

Characterized by systematic rescue and reinterpretation of past archaeological work, the period had a notable feature: authors left aside acid criticisms of former archaeological method. The work of pioneers was no longer used as a comparison to praise modern techniques or theories. At the end of the period came Willey and Sabloff's (1974) *History of American Archaeology,* which was the first full-scale history of New World archaeology and came at a time when several regional histories were published. Internal approaches, that is, the way nationals viewed work in their own countries, became common. One question was, are conditions the same for nationals and for foreigners doing archaeology in the same country? Beginning in the 1960s, national identity became a central problem in Latin America. Several works tried to explore the archaeological situation: Ignacio Bernal (1979) in Mexico; Luis Luján Muñoz (1972) in Guatemala; and Luis Casasola (1975) in El Salvador.

Beginning around 1975, the institutionalization of mesoamerican history of archaeology allowed it to be included in the world history of archaeology. Glyn Daniel's *Short History of Archaeology* (1981c) contains an extended section on Latin America. Also symptomatic of this period was the First Congress on the History of Mesoamerican Archaeology held in Mexico in 1983 in honor of Ignacio Bernal (Schávelzon and Litvak 1983). The translation into Spanish and the commercial publication of the much-criticized work of Brian Fagan (1984b) on the Aztecs and the outstanding historiographic study of the same culture by Benjamin Keen (1984) are examples of increased interest in this kind of publication.

In the last decade a variety of books on the history of "classic" personalities, for example John L. Stephens and Frederick Catherwood (Hagen 1974), and of others not as well known, for example Lord Kingsborough and his contemporaries (Graham 1977), have been written. Robert Brunhouse published much biographical material, including books on early travelers, antiquarians, and pioneer archaeologists (1975) and on Frans Blom (1976), which followed an earlier book on Sylvanus Morley (1971). The period has also resulted in works by Keith Davis (1981), who viewed Désiré Charnay as explorer and photographer; Augusto Molina (1978), who wrote about Palenque; and Lawrence Desmond, who wrote about the Le Plongeons (Desmond 1983; see also chapter 12), and many others.

A much more critical line has reinterpreted the past from controversial points of view that has had great impact on the countries concerned. An article written by Alberto Ruz (1978) on Morley's vision of the Maya was so disturbing that it was eliminated when his collected works were published posthumously (Ruz 1982). Other critical reinterpretations have been written by Andrés Medina (1976) on the works of Miguel Covarrubias, by Carlos Navarrete (1982) on those of Modesto Mendez at Tikal, by Carlos Echánove Trujillo (1975) endeavoring to rescue the image of Teobert Maler, by Eduardo Matos Moctezuma (1972)—with an ideological position—on the works of Manuel Gamio and other issues, by Manuel Gándara (1978) on the Mexican government's archaeology, by Marshall Becker (1979) on the emergence of the model of Maya ceremonial centers, by Bernd Beyer (1986) on those of Oaxaca, and by myself on archaeological restorations (Schávelzon 1984) and the work at Zaculeu (Schávelzon 1988).

There are other notable changes taking place in the writing of the history of mesoamerican archaeology, and although it is always difficult to understand processes that are current, one notes the absence of interest in some determinant issues. My intention is not to criticize the selection that history always implies, not even the methodological arbitrariness this selection represents. But different lines of historiographic acceptance or rejection are apparent. For instance, archaeologists work not only in the field and in the laboratory but also are involved in many other activities that are part of their professional lives: teaching; searching for financial support; dealing with institutional struggles and personal confrontations; defending ideas; participating in the sacred ritual of congresses, lectures, and seminars; finding editors; maintaining relationships with their colleagues; or even avoiding important political issues that could interfere with their work in a foreign country. The list is endless and, in general, our histories often leave such topics untouched. We fail to examine national, institutional, or personal struggles and controversies except when they have to do with different paradigms or interpretations supported by scientists (see chapter 14).

A few examples of these subsidiary matters help clarify my point. When the Peabody Museum of Harvard University undertook fieldwork at the ruins of Copán between 1891 and 1899, a heated controversy arose in Honduras. In short, the excellent scientific work performed was viewed politically; opposite points of view were taken by the liberal and conservative governments. Foreign archaeologists were tied closely to the dramatic economic problems created by American corporations. As a consequence of the Copán archaeological work, some authorities and ministers were removed, scandals occurred, and contracts were more than once cancelled. At the same time, these foreign archaeologists left the country in possession of rich archaeological collections—with the government's authorization, it is true—creating a situation of diplomatic and economic pressures. The events can be interpreted in different ways; certainly the people of Honduras and the American museums have very different views. These issues clearly had more significance than the archaeological works themselves.

As another example, when in 1923 the Carnegie Institution initiated work in Mexico, the situation was quite different. The authorization to excavate Chichén Itzá was mainly political. A committee that had been discussing the possibility of reinstating diplomatic relations between Mexico and the United States made the decision to allow excavations to commence as a cultural approach to facilitate negotiations. As a part of this strategy, the School for Foreign Students was then created at the National Autonomous University of Mexico (UNAM), where Ramón Mena dictated his lessons on Mexican archaeology in English to American students who made the trip to

Mexico free of charge. It was also in this framework that Byron Cummings from the University of Arizona began his excavations at Cuicuilco (Schávelzon 1983a, 1983b).

There are no doubts about the capabilities of Sylvanus Morley and his staff, but their work took place in a special context. Chichén Itzá was in the middle of the most restless region of Yucatán, just pacified after the War of Castes and led by communist Felipe Carrillo Puerto, who wanted to declare Yucatán a republic independent of the central Mexican government. The significance of Chichén Itzá was obviously different for Carrillo Puerto than for the Carnegie Institution or even for the Mexican government (Schávelzon 1984). Again, archaeology had different meanings to the different groups involved.

Another case involves the endless confrontations between Edward Thompson and the Mexican government between 1890 and 1915. Thompson, an amateur archaeologist and consul for the United States in the Maya region, played for American historiography the part of a pioneer, a man of courage who had to overcome difficulties common in those times and in that land (e.g. Echánove Trujillo 1975; Fagan 1977). But in Mexico he is considered a looter, someone who unmercifully destroyed archaeological sites and exploited the Maya Indians. His name is usually recalled when Mexicans want to refer to some lunatic exercising political and intellectual power. In his official activity he was consul and representative of the American corporation that controlled the monocultives on which the lives of thousands of Maya Indians depended. The Carnegie Institution even had to pay Thompson to work at Chichén Itzá, as he remained the legal owner of the ruin for another 30 years, until he was tried and destituted and the area nationalized. It does not matter who was right or wrong, but it is important to understand that confrontations such as these are examples of greater conflict in the cultural field and that recognizing this wider context is necessary for the historian of archaeology.

The examples above were chosen at random—they seemed to me to be representative and have been prominent in the literature. Modern studies of the history of mesoamerican archaeology increasingly concentrate on conflict and paradigmatic change instead of on processes and evolution. Conflicts, among paradigms, personal positions, and institutional positions, are often more determinant of scientific change than periodic processes of growth. Also, the quality of ideas has not been as important as the academic or economic power of the scholars involved.

Archaeology is subject to different meanings and objectives in each country of the North American continent, and these meanings and objectives change continually. Archaeology for an aboriginal, ethnic, or popular group is not the same as for scholars with their academic and learned viewpoint. Thus, the history of archaeology varies depending upon which side of the road the historian stands. Mesoamerica has more than 400 million individuals, with a sophisticated cultural legacy, and their search for an identity is closely linked to archaeology and ethnology. The recent publications in the history of mesoamerican archaeology are beginning to recognize the social and political context of archaeology, and we can expect it to be a major trend of future research.

10

Prejudice and Context: The Anthropological Archaeologist as Historian

Donald McVicker

Most university-educated archaeologists in the United States receive degrees in anthropology. As a result future archaeologists first encounter the history of their field in the context of anthropological theory. The early history of archaeology is buried in anthropology's own mythic history and obscured in the biographies of early anthropologists. The contributions early professionals made to ethnography and ethnology are emphasized in the history of anthropology, and their interests and activities in archaeology are neglected, which is curious because contemporary anthropology as a discipline is presented to students as a fourfold field in which sociocultural, physical, linguistic, and archaeological subdisciplines are given equal weight. Consequently, the students can only conclude that past archaeologists made few contributions to mainstream anthropology or that until recently archaeology was indeed but "the handmaiden of ethnography."

However, the idea of anthropology as an equally weighted fourfold field was taken to heart by many early anthropologists. For example, Lewis Henry Morgan, through his surrogate Adolph Bandelier (1884; White 1940:x), was deeply interested in central Mexican prehistory, and even E. B. Tylor, 50 years after his one visit to Mexico, was still looking for pots to add to the collection of the Pitt-Rivers Museum (Tyler to Starr, 11 August 1903, Starr Papers general correspondence [SPGC]).

Although Franz Boas, the "architect" of early twentieth-century anthropology (Lesser 1981:3), promoted a partnership among the four anthropological subdisciplines, he also emphasized that archaeology should be guided by ethnography. Archaeologists should provide data to support the historical and descriptive objectives of his "new ethnography." As a result, Boas's own contribution to ethnography is most widely heralded, and his involvements in archaeology and physical anthropology (Cole 1985), are relegated to a footnote concerning the founding of the International School in Mexico (Godoy 1977).

Because archaeologists are educated in the history of anthropology, archaeology as anthropology has become the standard by which past archaeological research is judged (Trigger 1985 : 225). In the context of anthropology's view of its history and of the use of standards established by anthropologists for judging past archaeological research, how are the archaeologists as historians to develop independent standards of judgment to assess past research in its own terms? First, how are they to decide whose archaeological contributions are significant enough to be admitted into the history of the field? Second, by whose standards are they to judge these contributions?

The development of independent standards of judgment by archaeologists is made more difficult by anthropology's historical ethnocentrism. It is ironic that anthropologists, who are the first to teach that cultures must be judged in their own terms, are often the first to condemn the careers of their predecessors out of historical context. Turn-of-the-century American anthropologists and archaeologists should be judged in the context of their own culture. Unfortunately they are usually judged instead in the context of European political and scientific enlightenment, which Franz Boas brought to capitalist America.

This chapter examines the careers of Frederick Starr and Marshall H. Saville, two turn-of-the-century professionals who engaged in archaeological research in Mexico. They could be classified as Americanists, but they placed themselves in somewhat different categories. Starr considered himself an anthropologist regardless of the subdiscipline within which he worked. At the University of Chicago, he adhered to a Tylorian definition of anthropology that encompassed all four subdisciplines. He viewed archaeology as only part of anthropology, as necessary for education and for attracting both public patronage and financial return. He refused to accept F. W. Putnam as an anthropologist and arrogantly referred to him as only a "Harvard archaeologist" (Starr to Harper, 29 June 1892, William Rainey Harper Collection [WRHC]). As an evolutionist, Starr was never comfortable with Boas's "new ethnography."

Marshall H. Saville identified himself as an archaeologist despite having worked closely with Boas first at the American Museum of Natural History and later at Columbia University. So uncongenial was Boasian academic anthropology to Saville that he vacated the prestigious Loubat Chair of American Archaeology that had been established for him at Columbia and returned in 1917 to museum archaeology at the newly founded Museum of the American Indian ("The Matter of Saville," 1916, Museum of the American Indian Archives [MAIA] correspondence).

Today those contemporaries of Boas who failed to accept his cultural relativism, inductive methods, and view of anthropology as a "natural science" (Smith 1959) are usually ignored. For Boas, material culture was an expression of a culture's social organization, not a technological marker of its evolutionary stage. An object's museum display value was secondary to its value as a cultural marker (Boas 1955). The reputation of men like Starr and Saville who adhered to a nineteenth-century museum-collecting philosophy and who sought with equal fervor archaeological and ethnographic specimens, has faded. These men are also condemned because their philosophy is thought to have encouraged the expropriation of cultural property, and their orthogenic evolutionary perspective is thought to have supported imperial expansion (Stocking 1985).

To the historian who is familiar with the late nineteenth-century context of anthropological careers, however, today's assessment of these early careers appears prejudicial. Although Boas consolidated his power and finally achieved many of his goals in the twentieth century, at the end of the nineteenth century his anthropological practices were quite similar to those of his now-snubbed contemporaries. Like Starr he was a professional anti-imperialist, yet under the pressures of career and patronage, again like Starr, he personally expropriated the cultural property of other nations (McVicker 1987).

To assess objectively the sources of prejudice leveled against certain early professionals, the career of Frederick Starr will be presented as a case study. His career will then be compared to that of Marshall Saville. Finally, the contributions of Starr, Saville, and their contemporaries will be evaluated against the background of turn-of-the-century American society and of twentieth-century professionalization of anthropology.

Frederick Starr

Frederick Starr (1858–1933) was the first anthropologist at the University of Chicago. On twelve separate trips to Mexico between 1894 and 1904, he measured Indians, recorded vocabularies, noted customs, and amassed artifacts. Starr's wide-ranging anthropological interests brought him international fame during the first decades of the twentieth century.

He came to Chicago with a vision: to establish one of the first departments of scientific anthropology in the United States and to create a great museum at the university. All of his grand plans were to be frustrated. He was placed in a joint department of sociology and anthropology. Sociology grew rapidly and became more professional. Anthropology, under Starr, never broke free and remained stunted.

The Walker Museum of Natural History was built at the University of Chicago, and Starr directed its development. However, he could not compete with the collection patronage and research potential of the newly founded and better-funded Field Columbian Museum (McVicker 1986). As a result, by 1896 Starr had defined the collections in "his" museum as only needing to be "formed with reference to their actual teaching value" (Starr, quoted in Miller 1978:57).

In Starr's circumscribed academic setting he developed into one of the university's most popular and controversial undergraduate teachers, and he became one of the Midwest's most effective popularizers of anthropology (Evans 1987). As his self-chosen professional isolation grew, he began to refer to himself as "The Lone Starr"—a label that also characterized his labors in Mexico. His extra-academic research was largely self-funded and conducted without the cooperation of the many professional colleagues he knew. In fact in his collecting endeavors, Starr usually thought of himself as being in competition with his colleagues as well as with private collectors and Mexican officials.

During the summer of 1894, Starr traveled to Mexico for the first time (Starr 1894) and he returned in December of that year. On 28 December, a fateful meeting took place in Mexico City. W. D. Powell, the first appointed Southern Baptist missionary to Mexico, was in town for an ordination. Starr and Powell were introduced, and the two men soon became fast friends and business partners. After their first meeting, Starr describes Powell as a "genius," turning the worldly minded into helpers (Starr Papers Field Notebooks [SPNB] 4:26). The next day Starr went to Toluca to stay with Powell. There he was shown "some specimens of pottery he has lately dug upon a hill nearby. They are good" (SPNB 4:28). After a trip to the state museum and dinner, a deal was struck. At this point Starr did not reveal what their plans were.

Starr returned to Mexico during the summer of 1895 on what he refers to as a "photographic expedition." On 5 August he was again in Toluca where Powell met him at the station and took him to his house. According to Starr, "We first looked over 'the result,' which was far more than I had anticipated. Mr. P. estimates it at a hundred dozen pieces: there are curious ball rattles, good flutes, two good labrets, one carved wolf figure, *many* tripod vessels, vases, curious ball cups, bones remarkably notched, spindle whorls galore, etc., etc." (SPNB 6:55; emphasis in original). After lunch Powell, Starr, and a Mr. Hubert Brag went by horse and buggy

> up an ascending road to a mean little village which lies on the barren flanks of the hill [Tlacotepec]. In this district some four or five spots have been excavated by Mr. Powell's direction. The objects are found at several feet depth. Two yards of Indians have been quite completely excavated and, at one place in a cornfield very curious conditions were found—seven bodies, one over another, were taken out all with notched bones. In one yard seven dozen pieces of pottery were taken out in one hour. In one place a skeleton was found clutching two obsidian knives in hand. We set a woman to work digging that I might see how things lie. It was a place where the whole yard had been dug over, so she dug up her kitchen floor! She used a digging hoepick, a sickle, and a gourd. The sickle was used for working the dirt fine when it was scraped out with the gourd. This was passed up to women above. At 3 or 4 feet down she came upon

stones quite solidly packing together. This is a sign for watchfulness and is always found at that depth. In a few minutes more she called out that she had found pottery and a minute later, bone. She uncovered the edge of the bowl so I could see it, then she worked it out. It was a handsome bright red (inside) tripod bowl with five black disks on it [SPNB 6:56–57].

From Chicago in December, Starr began a remarkable correspondence with Powell. Surprisingly candid letters from Powell reveal the intellectual, political, and financial maneuvers of Americans in Mexico at the turn of the century. Starr was evidently a willing participant in these maneuvers.

In Powell's first letter dated 1 January 1897, he informed Starr that he had been appointed special commission to Mexico from Nashville's Tennessee Centennial Exposition. Powell then revealed how he planed to use his position to move their collections across the Rio Grande.

> Now I mean to give more attention than ever to our work at this end of the line and I am depending on you to do the principal part in arranging our Mexican Exhibit. It is understood with the Centennial people that they are to be liberal with your medals, awards etc. We will have *Ancient* and *Modern* Mexico. I am going to make a great effort to get all the best things in the Toluca Museum, I shall depend on you to tell me what we shall strike. This will be a golden opportunity for us to get our material as far as Nashville free of cost, or nearly so. We must take full benefit of it [Powell to Starr, 1 January 1897, SPGC].

In his letter of 23 January Powell first mentioned the Peñafiel collection (Peñafiel 1890, 1900). "He asks only $6,000.00 gold for his entire collection! This, of course, is entirely too much, but he is very anxious to sell it to get some money to finish his residence, and I believe it might be possible to get it for $6,000.00 silver" (Powell to Starr, SPGC).

Powell's next letter is particularly candid. In a burst of feeling, Powell expressed his attitude toward Mexico and its cultural property. "We must push matters this year for all we are worth. I wish I could ransack the State of Guerrero. I have never been well of the sickness contracted there. Possibly if I would go back I would find my health where I lost it" (Powell to Starr, 26 January 1897, SPGC).

On 27 March 1897 Powell announced that he had purchased Peñafiel's collection and that he wanted "$3,000 in U.S.C. for the things delivered beyond the Rio Grande." Powell then went on to seek Starr's advice about selling the collection and assured Starr that he "will do nothing until I hear what you think best for me" (Powell to Starr, 27 March 1897, SPGC). Powell urgently needed to sell the collection as charges had been preferred against him by his fellow Baptist missionaries, and he had tendered his resignation (Patterson 1979:45).

Starr apparently took this as a golden opportunity. Included in Starr's papers is a bill of sale.

> I hereby sell and convey to Prof. Federick Starr, of Chicago University, of Chicago, Illinois, U.S.A. the entire collection of Mexican antiquities, made by the noted Mexican Archeologist, Dr. Antonio Peñafiel during the past thirty years and consisting of idols, house decorations, pottery, gold ornaments, bronze casts, etc., being some two thousand pieces, all told . . . in the sum of SEVENTEEN HUNDRED DOLLARS ($1700) . . . . The goods to be delivered in the Tennessee Centennial, where they are now on exhibition, and it is agreed that all medals and awards given said collection shall be the property of Prof. Starr. W. D. Powell [20 August 1897, SPGC].

Apparently the Peñafiel collection had joined the Tlacotepec collection in Nashville under the guise of an official Mexican exhibit at the Tennessee Centennial.

Starr and Powell remained friends and continued dealing into 1898 when their correspondence ended abruptly. In the last letter on file, dated 25 April 1898, Powell was still carrying valises, trunks, and baskets of objects across the border for Starr. However, when Starr returned to Mexico for a brief visit in June 1898, he simply recorded that "Powell is in the States, I suspect on account of mission troubles" (SPNB 20:7).

Following Powell's fall from grace, Starr never again involved himself directly in excavations. He continued his Mexican researches until 1904, primarily devoting his time to measuring and "busting" Indian tribes. During these years, however, he did not neglect to purchase antiquities whenever he could at a "good price."

In 1905 he left for Africa to study the Congo Pygmies. Although he later returned to Mexico many times on personal business, for the remainder of his life, his research centered on Africa and the Far East. To finance his new research interests, Starr decided to dispose of his personal Mexican collections. Ironically his most likely customer was his chief rival, George A. Dorsey at the Field Museum. On 1 August 1905, Starr wrote to Dorsey:

> I have finally decided to dispose of my collections from Mexico. You already know something of these collections which represent the work I have been doing in that country during the last ten years. . . . My price for this collection is $12,000 cash. I shall be glad if the Field Columbian Museum may purchase the collection. I should have wished that it might remain at the University, but if it must be sold outside it would be more than agreeable to me that it should be with your people than with any others [Field Museum of National History (FMDA):AF 947].

An agreement was struck in late August between Starr, the Field Museum, and its benefactors. The museum paid Starr 9,000 dollars for the material results of ten years of exploring, collecting, and expeditioning in Mexico. Today these are the artifacts and objects that represent Starr's tangible legacy to modern anthropology.

Context

Although the activities of Powell and Starr in Mexico may be harshly criticized today, they were both very much men of their time. They viewed the world from a pinnacle of Waspish superiority, and yet at the same time, they were dedicated to "saving" the natives and serving their clients.

Starr's own statements indicate that he was caught between global anti-imperalism and personal colonial behavior. With fervor Starr could state: "It is my belief that every people is happier and better with self-government, no matter how unlike our own from that government may be. I feel that no rationale is good enough, wise enough, or sufficiently advanced to undertake the elevation and civilization of a 'lower' people. Still less do I approve the exploitation of a native population by outsiders for their own benefit" (1907:4). Yet Starr's own personal behavior, as documented above and as expressed in his own accounts of his field expeditions, could very well be described as "the exploitation of a native population by outsiders for their own benefit."

Both Powell and Starr clearly recognized a basic humanity in all mankind. Both supported schools, and Starr throughout his life provided scholarships for needy boys who showed promise. Yet, like many Americans, Starr and Powell were caught between their belief in theoretical equality and their commitment to practical exploitation. Perhaps this contradiction between theory and practice can also lead to a better understanding of the friendship between Powell and Starr. On one level, their friendship appears to have been a mutually exploitive relationship, centered on money to be made in the antiquity trade. On another level, their relationship was one of Starr collecting for Science and Powell profiting for Salvation. On yet a third level, the friendship appears to have been genuine: two Christian gentlemen sharing good works in the land of papists and pagans. Their friendship stopped abruptly, however, when Powell was discredited and forced to leave Mexico.

How typical were Powell and Starr? It appears that many of the missionaries were collecting, as indeed were the businessmen. All interest groups were equally concerned with manipulating the political situation in Mexico. However, as critical as one may choose to be of the missionaries' and the businessmen's activities, Starr's activities are open to more serious criticisms. Starr was an anthropologist and viewed himself as a scientist.

And yet, his attitudes toward the cultural property of other nations, his manipulation of the political system, and his "evolutionary" ranking of Indians are an embarrassment to anthropologists today.

How typical was Starr of other museum-oriented Americanists operating in Mexico at the turn of the century? The evidence indicates that, though Starr may have been somewhat extreme, he was not atypical.

Marshall H. Saville

Marshall H. Saville (1867–1935) was the most prominent mesoamerican archaeologist at the American Museum of Natural History in New York until 1903, when he was appointed to the Loubat Chair of American Archaeology at Columbia University (Weitzner: n.d.). Saville's professional training began at the Peabody Museum of Harvard University under the guidance of F. W. Putnam. He served as assistant curator at the Peabody from 1889 to 1894. Saville's career in mesoamerican archaeology began with a collecting trip to the Yucatán Peninsula in 1890. In 1891–1892 he was sent to Copán, Honduras, to gather material for an exhibit at the Chicago World's Columbian Exposition. Subsequently he led many expeditions to Mexico for the American Museum.

It would appear that Saville was as adept as Starr and Powell were in manipulating the Mexican political system. Throughout 1896 Saville fought long and hard to assure passage of a law in Mexico that would be favorable to the American Museum's desired excavations and exportations. Despite the backing he received from President Porfirio Díaz, Saville was frustrated in his endeavors by the maneuvers of Inspector of Monuments Leopoldo Batres. He did, however, eventually win a liberal interpretation of the Mexican antiquities law. This interpretation enabled him to conduct his excavations at Mitla and at other sites in the Valley of Oaxaca and in the southern Maya lowlands.

As "inspector," Batres accompanied Saville to Oaxaca and subsequently claimed that he, not Saville, was responsible for the major excavations. Thus began a lengthy battle over the issue of Mexican versus American priority in Oaxacan archaeology. At the 1902 International Congress of Americanists in New York, Batres created such a scene over this matter that he was recalled to Mexico in disgrace.

The battle between Saville and Batres culminated in 1910 when Batres published an article in the *Mexico City Herald* that pressed his claims to the Oaxaca excavations. Saville replied in a privately printed broadside that accused Batres of every possible archaeological sin (1911).

Saville's "holier than thou" debates with Batres should be viewed in the light of his earlier actions in Mexico. Saville, German scholar Eduard Seler, and the duke of Loubat seem to have been as busy collecting and dealing as were Starr, Batres, and Powell. Duke of Loubat Joseph F. Loubat, was one of the most important early patrons of the American Museum and was also Saville's special patron (Duc de Loubat 1912).

In 1896, in the middle of his struggle to assure passage of a favorable antiquities law, Saville received a letter from Loubat asking him to look at the Sologueren collection. Starr had first seen and coveted this collection in 1894 and in 1895 had described and photographed it (SPNB 7 : 10–28, 36). "The collection which Dr. Seler bought I am told by Dr. Peñafiel is an exceedingly valuable one and will give us many fine things" (Saville to Winser, 23 April 1896, American Museum of Natural History [AMME]). In May Saville saw the collection and reported that it was "probably the most important collection in Mexico . . . more beautiful than any we have in the Museum" (Saville to Winser, 11 May 1896, AMME).

With Loubat's money and Seler's cooperation, despite the new antiquities law, the Sologueren collection was purchased for the American Museum of Natural History at the "lowest price." In 1896 it was presented to the Museum by the duke and placed on exhibit (Weitzner n.d. : 9). In the competition for collections, which typified museum policies of the time, Saville got Sologueren's collection for New York and Starr got Peñafiel's for Chicago.

Although Saville was clearly the American Museum's man in Mexico, his early research appears to be about as systematic as Starr's. Concern about controlling the quality of Saville's research was expressed by the American Museum's curator of anthropology, F. W. Putnam. Putnam's concern also offers an early contrast between Boas's ethnography and Saville's archaeology. "Boas and Smith send weekly accounts of work done . . . should like to have you do the same . . . a brief summary of the week's work every Saturday is what I would like" (Putnam to Saville, 23 July 1896, AMME).

Despite Putnam's concern and the growing importance of Boas, the museum's commitment to nineteenth-century collecting goals remained strong. In fact, until Saville's departure for Columbia University in 1903, "Only the work on North American Indian tribes . . . [was] reported under a 'research' caption; all other work [in anthropology was] . . . described under 'explorations' and 'expeditions'" (Weitzner n.d. : 20).

Saville remained a museum man to the end. His publications were not numerous but were, for his time, accurate in their descriptions (e.g., Saville 1900). He took no interest in theory or in advancing field-research technology. Yet he was one of the best-informed archaeologists on artifact types and their distribution in Latin America. In addition, he had a remarkable memory for the titles of books and memoirs in his special field (Wissler 1944). In his final days, after his return to the American Museum, he became a resource for future archaeologists (Gordon R. Willey, personal communication 1986).

Contrasts

Collier and Tschopik (1954:769) have described nineteenth-century museums as "concerned mainly with the acquisition of objects by purchase or gift, and the cataloging, preservation, and display of specimens." This seems to describe the program of Starr and Saville, even though they included fieldwork as a means of acquiring objects. Their fieldwork, however, differed sharply from that of Boas.

For Boas, fieldwork was a means of meticulously gathering facts about a culture and its history. He recognized that only careful excavation would permit the archaeologist to gather facts for culture history. Boas's view of history and fieldwork led him to establish the International School in Mexico (Godoy 1977); he inspired Manuel Gamio to undertake the first stratigraphic excavations in the Valley of Mexico (Gamio 1959). Starr's and Saville's fieldwork was guided by the acquisition of objects. Starr's evolutionary view placed all his "tribes" on the same level and hardly inspired him to expect stratigraphy to reveal a sequence of cultural development. Saville's early work among the Maya reinforced the then-current view (Hinsley 1985:34–35) that civilization had peaked early in Mesoamerica and had declined by the time of the Conquest. This view also discouraged the search for developmental sequences in the ground.

Since Boas, systematic collection and careful documentation have been the hallmark of material-culture studies in anthropology. Starr and his colleagues clearly failed to collect systematically. Unfortunately they also failed to document, let alone classify.

On 15 June 1907 Dorsey wrote a brief note to Starr: "I doubt if you realize the great importance to us of your giving us such assistance as you can, at your earliest convenience, in the matter of completing the catalogue of the collection which we purchased of you last year" (FMDA). On 17 July of that year Starr remarked to his mother that he finally did some work on his collections, "giving them data regarding my Mexican stuff that they bought before I went to Africa" (SPGC). Starr's scant "data" are presently on file on 5 by 7 in. cards that resemble the labels from the Walker Museum displays. The most informative read like the following example: "The great bulk of the present collection is from graves at Tlacotepec, a small place near the city of Toluca, and was excavated for Dr. Frederick Starr of the University of Chicago" (FMDA:AF 947).

Ironically, in the same year that Starr gave the Field Museum the "data" for his "Mexican stuff," Boas was establishing academic anthropology at Columbia University. In 1907 Boas publically questioned many of the assumptions that had guided his own earlier museum work. "The strong tendency to accumulate specimens has often been a disadvantage to the development of anthropology, because there are many aspects of this science in which the material objects are insignificant as compared with the actual scientific questions involved. . . . Anthropology requires a broader point of view for its fieldwork than that offered by the strict requirements of the acquisitions of museum specimens" (1907:931). Boas's new attitude toward museum policies was bound to affect the reputations of his anthropological colleagues who still accumulated specimens. Just as ethnography was to dominate archaeology, so the university was to dominate museum anthropology (Kroeber 1954:765).

Conclusions

Today, anthropologists not only demand that Boasian collection and documentation of material culture be the norm, they also insist that cultural context is more important than the objects themselves. Today, anthropological archaeologists declare that excavations without the guidance of hypotheses are little better than pothunting. In the extreme, archaeological positivists like Schiffer (1976:193) have argued that students should concentrate on defining the known principles of the discipline and designing future lines of research rather than studying previous lines of thought. As a result, collections like Starr's are ignored and almost forgotten, and their collectors are held in little regard.

In the context of the late nineteenth century, however, Starr did have an idea about what scientific anthropology should be. In a letter written to Frank B. Logan shortly before his retirement from the University of Chicago, Starr clearly sums up his view of anthropology.

> In my own work here at the University I have taken Anthropology in the broad sense in which it is used in Tylor's little book that bears the name. I divide the field into four minor fields. . . . Somatology or Physical Anthropology, Ethnology, Ethnography, and Culture History (including Archaeology). . . . In my teaching *evolution* is fundamental. It runs through every course I offer. It is what gives life and value to the work. It would be evolution of man, of human types, of ideas, customs, arts and industries that would be illustrated and studied [7 August 1922, FMDA].

Starr maintained his enthusiasm to the end, despite his failure to develop anthropology at the university (Stocking 1979a). Unlike Saville who apparently disliked teaching and showed no interest in graduate students, Starr viewed himself as a "missionary for anthropology" (Evans 1987). Starr's frustrations at the University of Chicago are brought to light in his response to Boas's request for information about anthropology at Chicago.

> I lay especial emphasis upon the disciplinary and educational value of our work at Chicago for all professional workers in whatever field. The result is that we have aimed to reach undergraduates and to serve them. More than that the limited facilities that have been given and

the expressed non-intention of developing the Department have all prevented my making the opportunities for advanced workers what I would wish. The nearness of the Field Museum and the consequent lack of interest in collections and to some degree in laboratory have operated in the same direction [26 February 1910, SPGC].

Starr's professional problems provide a personal context that may lead to a better understanding of the man. However, archaeological historians must go beyond the personalities and experiences of their predecessors and judge the actions of these men in the context of nineteenth-century American culture.

Turn-of-the-century America was a society under great tensions. Rapid industrialization was undermining traditional values and the prerogatives of the social classes that promoted these values. In this historical context the social sciences were becoming professional. As Ross has remarked, "In American academe . . . the professional ideals of the genteel culture could not withstand the inroads made by the aggressive, competitive, professionalizing activities of the research-oriented newcomers" (1979:121). The "genteel" culture to which Saville aspired was rapidly being discredited by the forces of materialism and imperial expansion. The absolute moral force of Starr's missionary vision was being attacked by impersonal relativism (Hinsley 1981:84). Caught between the past and the future, neither the eastern Saville nor the midwestern Starr would leave a lasting impression on his profession.

As products of their time, however, Starr and Saville left a legacy that should not be ignored. Their artifacts and descriptions can still provide basic data for present-day research. Their specimens are sometimes the only objects remaining to represent destroyed sites and acculturated tribes. Without their collecting efforts, the shelves of storerooms and the halls of display cases of many major museums would be bare. To ignore Starr's and Saville's legacy would prove a loss not only for comparative research but also for education.

Of equal importance is the background that Starr and Saville provide against which to judge the "progress" of archaeology. Anthropologists take the stand that only through comparison can we know ourselves; only if we know our origins can we glimpse our future. If we can objectively view the attempts of anthropologists of the late nineteenth century to establish a science, then we can learn from their failures and build on their successes. As Trigger has remarked, "Knowing more about the social factors that influence archaeological research should increase the self-awareness of archaeologists and permit a more objective understanding of their interpretations" (1985:232).

Recent publications (Arnove 1980; Hinsley 1981; Meltzer 1985; Patterson 1986; Rydell 1984) have examined the history of American anthropology and archaeology in the context of American society. These studies conclude that, in the late nineteenth century, anthropology reflected the growth of American nationalism and the values underlying capitalist expansion. In turn they suggest that archaeological research was used to support popular ethnocentric ideologies and to justify imperialistic expansion, both internally and abroad.

In the careers of Starr, Saville, and their contemporaries, we can discover the context out of which American anthropology and archaeology emerged. American society today still carries on the traditions of archaeological imperialism and social Darwinism that crystalized at the turn of the century. In the context of these traditions, that Franz Boas, despite his imperfections, managed to lead anthropology into its academic future appears all the more remarkable (Stocking 1979b:48).

To accomplish his ends Boas had to discredit the past. Early in his career he had questioned the value of museum displays that presented evolutionary stages. In the 1880s Boas and Otis T. Mason, the first curator of ethnography in the National Museum, engaged in a debate in which "Mason preached the unity of human cultural development in all its varieties, [and] Boas was already implying cultural relativism and pluralism" (Hinsley 1981:100). Throughout his career Boas fought against classic evolutionary theory, which he felt provided the justification for racism and ethnocentrism.

Despite Boas's success in establishing his university-based liberal relativism, however, evolutionary theory did not die. Developmental stages were resurrected in the 1950s (Steward 1955; White 1959; Willey and Phillips 1958). Under the guise of cultural ecology, evolutionary approaches gained a renewed respectability in the 1960s. Cultural ecology, as a theoretical perspective, once again joined archaeology and ethnology as equal partners in the study of cultural processes. As a result of this partnership, many anthropologists have now reevaluated the contributions of Tylor and Morgan and have granted them an honored place in the history of anthropology (Harris 1968).

In the context of the anthropology of the late nineteenth century, present-day archaeologists should also now reevaluate without prejudice the contributions of their predecessors. Archaeologists as partners in the development of current anthropology should not forget that they were equal partners in the establishment of anthropology as a discipline, well before Boasian ethnology established its early twentieth-century hegemony.

Acknowledgments

This chapter was made possible by a professional term granted by North Central College and a fellowship awarded by the Midwest Faculty Seminar Fellowship Program of the University of Chicago.

Various archival sources were made available to me during my research. Permission to use archival materials was granted by the Special Collections Department, Regenstein Library, University of Chicago; the Departments of Anthropology at the Field Museum of Natural History and the American Museum of Natural History, New York; the registrar of the Field Museum of Natural History; and the archivists at Museum of the American Indian, Heye Foundation. All support is gratefully acknowledged.

11

The Role of Ideology and Institutions in Shaping Classical Archaeology in the Nineteenth and Twentieth Centuries

Stephen L. Dyson

In a conference devoted mainly to the history of North American and European prehistoric archaeology, a paper dealing with the development of the discipline of classical archaeology needs some explanation, if not justification. The fields of classical and anthropological archaeology have, in recent years, gone their own ways, and many archaeologists with an anthropological orientation regard classical archaeology as largely irrelevant to the development of a modern scientific discipline. Whatever the justice of this attitude may be in describing the condition of present-day classical archaeology, it should not affect an interest in the history of that subbranch of the discipline. Indeed, the history of classical archaeology should be of special interest to other archaeologists trying to understand how their particular fields developed.

Classical archaeology is the oldest branch of archaeology in the United States. Without exploring the prehistory of American classical archaeology in the early years of the nineteenth century or its development in Europe from the Renaissance onward, one can note that its professional society, the Archaeological Institute of America (AIA), was founded in 1879, that the *American Journal of Archaeology (AJA)* celebrated its one hundredth anniversary in 1985, and that the first meeting of the AIA was held in New Haven, Connecticut, in 1900 (Donahue 1985; Sheftel 1979). Therefore, in the United States as well as in Europe, classical archaeology as a profession has a time perspective and also an evolutionary history that are several generations older than those of Americanist archaeology. It makes classical archaeology and its professional organization, the AIA, the founders of professional archaeology in the United States. As such, they were important in the development of other emerging branches of archaeology in the United States including the North American field. The role of the AIA in assisting in early fieldwork in the Americas (Adolph Bandelier was an early research employee of the AIA) and in helping found such institutions as the School of American Research in Santa Fe, plus the role of classical archaeology, in general, in shaping the field methods and research goals in early Americanist archaeology deserve more consideration than they have received in the history of American archaeology.

Equally important for students of the history of academic disciplines in general and of archaeology in particular is that this longer time period allows a better evolutionary perspective. Few academic professions in the United States are more than 100 years old and have seen the passage of so many generations with their collective production and changing fashions of research. Study of American classical archaeology offers the potential for observing a number of paradigm shifts in the Kuhnian sense (Kuhn 1962). Moreover, it offers the opportunity to observe a discipline developing in relation to a whole range of changes in the larger society, both national and international. Thus by 1935 when the Society for American Archaeology (SAA) was founded, classical AIA archaeology in the United States had gone through the closing of the frontier; two major, highly nationalistic wars; the creation of formal graduate programs in the country; the boom of the 1920s; and the worst part of the Great Depression. While the SAA was just emerging as a professional organization and Americanist archaeologists were just beginning to carve out their niches in university anthropology departments, classical archaeology departments were absorbing a major influx of refugees from the emerging totalitarian regimes of Europe and would shortly have access to fieldwork in Europe and the Mediterranean, which had been cut off for nearly a decade. Each of these events gave special direction to the discipline of classical archaeology and provides more complex perspectives on the history of archaeology in general.

Other instances of the usefulness of the history of American classical archaeology for other branches of the discipline could be cited, but I would rather concentrate on the major issues highlighted in the title—that is, the role played by the complex interaction of ideology and institutions in the shaping of a discipline like classical archaeology. By *ideology*, I mean simply the larger justifications we provide for why and how we do what we do. For "new archaeologists" the statement that "archaeology is anthropology or it is nothing" (Willey and Phillips 1958:2) is an expression of ideology, firmly placing archaeology in a certain niche in a personal or collective intellectual universe that may or may not have strong empirical justification. For a classical archaeologist such an expression of ideology might be that classical art and culture represent one of the highest points in human achievement and that the humble task of the archaeologist is to recover and reconstruct as much as possible of these cultures for the general betterment of mankind. This belief is very different from the credo of the anthropological archaeologist but equally describes how a group of professional archaeologists views the world.

I would contend that all archaeologists have elements of an archaeological ideology buried within them and that these individual ideologies are intertwined in very complex ways with the collective ideology of the discipline whether the latter is well articulated, semiarticulated, or merely implied. Moreover, this ideology is a major motivating force for what they do. Otherwise, for many, the practice of archaeology would end up as an exercise little different from stamp collecting. Anthropological archaeologists have been active in examining the ideological as well as the theoretical basis of their discipline during the last twenty years. Classical archaeologists have been much less active in this pursuit but have subconsciously accepted the major elements of the late nineteenth-century founding ideology of their profession while dropping some of its most imaginative components and not replacing them with any new paradigms drawn from the social and intellectual experience of the last 75 years. This theme of isolation and, hence, theoretical impoverishment in classical archaeology is one that I have explored before; for I think it is crucial to the understanding of the evolution of that branch of the discipline (Dyson 1981, 1985).

In the world of modern academics, ideology cannot be separated from institutions, especially in the discipline of archaeology whose practitioners work in a complicated and expensive field where activities are increasingly based in collective operations. Archaeologists join a range of professional groups. Their approach to the discipline is shaped by their graduate training, most notably by seminars and field programs. Success in the profession, especially at the early stages, results not only from the mastery of data and the understanding and criticism of theory but also from the ability to absorb and articulate the prevalent ideology of the graduate institution of which they are a part. These conditions affect their ability to become employed, to be funded, to publish, and to get favorable reviews. Obviously institutions also affect power relationships. In competition, they like to collect kudos but also to use power positions to reinforce ideology.

Certainly the study of ideology and institutions as they have evolved historically in a profession as old as classical archaeology is the proper theme for an entire book, not for a single chapter. Moreover, the moment for such a full consideration of these questions is premature, for surprisingly, relatively little work has been done on the history of classical archaeology in the United States, and most of what has been done is historiographically unsophisticated. Useful histories of some major institutions, such as the American School of Classical Studies in Athens (Lord 1947; Meritt 1984) and the American Academy in Rome (Valentine and Valentine 1973), have been written, but they are generally cast in a rather old-fashioned positivistic mold, if they are not downright hagiographical. Except for some of the earliest figures like Charles Eliot Norton, biographical studies of major

American classical archaeologists are generally lacking (Edlund et al. 1981; Valentine 1959). Overviews of the history of major excavations are just beginning to appear (Camp 1986; Hanfmann 1972; Hopkins 1979). Except for a few articles, the history of neither the AIA, nor the major journal, the *AJA,* has been written (Donahue 1985; Sheftel 1979; Thompson 1980). Oral history has not been pursued, even though many important figures of the last two generations of classical archaeologists are still alive. Archival work both on the history of major institutions and on the collected papers of major figures in the field has just started. While I have set myself the long-range task of writing such a history of classical archaeology in the United States, I realize that my work is only in the most preliminary stages. What I want to propose in this chapter are some directions that I consider important for my own research and also a few sample areas where more detailed investigation has yielded some interesting results.

The ideology of classical archaeology as an American academic discipline was firmly stated from the beginning. The early publications of the AIA contain a number of position papers and often highly rhetorical statements of the institute and its members, largely, if not exclusively, classical archaeologists. Among the founding group, one of the most influential and outspoken was Harvard's Charles Eliot Norton (Valentine 1959). Not only did he help found the institute but he was a very active figure in its early development. In 1899, at the first general meeting of the AIA, he gave a speech that is today well suited for describing the ideology behind the creation of the institute and, to a very large degree, the classical archaeology profession in the United States (Norton 1900). It is vintage, highly rhetorical, late nineteenth-century prose, but for that reason it highlights major themes and makes the task of the intellectual historian easier.

One of the first issues Norton discussed was the need for American scholars in general and people in the field of classical archaeology in particular to prove themselves in relation to European academics. Norton noted that American professionals got started later and worked for too long with very limited resources, especially in the area of scholarly materials. However, he felt that by the end of the nineteenth century, some 20 years after the founding of the AIA, our scholars were making worthwhile contributions to an international field, which expressed the international quality of the discipline of classical archaeology—something much more pronounced in this subbranch of the discipline than is found in North American archaeology. It also is an expression of a strong sense of insecurity, even inferiority, in American classical archaeology, something that has been reinforced by the regular importation of European professors throughout the history of the discipline and particularly by the massive influx of Europeans in the period just before and after World War II. While these new arrivals have made many very important contributions to our discipline, they have complicated the creation of a distinctively American form of classical archaeology and have set up distinctive lines of communication within American academic institutions, which have helped to cut off classical archaeology from other more dynamic branches of archaeology in the post–World War II period.

Norton developed other themes that reveal continuing shaping forces in classical archaeology. One of these themes is the inherent worth of studying classical civilization. He sums this up nicely in discussing Greek and Roman civilization. "Together they represent the full circle of human affairs and interest. To them all the previous life of man contributes, from them as from their head all the varied full currents of modern life derive" (1900:14). For Norton, the study of classical archaeology contributes not only to our comprehension of the Greek and Roman past but also to an understanding of "the origins and goals of our own civilization" (1900:15). In fact, the goals of archaeology as with any humanistic branch of scholarship should reach even higher to encompass "a fuller acquaintance with life in its higher ranges, . . . a juster appreciation of the ways and works of man, and of man's relation to that inconceivable universe, in the vast and mysterious order of which he feels himself an infinitesimally small object" (1900:12). In asserting the superiority of Greek and Roman culture, the classical archaeologists were claiming a special position for themselves as the interpreters of an especially important civilization. In this assertion they recalled the biblical archaeologists. Each in a particular way dealt with a civilization considered "sacred" by the West, and each could justify his or her activities as much on the basis of what was studied as by what approach was taken. In a variety of ways both positive and negative, this sense of being special has shaped the development of classical archaeology during the last 100 years.

Another parallel with biblical archaeology is that sacred objects are closely associated with sacred texts. Norton emphasized the need to interrelate carefully the study of classical archaeology and classical literature. This aim is admirable in some respects, not least because until the development of American historical archaeology, the classical archaeologists were the group that could call on the most complete written record to test results obtained from the analysis of material culture. However, the existence of this rich, abundant, and intellectually powerful body of literature has prevented the emergence of a modern discipline of classical archaeology that asks questions independently of texts written by and for elites. It is an issue that I have explored in more detail elsewhere, but one that should be kept in mind whenever the past, present, and future of classical archaeology is considered (Dyson 1981).

Norton did not see the activities of the AIA-oriented archaeologist as limited to the Mediterranean. His speech called attention to the role of the AIA in sponsoring early research in the archaeology of the New World. Part of this work developed out of an interest in North American monuments and their preservation but also involved larger questions of archaeology as a discipline involved in the study of mankind. As Norton put it, "the larger questions which are included in it are the same as those which concern the prehistoric periods of man's life in whatever region of the world, while the actual conditions of the existing remnants of the tribes who occupied the continent in ancient times afford peculiar opportunities for ascertaining facts which illustrate, nay which in a sort actually represent the antiquity of mankind" (Norton 1900 : 5).

Even with its quaint, late Victorian self-confidence and even its less than appealing prejudices, Norton's speech does provide a real sense of ideology, a justification for how and why his generation did archaeology. To see how these overviews of the profession changed, I decided to look at other anniversary speeches. For the fiftieth anniversaries of both the AIA and of the *AJA* in 1929 and 1935, respectively, relatively little fuss appears to have been made. An anniversary plenary session was held at one of the meetings, but the speeches were not, as far as I know, printed. During the Great Depression, our colleagues were more interested in finding the financial means rather than the rationale for doing archaeology (Donahue 1985 : 22–26; Sheftel 1979 : 13). For the one hundredth anniversary of both institutions, considerably more fuss was made, and the events were celebrated with several publications (Donahue 1985; Dow 1980; Sheftel 1979). The essay that was probably the most comparable to the speech by Norton was the address "Pursuit of the Past" given at the AIA centenary celebration by Homer Thompson (1980).

The Sheftel and Donahue articles are basically archival in approach. They contain much useful information about the early history of the AIA and its journal, Norton's contributions and prejudices are laid out in considerable detail as are institutional history and finances, but little is said about the larger directions and goals of the AIA or the *AJA*. Occasional side observations suggest failure of nerve. Thus, when the trustees of the AIA initially refused to support the foundation of the American Research Institute in Turkey because it was an organization "little connected with the direct purposes and activities of the AIA," the author notes sadly that "this represented a considerable change in attitude from the late years of the nineteenth century when nearly every meeting of the Institute saw lively discussion on the hopes of founding an American school of archaeology somewhere abroad" (Sheftel 1979 : 16), but no effort is made to relate this change to larger questions of the restricted vision of the archaeologists directing the institute.

The essay by Thompson has a wide sweep and an elegant presentation. The author is one of the best classical archaeologists of his generation and a humanely educated scholar. Themes developed by Norton, such as the close relation between the artifact and the text and the complex interactions of American and European classical archaeology and archaeologists, are explored, and an excellent review is provided of major excavation projects undertaken by American groups. The splintering off from the AIA of various archaeological groups is noted, but no effort is made to explore the intellectual implications that this narrowing of archaeological focus may have had for the discipline of classical archaeology. Indeed it is striking that

20 years after the birth of the so-called new archaeology and the ferment it caused in so many areas of archaeology, no issues of theory or the general direction of classical archaeology are raised.

This lack of interest in questions of new method and theory and the way that changes in other branches of archaeology might effect classical archaeology is not limited to anniversary speeches. Elsewhere I have looked at certain major topics represented in articles published in *AJA* as contrasted with *American Antiquity* and noted that *AJA* showed almost no interest in either theory, method, or such innovative approaches to archaeology as survey and environmental analysis (Dyson 1985). Moreover, while fashions in articles have changed dramatically over the last few years in *American Antiquity*, these changes have been minimal in *AJA*. The same patterns can be observed in the papers presented at the annual meeting of the institute. From the 1930s through the 1960s topics related to areas like Greek material culture (i.e., sculpture and vase painting) dominated while almost nothing was said about method, theory, geoarchaeology, or floral and faunal analysis. By the 1980s some papers in those areas had begun to appear, but such topics as Greek material culture still dominated. A 1985 program of the AIA was not materially different from one in 1935 both in the format and in the topics covered by the papers.

The natural question that grows out of this analysis is, What has caused this ossification of a subdiscipline that was once a leader in the field? The answer is naturally complex, but it leads back to questions about institutions and how they shape the discipline. In the remainder of this paper, I would like to explore this issue in a very preliminary fashion, concentrating on the topics of access to new ideas, the shaping of graduate and field training, and the control of key power positions in the profession. Regarding access to new ideas, I have been exploring the development of the book review section of the *AJA* and have made some trenchant comments on the topic elsewhere (Dyson 1981). A more detailed analysis of reviews published in the 1930s and the 1960s shows much the same pattern as that found in articles and convention papers. In fact books related to material-culture analysis took up only 11% of the reviews in the 1930s and 22% in the 1960s. The generation of graduate students in the 1960s (who are now emerging as the leaders of the profession) were being guided in their reading by an *AJA* book review section that was, in some respects, more conservative than that of the 1930s and this at a time when their anthropological counterparts were being shaken by the new archaeology revolution.

If they did not find new horizons in the book review section of *AJA*, they might have found them in graduate school. Clearly a detailed analysis of the history of the major graduate schools, their faculty, and especially their seminar programs is needed. It is a task I have only just begun. However, it is clear that major programs during the 1960s, such as those at Bryn Mawr, Harvard, and Princeton, were conservative in their approach to archaeology. Many of their faculty were European trained and more inclined to establish links with classics and fine arts than with anthropology. Some universities, such as Boston University, Indiana University, and the University of Minnesota, have attempted to develop archaeology programs oriented toward the Old World that break with the traditional mold and orient their students toward new directions in anthropological archaeology (Wilkie and Coulson 1985). While their students are beginning to make some impact in the profession, they have not broken the domination of the older, more conservative graduate programs whose students were placed in a large number of departments during the boom period of the late 1960s and early 1970s.

Classical archaeology students tend to be trained in a limited number of relatively conservative graduate programs. From there the most successful enter one of the major overseas schools. For classical archaeology, the most important of these has been the American School of Classical Studies in Athens. By late in the course of his or her graduate program, this same promising student has probably become associated with one of the major excavation programs. Throughout its history, classical archaeology has been associated with large-scale excavations, usually at major urban or religious centers, especially in the 1950s and 1960s when funding was relatively abundant, and each graduate program felt it needed an excavation. In Greece, this direction is encouraged by the government, which allows each foreign country only a limited number of permits. Some of these excavations, such as that of the American School in the Athenian Agora and at Corinth, go on for decades or even generations. Tradition pervades. Students are confronted with rows of field notebooks bearing the names of greats of the past. Through the library and tearoom of the American School and the American Academy in Rome pass not only the greatest scholars of the present generation but many retired luminaries who spent their post-teaching years in Athens and Rome. Moreover, most excavation staffs are large and arranged in a strong hierarchical fashion. The new arrival soon learns his or her place and sees that success comes from accepting and using the system rather than from challenging it. Few students are encouraged to strike out on their own with radical new projects, and few do so. In such a system with its strong stress on tradition, innovation is about as likely as in the Chinese bureaucracy in the age of Confucius.

Even if the emerging scholar is inclined to offer radical alternatives in classical archaeology in spite of earlier training and professional acculturation, that individual, if at all politically sophisticated, will see rapidly that the power elite in the profession is strongly entrenched in a limited number of institutions that have held power for long periods of time. As an example, the editorship of *AJA* has never left the east coast of the United States and has never migrated north of Cambridge or south of Philadelphia. The contrast with *American Antiquity* is immediate and striking (Dyson 1985:461). I am in the process of gathering data on such topics as program committee membership, review panels of major granting agencies, and other similar power groups. From personal experience, I suspect that the same pattern of control by a limited number of interlocking people and institutions will emerge and that few of these will be scholars who encourage challenge of the status quo. Moreover, I suspect that the data will show a strong correlation between power control in one generation and the success of younger scholars with the correct institutional and ideological orientation in the next.

In this chapter I have laid out an agenda for future research rather than a history of my discipline. My interest in such topics as the role of certain institutions in shaping an intellectual and professional outlook and the need to study professional acculturation in its systemic context are clear. Many of my concerns are related to internal issues of classical archaeology. However, I believe that they also relate to large questions that should interest all historians of archaeology. Classical archaeology is the oldest of the archaeological subfields and therefore the most "mature." One can ask whether such developments as the concentration of power in a limited number of institutions and the loss of ideological vigor are special to classical archaeology or whether that loss is inherent in the maturing of any large professional group. I suspect that the correct answer relates more to the second rather than to the first proposition. Certainly, I have observed the subfield of historical archaeology move, in the last 20 years, from a small, informal band of feuding Deetzians and Southians to a much more formal, somber, bureaucratic group. If such trends are likely within any bureaucratically organized profession and if they are considered undesirable, then a discipline's historian has a mission to study and understand trends that may lead to intellectual ossification. This concern is only one of the many ways in which the history of archaeology becomes interesting and important for its practitioners in the last years of the twentieth century.

Part III

Researching and Presenting the History of Archaeology

Introduction

In some ways, the methods of history come naturally to archaeologists who, as prehistorians, are faced with many of the same problems of constructing interpretations of the past by evaluating data from several, sometimes conflicting, sources. The specific types of data and methods of data collection, such as using texts and interviews, and the specific forms of interpretation and presentation, familiar to historians may be unfamiliar to archaeologists. A number of historical research methods have already been discussed—questionnaires and analysis of curricula vitae by Embree, analysis of illustrations by Hinsley, and textual analysis of speeches by Dyson. In part 3 further information about researching and presenting the history of archaeology is provided.

Desmond (chapter 12) provides a detailed account of his encounter with the lives of Augustus and Alice Le Plongeon. The Le Plongeons conducted pioneering work at Mayan ruins in the Yucatán, but because they were on the losing side in the debate about the origins of mesoamerican civilization, they were relegated to the lunatic fringe by later historians until Desmond decided to reevaluate their contributions. Anyone who anticipates researching the life of an archaeologist should read Desmond's account to understand the level of commitment required to accomplish such a task.

Chapman (chapter 13) discusses some of the research issues involved in studying a community of scholars, a subject touched upon by Embree and Dyson. Using British archaeology in the mid-nineteenth century as an example, he argues that by looking at the institutional framework within which archaeology was done, one gains a clearer understanding of why research took the directions it did. As did Embree, Chapman takes a sociology of science approach to emphasize relationships between archaeologists (for another example, see Kurtz 1979).

Continuing the issue of context from part 2, I argue (chapter 14) that archaeologists as historians of recent archaeology may be limited in what or who they may write about. Sabloff and Embree have discussed some aspects of studying recent archaeology from an intellectual or a sociological perspective, but I consider the more personal or biographical level that could be harmful to the career of an archaeologist who discusses certain sensitive, but historically relevant, events.

Jeter (chapter 15), like Reyman and McVicker, is involved in research on old collections and records. He provides examples from his research in Arkansas about how early archaeological work can be used for current archaeological research. Jeter's chapter illustrates how research on the history of archaeology done for archaeologists can differ from that done for other audiences. For example, he found that Edward Palmer suffered from directional dyslexia (i.e., writing north when he meant south). Such an idiosyncrasy may be of little interest to a historian, but to an archaeologist trying to use the subject's collections and records it may be critical.

Until recently the history of archaeology has been presented in written form; however the expansion of the television and video industries has opened a vast new outlet. Tarabulski (chapter 16) shares his experiences of producing a video about a 1930 archaeological expedition. He takes the reader step by step through the production process and explains how the combination of old film footage, interviews, period music, and symposium presentations can be used to share the adventure of archaeology's past with a wider audience.

Writing the history of archaeology is not possible unless evidence remains for historians to interpret. Idea histories, such as those of Daniel (1950, 1962, 1981c), are possible using primarily the published literature, but many of the questions of increasing interest to historians of archaeology can be answered only by using the evidence contained in personal papers, archives, and archaeologists' memories. Lyon (chapter 17) presents a plan for the preservation of these unpublished sources in public repositories so that they are available to those who wish to use them. Other disciplines have established documentation programs for preserving their histories, and archaeologists must do the same before more important records are lost.

One method of research of the history of archaeology that has not been mentioned (except by Meltzer, who quotes Sackett about excavating the back dirt of previous archaeologists) is the study of artifactual remains left by archaeologists themselves. A study of archaeological field technology in the form of field vehicles, excavation tools, and camping equipment could be highly informative. Study of the original items themselves would no doubt be a challenge and involve much grubbing in the back rooms of museums and universities. Perhaps somewhat easier would be the study of archaeological field camps that still survive. Such a study has already been done at one camp in the Southwest (Scott 1972), and there are many others in that region that are still visible. It is not often that archaeologists have a chance to excavate the home of an archaeologist, but there is at least one example, the house of Charles C. Abbott in New Jersey (Stanzeski 1974). One hopes that historical archaeologists will take an increasing interest in such remains.

12

Of Facts and Hearsay: Bringing Augustus Le Plongeon into Focus

Lawrence G. Desmond

> False facts are highly injurious to the progress of science, for they
> often long endure; but false views, if supported by some evidence,
> do little harm, as every one takes a salutary pleasure in proving their
> falseness; and when this is done, one path towards error is closed,
> and the truth is often at the same time opened.
> —Charles Darwin, *The Descent of Man,*
> *and Selection in Relation to Sex*

Searching for Augustus Le Plongeon

It is hard to find a person with a less attractive image in the history of
American archaeology than that of Augustus Le Plongeon. He was thrust,
suddenly, into my life in 1977 when I was teaching a class on mesoamerican archaeology at Foothill College in California. I thought it important that
my students should have some background on the history of Mayan studies,
so in preparing for a lecture, I read Robert Wauchope's account of Le Plongeon in his book *Lost Tribes and Sunken Continents.*

According to Robert Wauchope, Le Plongeon's "arrogant flaunting
of his own ego produced a lurid epoch in the history of American archaeology" (1962:8). The idea that a "lurid epoch" could be produced by one
archaeologist seemed an overstatement, but, intrigued, I looked for more
background material.

Robert Brunhouse's book about eight archaeologists, *In Search of the
Maya,* published a decade later, gave a somewhat more balanced view of
Le Plongeon. He stated of Wauchope's work that it "gives the best introduction to the story of the Le Plongeons" (1973:229). The activities of Le Plongeon's wife, Alice, were noted; however, her contributions were minimized
by the suggestion that her husband was the source of all her ideas. Le Plongeon was summarized as "mysterious, preposterous, opinionated, haphaz-
ardly informed, reckless, and a remarkable person" (1973:137, 164).

Brunhouse cited a letter about Le Plongeon written in 1931 by Sylvanus Morley, director of the Carnegie Institution's Chichén Itzá project, to Carnegie director John C. Merriam. I wrote for a copy of the letter and received it two weeks later. The letter hooked me. It was Morley's account of his daylong interview with a friend of the Le Plongeons, Maude Blackwell, in whom they had entrusted their lifework (10 October 1931, Carnegie Institution of Washington). Blackwell told Morley and archaeologist Karl Ruppert that she had in her possession all the Le Plongeon photographs, notes, and unpublished manuscripts and that she was interested in passing those materials on to the Carnegie Institution. In the letter Morley also stated that Blackwell knew about the Le Plongeons' discovery of Mayan codices in the Akab Dzib at Chichén Itzá and in the Adivino Pyramid at Uxmal. Unfortunately, because Morley criticized Le Plongeon's theories about cultural diffusion too strongly, Blackwell was offended and refused to sell the collection. She then turned to a more sympathetic person, Manly P. Hall, president of the Philosophical Research Society in Los Angeles, and in the fall of 1931, the society bought the collection.

I began to dig into the Le Plongeon archival materials in earnest and naively imagined that it would not take long to come to some incontrovertible conclusions about the "Old Doctor" and Alice—it was time to clear up the so-called mysteries about them. I soon discovered, however, that it was too early for any meaningful interpretation. So instead, I collected articles, purchased or copied their books, dug into archives and libraries, and read all the correspondence to an from and about them I could find. I also interviewed scholars for their opinions on the Le Plongeons and placed ads in newspapers for lost Le Plongeon materials as well as for leads about Augustus's childhood on the island of Jersey and Alice's in London. My enthusiasm was somewhat dampened by the negative reaction of some archaeologists to my research subject. They wondered how I could possibly want to pursue research on such a loser. It appeared that for most archaeologists, the Le Plongeon case was closed.

Augustus Le Plongeon, one of the earliest individuals to investigate extensively the Maya, had been dismissed since the turn of the century by nearly all Mayan scholars as little more than a troublesome eccentric. He had spent considerable time working in Yucatán, but his theory that the Maya founded world civilization never found support in the scholarly community. His extraordinary record of Mayan sites documented by photography, drawings, and plans was all but forgotten.

Alice Dixon Le Plongeon has been characterized by writers of late as no more than a faithful follower of her husband, a "young and lovely bride" parroting his bizarre theories (Brunhouse 1973:137; Wauchope 1962:8). But Alice was a true pioneer in the study of the Maya (Desmond 1988). She went to Yucatán in 1873, fresh from London, and spent 11 years among the Maya and the ancient ruins, learned the language and local customs, and published books and numerous journal articles. Around the turn of the century, her contribution to understanding Mayan civilization was noted in the *Scientific American* (A Woman Archaeologist 1895), but within 20 years she was all but forgotten, except for a few minor notices by the last defenders of the Le Plongeons.

Fortunately, I had been corresponding with Dennis Puleston at the University of Minnesota. He encouraged me to continue my investigations into Le Plongeon and agreed to spend time with me, after the 1978 Palenque Mesa Redonda, at Chichén Itzá to search for evidence that Le Plongeon had found Mayan codices in the Akab Dzib. Lewis C. "Skip" Messenger, his graduate student, and Phyllis Messenger also assisted in the work at Chichén Itzá. After no more than a visual inspection of the Akab Dzib, however, our project abruptly ended when Puleston was tragically killed by lightning atop the Castillo Pyramid. Stunned, but determined to continue my work on Le Plongeon, I drove from Mexico to Washington, D.C., stopping on the way at Tulane University's Latin American Library in New Orleans. To my delight I found that the correspondence from Maude Blackwell to Frans Blom about the Le Plongeon photographic collection had been preserved along with a few photographs and Le Plongeon's plans of the Akab Dzib at Chichén Itzá and the Governor's Palace at Uxmal. In her letters to Blom, as in her interview by Morley, Blackwell revealed that, on her deathbed, Alice Le Plongeon had told her the location of Mayan codices (Blackwell to Blom, 1931, Latin American Library, Tulane University). According to Blackwell they had been found and then reburied at Uxmal and Chichén Itzá, but she gave Blom only vague instructions about their location.

My next stop was the American Antiquarian Society in Worcester, Massachusetts, where I read the hundred or so letters from Le Plongeon to his patron at the society, Stephen Salisbury, Jr. The letters gave Salisbury an accounting of the Le Plongeons' theories, travels, and discoveries; complaints about rivals; and in one letter Le Plongeon offered for sale 70 "views" of Belize for 10 dollars each. Today only 15 of his photographs of Belize are known to have survived.

In Washington, D.C., I visited the Library of Congress which contained letters to Ephraim G. Squier from Augustus, and also the Smithsonian Institution where there were a number of letters to Spencer Baird and William McGee. The letters to Squier had originated from Lima, Peru, where Le Plongeon was attempting to find a permanent position in the diplomatic corps and asked Squier for assistance. In addition to a medical clinic, Le Plongeon had a photographic studio in Lima and may have taken a significant number of Squier's Peruvian archaeological photos. Le Plongeon's letters from Belize in the late 1870s bitterly complain to Salisbury that Squier had published his photographs without his consent and without giving him credit or financial compensation. Le Plongeon had written to Baird asking for funding to build a Mayan temple from his molds at an exposition in New

Orleans, but high fire-insurance rates caused them to decide against the project. A letter to McGee answered his inquiry about a Mayan dictionary that they were preparing to publish.

Because most of the Carnegie Institution's archival holdings of archaeological materials had been transferred to the Peabody Museum at Harvard University, I realized there would be little of direct relevance for me there. All the same, I spent an afternoon going through their archives with the hope that something might turn up, but I found nothing on the Le Plongeons.

All the institutions I visited were extremely helpful, and I found the limited photocopying rule, 10 pages per day, at the American Antiquarian Society a small inconvenience. Their curatorial staff, then headed by William Joyce, was of great assistance and always kept a watchful eye. On one occasion, racing to finish reading materials before closing time, I had not placed the Le Plongeon letters squarely back in their folders and was reminded of the proper way!

At this early stage in the research, my interests were divided between determining the nature of Augustus's contribution to American archaeology and finding out if he had actually uncovered Mayan codices. While I suspected a hoax, I must admit that it was more exciting to look for clues leading to the location of the Mayan "treasure" than to wrestle with Le Plongeon's theories and lifetime of scholarly maneuverings, and this possibility kept me reading his rambling handwritten letters.

Augustus had several professions during his life, including photography, medicine, and archaeology, that gave me logical paths of inquiry. An evaluation of his photography and archaeology was far easier than an evaluation of his medical career. It took some digging into the history of the medical profession to find answers to how Augustus might have been trained as a doctor, and how useful his "electro-hydropathic" clinic in Lima was.

The search for every trace of Le Plongeon took me to evermore obscure corners. He was a Freemason, and during her last years, Alice had contact with the Theosophical Society founded by Madame Helena Petrovna Blavatsky. In 1890 Alice delivered a lecture titled "The Mayas" to the Blavatsky Lodge of the society (Le Plongeon 1890). In 1913, *The Word Magazine,* another publication of the society, published posthumously Le Plongeon's key work on the founding of Egypt by the Maya, "The Origin of the Egyptians" (Le Plongeon 1913–1914).

In New York I visited the Theosophical Society of America, the Olcott Library, and the United Lodge of Theosophists; in Worcester, Massachusetts, the Masonic Temple; in Washington, D.C., the library of the Supreme Council 33, Scottish Rite; in Spring Valley, New York, the Anthroposophical Society (they had published a paperback reprint of Le Plongeon's book on Mayan cultural diffusion, *Queen Móo and the Egyptian Sphinx*), and later in the year, the Theosophy Company in Los Angeles. I was never able to establish a direct connection between the Le Plongeons and Theosophy, and I have never been able to determine Le Plongeon's grade or lodge in Freemasonry.

While nothing turned up from those institutions, surprises often surfaced when least expected. In the basement of the Brooklyn Museum while looking at an assortment of artifacts from Mexico, I noticed an old, broken filing cabinet. The bottom drawer was open and a folder said "Spinden." The only letter in the folder was from art historian Herbert Spinden to a Mr. Linklater. In it he made a number of critical comments about Le Plongeon's theories, which he felt had "not the slightest archaeological justification," but he went on to say that "Le Plongeon did some really good excavating at Uxmal . . . and [at Chichén Itzá] discovered the famous Chacmool" (25 March 1947, Brooklyn Museum). I was encouraged to look further into Le Plongeon's fieldwork.

A second surprise occurred in New York during a visit to the American Museum of Natural History. I wanted to inventory artifacts that the Le Plongeons had sold to the museum around the turn of the century. Gordon Ekholm, curator emeritus of mesoamerican archaeology, stated he had received a trunk in the mid-1950s with Le Plongeon's negatives and prints. A storage company in Brooklyn had delivered the trunk to anthropologist William Duncan Strong at Columbia University, but Strong sent the trunk to the museum because he felt the contents were more appropriate to a museum collection. The trunk contained a few of Maude Blackwell's personal items and some of Augustus Le Plongeon's materials: 22 collodion glass-plate negatives, 118 albumen prints, and 29 lantern slides. This cache was an exciting find and a great motivator, keeping me on the trail of Le Plongeon materials in spite of my worries about funding to keep the project going—I had financed the project from my own resources.

In Brooklyn, I searched for the Le Plongeons' last residence at 18 Sidney Place, I found the building, but it yielded nothing. According to the landlord, it had been completely renovated in the early 1970s.

The Long Island Historical Society held a single-page "Memorial to Augustus Le Plongeon" written by Alice, which told the story of Le Plongeon's cremation at Fresh Pond and the scattering of his ashes at sea by a deeply grieving Alice. I had to copy the page by hand because the photocopy machine was not operating, and a year later when I went back for another look, I was told the memorial had been sold to a bookstore in Manhattan. When I raced to the bookstore I found the item had been purchased by an unknown buyer. My first review of archival materials in East Coast institutions completed, I returned to my archaeological job in California with my backpack full of photocopied materials and notes.

Late in 1978 I drove to Los Angeles to determine the extent of a collection of Le Plongeon photographs that were reported to be at the Philosophical Research Society. I asked the head librarian if they might have some old photographs by Augustus Le Plongeon. To my delight she said they had "quite a few," and then asked me if I would like to step into Manly Hall's office and talk with him. Hall was most enthusiastic about my interest in the Le Plongeon materials and asked if he might help me. I told him I was planning a book about Le Plongeon and would like to work with the photographs. He thought it was a splendid idea, encouraged me to put them to good use, and wished me well. Hall's generosity was important because it allowed me to check firsthand the quality of Le Plongeon's photographic fieldwork. With the exception of ethnohistorian H. B. Nicholson, few persons outside the Philosophical Research Society were aware of the collection or of its importance.

I spent the rest of the day looking at the 300 negatives and 234 prints. There were also 25 tracings of sections of the murals in the Upper Temple of the Jaguars at Chichén Itzá in the collection. The tracings, made in 1875, were the first copies of those important Mayan murals and were still in excellent condition. In addition, the collection included a few pages of the Le Plongeons' field notes from the excavation of the Platform of Venus at Chichén Itzá, some miscellaneous letters, and the original handwritten manuscript of Le Plongeon's book-length article "The Origin of the Egyptians" (Le Plongeon 1913–1914).

I was surprised at the thoroughness of Augustus Le Plongeon's photographic work. For example, at Uxmal, working from a ladder to prevent distortion, he recorded the magnificent 320-foot-long east facade of the Governor's Palace in 16 overlapping stereopticon photographs. He also made five-by-eight-inch close-up and stereo photos of all the intricate and important motifs on the west face of the Chenes Temple of the Adivino Pyramid. From the top of the pyramid, he created a stereo photographic panorama of the site from the Governor's Palace to the Nunnery Quadrangle—almost 180 degrees.

At Chichén Itzá, he created a photographic mural in stereo of the bas-reliefs in the Lower Temple of the Jaguars. He photographed all the major structures from a number of angles, all bas-reliefs in the central part of the site, and recorded his archaeological excavations of the Platform of the Eagles and Jaguars and the Platform of Venus with written notes and photographs. A number of the images show Alice working in pants with a skirt rolled up around her waist. When she was around the Mayan women, she rolled the skirt down to avoid offending them. Other photos depict friends of the Le Plongeons in the ruins and in Mérida, some ethnographic shots of the Maya, and a few photographs from their stay in Belize.

I left for Yucatán in February 1980 with prints of the negatives to identify each photo, prepared to photograph each scene in black-and-white and in color. Once at Chichén Itzá, the work of photo corroboration went smoothly because the site is now cleared of forest, and the buildings have been repaired and consolidated. The Le Plongeons had to have the vegetation chopped down to photograph the Mayan buildings in the 1870s. The immenseness of the work is apparent in his photograph of the Great Ball Court where only the west half of the playing field has been cleared showing the full height and density of the tropical forest. The bas-reliefs too showed considerable change over the last 100 years. In the Le Plongeons' photos whole motifs with sharp crisp lines are evident, where today the surfaces are rounded. In a few instances elements in motifs or parts of buildings are missing.

After my return from Mexico, I called on photographers Pirkle Jones and Ansel Adams for their opinions about the Le Plongeon photographs. Jones, a professor of photography at the San Francisco Art Institute, has had extensive experience with nineteenth-century photographs. His opinion was that while the negatives were technically excellent, better images would have resulted had I printed them using the nineteenth-century albumen printing-out process because modern photographic papers cannot reproduce shadow detail from collodion glass-plate negatives as well. Lacking the experience and time for such an ambitious undertaking, I decided that prints made on current photographic materials would have to suffice for publication purposes. Ansel Adams generously devoted an afternoon to looking over the Le Plongeon prints in his house in Big Sur, and both he and his wife, Virginia, fascinated by the story of the Le Plongeons and the conditions under which the photos were taken, encouraged me to have them published.

During the summer I decided to make another trip east because I felt my understanding of the Le Plongeon materials was still too superficial. My first stop was the American Antiquarian Society, and after reviewing the materials there, I traveled to the Peabody Museum at Harvard University. I learned of another collection of Le Plongeon photos at Harvard from Daniel Jones, curator of photography. There were 135 prints in the collection, and 124 had been mounted on large cardboard backings for display at the American Antiquarian Society and then transferred to the Peabody Museum around the turn of the century. Most were duplicates of photos at the Philosophical Research Society and at the American Museum of Natural History, but they were, nevertheless, in excellent condition and filled a few gaps in the other collections.

At Harvard two important events occurred. The first was my introduction to Gordon Willey by art historian Linnea Wren. She thought that I should discuss my ideas about Le Plongeon with him. Willey brought to my attention problems of "core and fringe" in archaeological scholarship and felt a thorough analysis of Le Plongeon's work might be a valuable addition to our knowledge of early pioneers in Mayan studies.

The next day, while I was at the museum again, Ian Graham gave me a letter written by Augustus Le Plongeon to Charles P. Bowditch, a patron of the Peabody Museum. Bowditch had been interested in Le Plongeon's interpretations of Mayan hieroglyphics and had attempted to get him to divulge where he thought Mayan codices might be hidden. Augustus answered:

> [I] may be induced perhaps, to mention some of the places where such records may still exist and where some years ago, I began to look, when my researches were interrupted by events beyond my control. I have no objection to tell you that, in my own mind, I am convinced that very ancient Mss. exist at Chichén. . . . If I had money of my own I would be willing to spend it to bring to light these ancient books [28 May 1907, Peabody Museum, Harvard University].

Now I had evidence that the Le Plongeons had never uncovered Mayan codices, and I understood why I had never found any archival evidence. The story had been contrived by Blackwell after all.

Elated that I was getting some results from all my research, I traveled to the American Museum of Natural History to search their storage rooms for molds made by Augustus Le Plongeon. A few months earlier at the Bancroft Library of the University of California, Berkeley, I had read letters from Alice Le Plongeon to Phoebe Hearst in which she stated that they had deposited 264 papier-mâché molds made at Chichén Itzá and Uxmal at the American Museum of Natural History. Also at the Philosophical Research Society, I had seen a photograph of Le Plongeon on a scaffold making a mold of the center motif of the Governor's Palace. So I wrote the museum asking to see the molds during my trip, but they replied that they had no Le Plongeon molds in storage. Because the molds were so important to my research, I was determined to look for them personally. I called Gordon Ekholm to see if he could help me. He invited me to spend the day with him searching, but we found no trace. The only remaining evidence was an inventory of the collection. Had I been able to see the molds, I would have learned more about Le Plongeon's fieldwork. Even his rivals had described them as "exquisite" and I wanted to see them for myself.

From New York I traveled to Minnesota and spent the next six weeks in the Messengers' basement study writing up my notes and trying to develop a basic chronology of Alice's and Augustus' lives. It was a good beginning.

Academic Text

How can one deal with so many facts—
so many and so many and so many?
—Virginia Woolf

In January 1981 I began my doctoral studies at the University of Colorado and early in the fall semester asked Russ McGoodwin to supervise my dissertation on Le Plongeon. I needed a scholar and strategist with McGoodwin's skills to supervise my work and steer it through the political labyrinth.

I proposed focusing on Augustus in the context of the history of archaeological studies of the Maya. It seemed to me that a study of his life could be a lens through which we might better understand the early development of Mayan studies. In my efforts to evaluate the theories proposed by Le Plongeon in *Queen Móo,* as well as in "The Origin of the Egyptians," I found it fruitful not to dissect every speculation but instead to maintain an intellectual distance to avoid being drawn into his ever-expanding web of speculations. So outlandish were some of his claims that it would seem his intention was mainly to stir up debate.

Another line of attack was to read what his contemporaries said of him. During the 1870s and 1880s, a battle had pitted Le Plongeon against scholars Daniel Brinton, Samuel Haven, and Philipp Valentini, over the issue of cultural diffusion. Brinton had accused him of being "eccentric" (1890:439). Le Plongeon was incensed that those he considered armchair scholars should criticize one who had worked so long and diligently in the field. He challenged Brinton to a public debate, but Brinton made no reply to the challenge. This event was the beginning of the end for Le Plongeon's credibility as a professional scholar.

I found Le Plongeon's proposal that the Maya were the founders of Egyptian civilization only a new twist on Charles E. Brasseur de Bourbourg's (1868) thesis that the New World was the source of world civilization. Brasseur had proposed his theory in the 1860s, and within a few years, it had been rejected by scholars as lacking evidence. Le Plongeon, convinced of the correctness of his own interpretation of Mayan iconography and murals by his discovery of the statue he called Chaacmol (now Chacmool), tenaciously held to the idea that the Maya had diffused culture throughout the ancient world.

By 1890, still writing and lecturing on Mayan cultural diffusion, Le Plongeon found that fewer and fewer archaeologists were willing to listen to him. Bitter at being ignored and unrecognized for his pioneering work by those in the mainstream, he became evermore isolated from the developing profession of archaeology, until finally he was totally rejected, although never completely forgotten. Since his death in 1908, stories about Le Plongeon, his theories, and his exploits, have passed from one generation of archaeologists to the next, and understandably, few writers have transcended basically anecdotal appraisals.

Manly Hall, however, in an article in *Horizon,* was perhaps the first writer to offer a more comprehensive assessment of the Le Plongeons' contribution to Mayan archaeology. He wrote: "Le Plongeon could not censor his discoveries by referring to the learned texts of other authors. He did not have the benefit of the works of the great institutions, which have since spent millions of dollars and sent dozens of experts to examine the field. He and his wife could report only what they actually found, but it was impossible for them to be in the presence of so many wonders without doing a little wondering themselves" (1948:29).

Wauchope's and Brunhouse's critical accounts were an important foundation for my work because they brought together the facts and the hearsay about Augustus and Alice. Brunhouse's bibliography, even if not all-inclusive, is still an important resource.

This phase of my research culminated in 1983 with the successful defense of my dissertation, "Augustus Le Plongeon: Early Maya Archaeologist," (Desmond 1983) before a committee of archaeologists, physical anthropologists, an Egyptologist, ethnologists, and a historian of religions.

Biographic Text

> It is perhaps as difficult to write a
> good life as to live one.
> —Lytton Strachey

Within a year I sent a revised manuscript to the University of New Mexico Press. Luther Wilson, director of the press, and editor Beth Hadas, who subsequently became director, were eager for a book on Augustus Le Plongeon. But my revision of the dissertation was not acceptable—I was told that a complete rewrite would be necessary. Practically exhausted at this point by Augustus and Alice, I dreaded the thought of additional years of rewriting the manuscript.

Then in 1984 the whole depressing situation was changed. During a break in the annual Society for American Archaeology meetings, Phyllis Messenger, a longtime friend and colleague, agreed, after some insistence on the part of Luther and Beth, to help me rewrite the book. Phyllis inherited what some writers might call an "academic narrative." Such narratives are "meticulous in . . . detail, and scrupulous in . . . documentation . . . inclusive, archival and comprehensive in detail acting as records rather than responses to life" (Nadel 1984:113). The narrative did not flow. Following Beth's advice, we decided to switch to a more biographical, hence chronological, style. Phyllis took scissors and file folders and literally cut my manuscript apart. Each folder was an episode or time period, and we began long discussions about the material assigned to each folder. We looked at the photographs as a kind of visual diary and found new clues.

As Phyllis began taping the manuscript back together, it became a mosaic of typed chunks held together by handwritten phrases. This was the skeleton of a new narrative that would be fleshed out over the next two and a half years in at least half a dozen major rewrites.

The reworking raised a number of new questions, and we both went back to the original sources to hash out new interpretations. As we got to know the Le Plongeons better, we added bits of personality to the story and made some assumptions about why they behaved in certain ways at certain times. We decided to paraphrase their writings to make the story read more smoothly and to reduce the number of footnotes. One conclusion we reached was that Alice made a major literary contribution and deserves more attention than she has received.

Somewhere in the middle of this process, Luther Wilson pointed out to me that Phyllis in reality was my coauthor, not an editor. After all, her contribution had become an essential ingredient in the book. He was right, and she readily agreed.

The serious rewriting began. We had lots of help and encouragement from our editor Claire Sanderson, though her limit of 50 photographs forced us into painful decisions. (Our first list of "absolutely essential" photos totaled about 140.) We added life to the finished product with new chapter titles and opening quotes for each chapter, to set the stage for a major event in the chapter, and with line-drawing figures from the Le Plongeons' tracings of the murals in the Upper Temple of the Jaguars, to illustrate subtly an idea in each chapter.

Our book *A Dream of Maya* (Desmond and Messenger 1988) is not excessively burdened with "meticulous detail," but it still retains the essential documentation. Phyllis summarized our intention when she said in the preface, "I hope that we have succeeded in helping them [the Le Plongeons] live again" (1988:xvi).

Conclusions

For ten years the Le Plongeons were the central focus of my research life, and early on my friends and colleagues noticed the all-consuming nature of my work. I became immersed, almost totally, in the subject; however, the volume of data and diversity of interpretive problems would have all but prevented completion had I not been single-minded.

Looking back, I am not unhappy with the pace and length of the project. From the beginning a good balance developed between acquisition of materials and my ability to interpret them. The collection of bibliographic sources from San Francisco area university libraries proceeded quickly enough, and visits to distant archives were not unduly delayed by my employment responsibilities or even by my lack of funds.

My dissertation, the product of the first phase of the project, is the centerpiece and holds as much about the Le Plongeons as could be uncovered. With so much misinformation and confusion about them, such a record was needed, but I was, at first, very reluctant to "dilute" it by a rewrite in biographical style. I soon learned a dissertation and a biography are not self-exclusive but can complement each other, and when properly set forth, they can provide readers with additional insights and a clearer picture of the lives portrayed.

A great number of persons have, in a cumulative sense, influenced my portrayal of the Le Plongeons by critically reading my account and making suggestions, but Russ McGoodwin and Phyllis Messenger have contributed most directly to the development of my overall conclusions. McGoodwin, with sharp pencil in hand, helped me in the early stages to find my way through "so many facts," whereas Phyllis has brought a literary dimension to the work and elaborated on it without diminishing the factual account.

This, then, is the summarizing analysis of the Le Plongeons that has emerged. Alice Le Plongeon arrived in Yucatán as a young woman, seeing the world for the first time. As one of the earliest European women to work in that area, she had to make her own rules as she went along. She quickly learned the skills she needed to be her husband's partner in their work. And on her own she made significant contributions to the understanding of the social history and living conditions of the Maya (Desmond 1988).

Augustus Le Plongeon was representative of many mid-nineteenth-century explorer-scholars, an educated man who was unencumbered by the geographic or disciplinary boundaries that were being forged at the time and that he chose to ignore if they did not fit his need or worldview. His experiences around the world must have led him to think that with a little research and experimentation he could discover or prove any hunch or perfect any process. This attitude served him well in his surveying and photographic careers, and similarly, he met with little opposition in his experiments and writings about earthquakes and "electro-hydropathic" medicine. But when he proceeded in this manner in his studies of world civilizations, he met with far less success. Refusing to compromise, he fought on until his death, suffering rejection by the very same established scholars whom he had regarded as lesser intellects.

13

Toward an Institutional History of Archaeology: British Archaeologists and Allied Interests in the 1860s

William Chapman

Problems of Method

I should stress immediately that I am a confirmed "contextualist" to use Trigger's (1985) term. I am less interested in what we might consider the growth and development of the field—the permanent contributions to knowledge—than I am in the preoccupations of British archaeologists during the 1860s. Many of the concerns of that time are just so much ancient history and have been left along the wayside, at least as far as archaeological research today goes. But such concerns, nonetheless, provide important insights into what was happening in archaeology at the time and, perhaps, into why certain things would continue to be important while others would not.

My main interest is the institutional history of archaeology. By this I mean anything that might be considered an organizational or professional locus for the field, specifically professional or amateur organizations, museums, universities, governmental entities of various kinds, and those middle grounds of affiliation—journals, friendships, and informal meetings.

Overall, this corporate aspect of the history of archaeology has been much neglected. There has been some research on the broader social background of the field. Stuart Piggott, for example, and, more recently, Kenneth Hudson have discussed the social milieu of archaeology—what both consider the broader currents of social and political life—and how they affect developments in archaeology itself (Hudson 1981; Piggott 1937, 1976). Both also have discussed early archaeological societies and affiliations, particularly the contribution of county archaeological societies in Britain during the nineteenth century.

From another direction, there have been a number of histories of individual societies, generally commemorative and written along strictly chronological lines. Joan Evans's studies of the Society of Antiquaries of London and the Archaeological Institute come particularly to mind (1949, 1956). In the 1930s Reginald Taylor discussed the beginnings of the Archaeological Institute and the British Archaeological Association. But his treatment, called "The Humors of Archaeology," has a decidedly anecdotal character despite its other, often surprising strengths (1932).

Museums, really the first professional homes for archaeology in that they actually paid archaeologists, have received more attention recently. Curtis Hinsley's study of the Smithsonian Institution is a fine example of this kind of work, placing the Smithsonian in the context of its times and tracing some of its contributions to the growth of archaeological interests (1981). To some extent, I have done the same with my history of the Pitt-Rivers Museum (1981, 1983, 1985). But all of these studies—my own included—tend to privilege certain material to the exclusion of other material, giving perhaps too much emphasis to institutional or organizational boundaries and not enough to factors that crosscut individual societies or museums.

What has been especially neglected is the pervasive character of institutional or organizational affiliations. Such associations set out, in a sense, the language and grammar of a discipline; they provide the very context for understanding or meaning. We often, especially in biographies, treat archaeologists as if they were independent agents working in intellectual or social vacuums. At best they drift into narratives as contributors to a particular line of thought or theme. What makes archaeologists' work meaningful, of course, is the intellectual framework, usually a contemporary framework, but sometimes one that develops later. Organizations or institutions provide forums for ideas and places for presentations, papers, and discussions. They are also sources for recognition, both of individuals and of ideas. At a deeper level, in accordance with what Michael Foucault and others of a long-standing critical tradition argue, organizational affiliations determine what is fundamentally meaningful, establishing not only what is worth studying but "how the tale will be told," how problems will be stated, what an answer will look like, that is, the structure and rules of a discourse (Foucault 1973).

The Nature of Institutional Affiliations in the 1860s

Even taking the pervasive character of institutional affiliations into account, the relative value of one context over another varies from period to period. Professional societies and universities probably vie for control of the field today; in the nineteenth century, it was amateur societies (which could be called professional for other reasons) and, at least toward the end of the century, museums that did so too. In the 1860s, professional societies controlled recruitment, publications, reports, what few small grants there were—nearly everything to do with archaeology, other than "mere spadework" as Woolley (1953) called it, which was carried out independently and, in many ways, part of another extra-archaeological tradition. There were rewards for successful participation: honors, positions, editorial assignments—even small grants. "Making it" in a professional society, then, was the only means of recognition, the only way one's work became meaningful.

Another factor that has been overlooked is the degree of overlap between societies and disciplines. While the societies, in a sense, controlled the discipline, the loyalties of individual members varied. Some members of archaeological societies were archaeologists only, but many more, financially and socially able as they were to join an archaeological society, could also join other organizations. It was not unusual for a Victorian archaeologist, especially one living in London, to be a member of one or more national archaeological societies, a county society or two, several other scientific or literary organizations, and to attend popular lectures sponsored by any number of institutions or organizations. The well-known nineteenth-century archaeologist Augustus Pitt-Rivers, for example, was (in successive order) a member of the United Services Institution, a progressive, scientifically oriented association of military officers; the Royal Geographical Society; the Ethnological and Anthropological Societies of London; the Society of Antiquaries; the Archaeological Institute; the Geological Society; the Royal Institution; the British Association for Advancement of Science; the Linnanean Society; the Wilts Archaeological Society; and several more (Chapman 1981). Some of his affiliations were little more than subscriptions to journals—significant, nonetheless, in themselves. Others were entered into more wholeheartedly. Working out which were important and which were not is a useful exercise in itself. It is more important, however, to establish what other archaeologists joined at the same time and how their interests coincided.

Surprisingly, historians of archaeology have been reluctant to play the numbers games common to the historians of the so-called hard sciences. The significance of statistics has long been understood—or at least applied—by sociologists of knowledge. There are, of course, limits to this approach. For archaeological historians the questions might be some of the following. How many archaeologists were also geologists? What percentage of county archaeologists were also elected to the more prestigious Society of Antiquaries? What were the institutional affiliations of the elected leaders in various societies? Who (or how many) voted for whom and for what office? Answers to these questions would do much to advance our understanding of what went on in archaeology at the time and also our understanding of how such factors continue to influence the field today.

Another point that should be stressed is the very political nature of organizational affiliations. Not only were archaeological societies forums for ideas, they were battlegrounds for individuals and special interest groups, which is, in a sense, the more "conscious" level of organizational participation. The actors were relatively aware of what side they were on (in contrast to the more implicit features, or really linguistic aspects, of organizational involvement touched upon before). Archaeologists such as Pitt-Rivers and his close acquaintances, Sir John Lubbock, John Evans, and Augustus Wollaston Franks of the British Museum, worked closely, and even conspiratorially, together to promote certain ideas and orientations within the archaeological societies of which they were a part. Each nominated the other to offices, made appointments to editorial committees, and helped exclude other, sometimes opposing interests. Societal involvement, as we all know today, is not always a positive and friendly thing, and there is an almost Machiavellian aspect that is often disregarded, at least in the historical context. Again, a closer look at membership figures as well as committee minutes and tallies of votes, are called upon to provide a more balanced picture.

Relationships among Societies and Disciplines: Archaeology and Ethnology in the 1860s

One point I want particularly to look at in my research is the relationships among different fields of interest. The statistical route has been useful in investigating this aspect of institutional life—determining who was a member of what, which people held offices, and so on. But there is also the problem of understanding what might be called coalescences of interest. The links, for example, between geology and archaeology as organizational and disciplinary entities, as well as the common interests of the members of each, have never been examined in depth. M. C. W. Hunter's (1971) study of the Royal Society's early contribution to archaeology, while particularistic in a sense, was useful; but there has been little follow-through, and some connections have been overlooked altogether.

The institutional ties between anthropology and archaeology, while implicit in the United States and recognized in the majority of present American university departments, have rarely been noticed by historians of anthropology or archaeology in Britain, whereas the actual links appear to have been very real ones. In large part, this omission is a factor of disciplinary shortsightedness; anthropologists (or historians of anthropology) write about the history of anthropology, archaeologists about archaeology.

In looking at British archaeology in the 1860s, I found not only a predominant but also a controlling archaeological interest in anthropology and in its predecessor, ethnology. A survey of membership revealed that the majority of archaeologists in the Ethnological Society of London were also members of the Anthropological Society during those crucial, formative years. Many more, lacking formal ties to archaeology, had fundamentally archaeological interests. A significant number of officers in both the Ethnological Society and the Anthropological Society had direct ties to archaeological societies. At the Ethnological Society during 1862, for example, two of four vice-presidents, one of two secretaries, and four of 19 members of the council were also Fellows of the Society of Antiquaries (Chapman 1981:177–178). Other members were also active at the British Archaeological Association and the Archaeological Institute.

The published papers of the Ethnological Society, once dominated by articles about race and language, also took on a noticeably archaeological character during the 1860s. More importantly, both the Anthropological Society and the Ethnological Society became implicitly archaeological in outlook, whereas before 1860 they had only been partly motivated by archaeological interests. This is to say that the program, or even more importantly the subject matter—that is, the study of indigenous or exotic peoples—became less a geographical, descriptive concern and more a reconstructive one, with exotic peoples standing in for ancient ones. For someone like Pitt-Rivers this was his only interest, and he said so explicitly (1867a:618). Other ethnologists of the 1860s had similarly archaeological orientations (e.g., Dunn 1867; Westropp 1866). This shift in orientation within both societies—even more so, within the older and more established Ethnological Society—would have important repercussions for later anthropological theory, an issue until recently only touched upon by historians of anthropology (Burrow 1966; Stocking 1971; cf. Stocking 1987).

The problem of ethnology or anthropology and the place of archaeology within that area of inquiry introduces another issue, that of continuity versus discontinuity. Narrative histories usually give an often undeserved impression of institutional progression. It is in part a problem of narration itself. Even when "ups and downs" or shifts in interest are discussed, the overall trajectory remains secure, based, again, on the narrative sequence. Looking now at archaeology and ethnology in the 1860s, both clearly were experiencing organizational crises. The 1850s had witnessed the beginnings of a revival with the Society of Antiquaries and other national organizations, but it was really only in the 1860s that ethnology reemerged, largely as a result of new interests in man's antiquity and its relationship to modern "primitive" peoples (Chapman 1981, 1985). The Ethnological Society of the 1860s, therefore, while stemming historically from an older society, was another organization altogether. It had different members, a different program, and a different agenda. Looking at the problem in context helps to underline this shift and allows us to see the problems more clearly.

Prehistory and Paleoarchaeology and the Archaeological Societies

Another advantage to looking at problems in their fuller context is that the emergence of specific interests within a discipline become more evident. When looking at British archaeological societies prior to the 1860s, one is struck by the absence of any sustained interest in prehistory. This absence may be surprising to many current archaeologists who assume that the germs of later interests can be found in the earlier work by their predecessors (see chapter 2). Again, the shift in interest was relatively abrupt, as my test case emphasizes.

The Society of Antiquaries of the 1830s was comprised of country clergymen and gentlemen scholars, of whom many were enthusiastic collectors and connoisseurs (Evans 1956). Classical studies still dominated, with only slight attention given to "Celtic" or "Primaeval" antiquities, most of which were seen as curiosities. Excavation itself figured little into the definition of antiquarianism. During the 1840s there was an increased interest in medieval antiquities. In fact, medievalists dominated both the Society of Antiquaries and the newly established British Archaeological Association and Archaeological Institute (Daniel 1976; Evans 1949, 1956; Radford 1961). Much of the medieval interest settled on buildings or medieval ruins. A number of archaeological societies, including that founded at Oxford in the 1850s, were really architectural organizations as we would now understand them (Eastlake 1872:703–704).

During the late 1850s the study of "Celtic" and "Primaeval" antiquities became more important, judging by the interests of individual members. Not yet labeled "prehistory" in the journal indexes, despite use of the term in Daniel Wilson's *Prehistoric Annals of Scotland* (1851), concerted interest in the prehistoric remains of Britain became evident only in the late 1850s when the number of articles and notes on early flints, bronze implements, and early fortifications increased significantly. "Prehistory" itself entered into popular usage in the late 1860s after Lubbock's introduction to the subject, *Prehistoric Times* (1865).

Interest in paleoarchaeology emerged within British archaeological societies at about the same time. The confirmed discoveries of Boucher de Perthes following the visits of Joseph Prestwich, Hugh Falconer, and John Evans to the Somme site in 1859 had a great impact upon the British public and the archaeological community (Daniel 1962, 1967, 1976; Grayson 1983). Again, the shift in interest was marked by increased memberships in British archaeological societies, as well as in societies with what might be considered parallel interests, most importantly geology and ethnology. It was paleoarchaeological interests that appears to have attracted Pitt-Rivers to the Archaeological Institute, the Society of Antiquaries, the Ethnological Society, and slightly later the Anthropological Society. Other British archaeologists and anthropologists of this time, including Edward B. Tylor, apparently joined for similar reasons (Chapman 1981:228, 232–233).

Interest in prehistory and in paleoarchaeology was promoted within British archaeological societies by enthusiasts such as Pitt-Rivers, Evans, and Lubbock. Many members of the newer group of prehistorians joined the societies during the period between 1859 and 1865 and moved quickly into positions of authority and influence. Pitt-Rivers was elected to the council of the Society of Antiquaries in 1867 and the same year served on the steering committee of the Archaeological Institute (Chapman 1981). Evans, Lubbock, and other prominent archaeologists with strong interests in British prehistory, including A. W. Franks, held similar offices. All worked together to promote prehistoric interests. In 1868 they helped organize the Third International Congress of Prehistoric Archaeology held in Norwich in conjunction with the annual meeting of the British Association for the Advancement of Science. Pitt-Rivers (1869b), in turn, edited the proceedings.

It was in the context of the archaeological societies, then, that what we now consider the subject matter of modern archaeology first came into prominence. Together with a greater emphasis on recording techniques and a pervasive sense of the need for scientific method, prehistoric and paleoarchaeological interests were the hallmarks of institutional life, published papers, lectures, and correspondence during the 1860s. It is really only by looking at the work of the societies, not at the individual contributions of those now recognized as founders of the field, that such basic concepts and areas of interest come into focus.

Archaeological Societies and Archaeological Museums

Another link worth pursuing is that between societies and other institutions. For the 1860s, it is the link between archaeological societies and museums that is the most useful for understanding developments in the field. Archaeological collections had been a part of the British Museum from the time of its foundation in 1759 (Hawkes 1962). A number of early prehistoric collections had been part of the core collection, and others were added periodically during the eighteenth and early nineteenth centuries. Administratively, archaeological collections had originally been part of Natural and Artificial Curiosities, and later becoming a separate Department of Antiquities under Henry Ellis (Kendrick 1954; Miller 1973). As of 1850, Oriental, including Egyptian and Mesopotamian antiquities, and classical materials and the British and medieval collections were all part of a single department, with little recognition of administrative subdivision. Prehistoric or "British" antiquities, including Romano-British collections, were established as a special subdepartment under Franks in 1851. In 1866, a separate and independent Department of British and Medieval Antiquities and Ethnography was organized, again under Franks's control, finally putting the newer archaeological interests, especially interests in prehistory, on a more secure footing.

The archaeological societies were particularly active in promoting recognition of British antiquities within public collections during this period. Both the British Archaeological Association and the Archaeological Institute had pressed for greater recognition of British antiquities at the British Museum (e.g., Evans 1949; Jerdan 1844). They had also promoted the idea of local museums and helped establish a number of smaller museums as a legacy of their annual meetings. During the 1860s, their efforts increased, and the newly reorganized British collections were, in part, a result of those efforts (Kendrick 1954:133; Wright 1866). The Society of Antiquaries, which had formed its own collection at Somerset House and reestablished it in their new home at Burlington House, also helped promote collections, stressing their importance for scientific advancement in the field (Evans 1956:250–257). The Society of Antiquaries also had considerable political influence, particularly over the national collections.

In the 1860s the connections between collections and archaeological theory became better recognized than they had been previously. British admiration for the Danish national collections had been expressed within archaeological societies during the 1840s and 1850s (e.g., Way 1844; Westwood 1858). The significance of the well-known Danish three-age system itself, had only been slowly accepted in Britain, however, even among the societies (Wilkins 1961). Classifications of British antiquities in national and local collections had avoided reference to the three-age system throughout the 1850s (Chapman 1981:157–158, 611). And even in 1866, when the British collections were reorganized by material, the official stance was that the new classification was for convenience only, disavowing any connection to the connotations of the Danish system (British Museum 1866).

During the 1860s, however, the majority of newer prehistorians within the British archaeological community had clearly accepted the basic concept of successive ages as represented by transitions from one material to another. There were recognized local differences, but the overall concept of process embodied in the system—suggesting a natural evolution rather than a particular sequence, as envisioned even by the system's founders, Thomsen and Worsaae (Thomsen 1937)—had gained acceptance among most of the newer archaeologists. Again, the idea of process was tied to the understanding that archaeologists had of the scientific character of their enterprise.

The interest shown in museums and systems of classification by archaeologists of the 1860s was paralleled in private collections. Collectors of prehistoric antiquities increased in numbers during the 1850s, which is best evidenced by the number of privately produced catalogs (e.g., Bateman 1855; Cuming 1860; Way 1859). Presentations by private collectors were a frequent feature of society meetings; inexpensive block prints provided easy communication (Klingender 1968:66–67). Private collections fit the mid-Victorian decorative ideals and the much-publicized concepts of self-improvement and education (Kerr 1871; Smiles 1859). Archaeological collections, as with collections of national history specimens, served as an expression of a Victorian gentleman's scientific commitment.

A number of collectors emerged as important figures in the archaeological community during the 1860s. A. W. Franks was a private collector as well as supervisor of the British Museum collections. Henry Christy, an active member of both archaeological societies, the Ethnological Society, and the Geographical Society, formed an extensive private collection, which was given to the nation following his death in 1865 to form a separate collection under the administrative umbrella of the British Museum (British Museum 1868; Christy 1862). John Thurman, an anatomist and field archaeologist, had a large private collection as did William Blackmore, who opened his Salisbury museum of archaeological and ethnographical pieces to the public in 1866 (Stevens 1867; Thurman 1850). Finally, Augustus Pitt-Rivers, who had been collecting ethnographic and archaeological pieces since the early 1850s, presented his collection to the public during this period, giving a number of papers on its system of organization (Pitt-Rivers 1867a, 1868, 1869a).

Museums and collections were important to archaeology in the 1860s; museums gave tangible expression to archaeological efforts. These collections were the scientific equivalent to those of geologists and botanists and helped improve archaeology's standing as a separate science. Museums in particular provided an acceptable institutional setting. Many perceived the establishment of museums and a national archaeological collection as an essential stepping-stone to further recognition of the field, a realization that was given initial expression only in the 1860s.

Collaborations among Specialists

I have suggested that there was a great deal of overlap among British, especially London, scientific and archaeological societies during the 1860s. Some societies recognized common interests, as in the case of the Ethnological Society and several archaeological societies (e.g., Mosley 1851:180; Tomline 1865:2). In other instances, the links were established through individual contacts. Societies or professional organizations, whatever the degree of institutional connection, provided opportunities for those with similar or complementary interests to meet and sometimes collaborate. John Thurman, for example, was a prominent member of both the archaeological and the ethnological-anthropological communities. He was also, together with J. Bernard Davis, the leading authority on British skulls (Davis and Thurman 1865). Thurman published the results of his archaeological work and his anatomical investigations (e.g., Thurman 1850). Others within the archaeological community relied on him and other specialists for advice in their own work—a typical pattern.

One of the best documented of such collaborations was that between Augustus Pitt-Rivers and a number of other specialists whom he knew through his archaeological and ethnological contacts. Early in his career Pitt-Rivers relied on Richard Owen, a close family friend and the director of the Hunterian Museum of Comparative Anatomy, to verify his findings of human and other faunal remains (Pitt-Rivers 1866). Later he relied on William Flower, Owen's assistant at the British Museum for the natural history collections (Pitt-Rivers 1867b). Occasionally he also referred to Thomas Huxley, whom Pitt-Rivers knew through the Ethnological Society of London. Pitt-Rivers's uncle, Albert Way, a leading figure at the Archaeological Institute, earlier introduced Pitt-Rivers to George Rolleston, the Linacre Professor of Human and Comparative Anatomy at Oxford (Chapman 1981: 192–194). Pitt-Rivers and Rolleston began this collaboration in the late 1860s, eventually working on a number of excavations together, with Rolleston serving as the expert on faunal remains and Pitt-Rivers the expert on excavation technique (Pitt-Rivers 1875; Thompson 1977:51). Both also collaborated with William Greenwell, another pioneering field archaeologist (Chapman 1981:252–253, 283–284).

Such collaborations were, in many ways, typical of archaeological work during the 1860s. Contacts were encouraged through society membership and activities. Partly by this means many archaeologists and the archaeological community at large were introduced to the methods and content of other disciplines and came to be allied increasingly with other sciences.

Professionalism

Throughout the mid-Victorian period there was no concept of professionalism as we now understand it. British archaeologists of that time were technically amateurs. Some, including Lubbock and Evans, were wealthy businessmen. Others were landed gentry or, like William Greenwell, country clergymen. Pitt-Rivers, as an aristocratic military officer, was unusual, though not exceptional. True professionals were encountered most in the scientific community. John Thurman was attached to a mental hospital in Devizes; James Hunt, founder of the Anthropological Society of London, had a similar hospital position. Thomas Huxley, William Flower, and George Rolleston held museum positions as did other naturalists with interests in archaeology. Among archaeologists of the 1860s, only A. W. Franks and a few other interested curators within various departments of the British Museum held professional posts in any way connected with archaeology. Even then, their professional responsibilities did not extend to the modern-day typical work of archaeologists, that is, excavating and reporting.

The close connections among the scientific and archaeological communities did much to advance the idea of archaeological professionalism. Also, museum positions helped make professionalism possible. Franks, for example, helped support the career of Charles H. Read, a young assistant in his department, who otherwise would not have had the means to join the ranks of amateur archaeology (Chapman 1981:537). Edward Stevens, curator of Blackmore's Museum in Salisbury, also established a reputation through his museum work (Stevens 1947). Similarly, secretarial or librarian positions with the societies, while generally occupied by unconnected clerks, increased in status as the archaeological societies grew larger and wealthier. Eventually, a number of individuals would be recruited to serve as archaeological professionals, working as excavators or draftsmen for wealthier archaeologists like Pitt-Rivers (Chapman 1981; Thompson 1977). The growth of the field in the 1860s laid the foundations for professionalism, and the close connections with the increasingly professional scientific community helped establish the precedent for later paid university and museum positions.

Conclusions

The 1860s were years of profound growth and change within the British archaeological community. It was a period of new relationships between archaeologists and other scientific groups, new interests and commitments, and new organizational expectations. It was not only a period of change for archaeology but a period particularly illustrative of the way in which shifts within a scientific community can redefine what a discipline is to become.

The organization and development of a discipline is obviously far more than the successive or even cumulative efforts of individual practitioners. Such an approach to archaeology's history has been one of the shortcomings of traditional treatments of the subject. Most historians fail to take the collective character of any scientific enterprise into account. A look at institutional or organizational contexts provides a way to understand that collective character—to discover concepts, expectations, prejudices, even commonalities of language that are general to a community at any time. Basic archaeological ideas, such as prehistory, came into usage in much the same way a word enters into speech. It was not so much introduced by one of the members, as arrived at by several, as closer analysis reveals.

A closer look at institutional contexts also emphasizes the political choices involved in disciplinary changes or advances. Prehistoric and paleoarchaeological interests not only became a part of the archaeological language but also were consciously promoted by adherents within the archaeological community. The societies of the 1860s, in this instance, provided the context in which such battles could be fought.

Other periods in archaeology's history can also be better understood through a closer look at institutional contexts. An examination of the relationship between museums and archaeology in the late nineteenth century, for example, when archaeology became more fully professional, would be a useful study. The relationship between professional archaeologists and governmental agencies more recently would be of equal interest. As part of their own historical efforts, archaeologists need to understand how shifts in orientation occur, how their own discipline has changed and continues to do so. It is time for historians of archaeology to get to work, to examine the trove of information available in their own institutional and organizational records. Only then can they begin to understand how the discipline has become what it is.

Acknowledgments

For their help and comments in the course of researching and writing this chapter, I would like to thank Steve Kowalewski; Andrew Christenson; my wife, Betty Ausherman; Yvette Neal; and the many archivists associated with the following institutions: The Royal Anthropological Institute, the Society of Antiquaries of London, the Ashmolean Museum, the British Library, the Salisbury and South Wilts. Museum, the Royal Geographical Society, the Imperial College of Science, and the Public Records Office, Kew. I would also like to thank those institutions for permission to refer to manuscript materials cited indirectly in this paper by reference to my doctoral dissertation (Chapman 1981).

14

The Past Is Still Alive: The Immediacy Problem and Writing the History of Archaeology

Andrew L. Christenson

In one of the most famous sociology of science publications, Derek Price estimated that 80% to 90% of the scientists who ever lived are alive today (Price 1986:7). This surprising figure is possible because of the exponential growth of science over the last 300 years and a similar value would be true of any exponentially growing subdiscipline of science as well. He labeled this phenomenon the immediacy of science.

The rapid rate of growth of archaeology in the last few decades has been obvious to all who have been a part of it. The story of the entire membership of the Society for American Archaeology meeting in one small room is only one of a class of archaeological lore that indicates the enormous growth of the discipline within living memory. Using such indexes as the number of Ph.D.'s awarded and the size of the membership of the Society for American Archaeology, Rogge (1976, 1983) has shown that American archaeology has been undergoing exponential growth since the end of World War II. Although this growth may be slowing, the period of exponential growth is so recent that it is probable that 90% of the archaeologists who have ever lived are alive today. Thus for archaeology, as with most other sciences, the past is very much alive.

The immediacy of archaeology has a variety of implications, but the ones I consider here pertain to the writing of the history of the discipline. The most obvious benefit of the immediacy of archaeology is that there are many living informants help to reveal the past. This activity, which has been misnamed oral history, can provide significant information for the archaeological historian.

If we use 1865 as the beginning date for professional archaeology, then perhaps one-half of the history of the discipline is still accessible to some extent from living sources. Thus, we need not rely upon occasional comments in site reports to reconstruct the past; we can gain significant insight directly from the participants, keeping in mind, of course, that reminiscences must receive the same healthy skepticism that any other historic data source receives (Cutler 1984).

Perhaps more important than verbal information is the written, photographic, and artifactual record that living archaeologists have or know about. Diaries, photographs, field notes, unpublished manuscripts, artifacts, field equipment, and other material remains from past archaeological work often provide more believable and useful information about archaeology's past than any quantity of reminiscences, but these remains may be uninterpretable or unavailable once the archaeologist who owns them dies.

The immediacy of archaeology presents serious problems for the historian of archaeology as well, especially if, as is usually the case, the historian is also an archaeologist. A truly convincing archaeological history, whether a biography, an account of an event, or a consideration of the development and influence of a particular institution, must examine the pertinent personalities and personal relationships. Such examination must include questions about bias and jealousy, vanity and modesty, friendship and hate—all dimensions of the human personality. To understand archaeologists' professional behavior, their view of the world, their research decisions, their success in getting grants and promotions, and their contributions to the discipline, historians must grapple with many aspects of behavior that are considered sensitive. Furthermore, to write convincing histories of archaeology, one must be prepared to deal with villains and villainy as well as with heroes and heroism.

The archaeologist-historian writing about the recent past is in a bind; the subject may still be alive and in a position to influence that archaeologist-historian's career. Potential subjects write articles, they review manuscripts and grant proposals, and they usually play other roles that give them some power over other archaeologists. No archaeologist can afford to offend such people by writing about sensitive past events or looking critically at personalities and personal relationships. This concern becomes particularly important when the academic community is small and strongly hierarchical and when members are easily offended (Leach 1984:3; Trigger 1985:221).

This fairly simple idea can be formalized: archaeologists will not compromise their professional standing for the sake of historical accuracy or completeness. This axiom could be generalized to anyone writing a contemporary history of his or her own discipline.

An example of what can happen when an archaeologist offends those in positions of power is provided by Walter Taylor and his dissertation published as *A Study of Archeology* (Taylor 1948). Although this work was not a history in the strict sense and did not concern itself with personalities, it did critically examine the recent work of living archaeologists to make points about the method and theory of archaeological research. When it was published, Taylor became persona non grata in American archaeology and his career suffered. Such ostracism was made easier because Taylor criticized archaeology from a position of weakness—he was too young and he lacked an effective power base. An established scholar would have been much more likely to get away with such critical assessments without harming his own career, although the reaction to James Watson's personal account of the discovery of the structure of DNA, *The Double Helix*, demonstrates that even a Nobel Prize winner can come under extreme attack from his colleagues for revealing the "naked truth" (see Stent 1980).

The writing of and reaction to *A Study of Archeology* deserves careful examination, not only for what it tells about the structure of archaeology in the early 1950s but also for how it contrasts with what happened when Lewis Binford criticized archaeology in the 1960s (see Schwartz 1978). Unfortunately, for the reasons discussed above, such a consideration will probably have to wait until the principal people involved die.

An additional factor influencing the archaeological historian's ability to study recent history is that he or she is part of that history. The need for objectivity and distance has often been presented as an impediment to writing good recent history. On the other hand one historian, Arthur Schlesinger, has made the involvement of writers in the events they are describing a virtue—"trapped as they may be in the emotions of their own age, [contemporary writers] may still, or in consequence, understand better what is going on than later historians trapped in the emotions of a subsequent age" (1967:74). He also makes the interesting point that "contemporary history can be more exacting in its standards—of evidence, of precision, of judgement, of responsibility—than the history of the past, for [it] . . . involves the writing of history in face of the only people who can contradict it, that is, the actual participants" (1967:74).

The problem of immediacy is certainly not unique to archaeological history. In fact, even historians outside a discipline would be under some pressure to be discreet when writing about certain recent events to avoid offending the practitioners. The issue of potentially offending living people has not been too significant to historians until fairly recently because past historians created a clear wall between the past, their realm, and the present, the realm of journalists. But the accelerated rate of change in this century has made contemporary history more acceptable and more important to mainline historians (Schlesinger 1967:69). A consequence of this change has been an increase in the number of current histories and the concern for the problems of writing about living persons.

As one biographer, James Clifford, puts it, decisions about what to include in a biography must be centered on historical truth. But when carefully hidden details are involved, he admits that the historian must evaluate and weigh the importance of such information to the reader against the anguish of those involved (1970:125). Balancing of pressures and contingencies becomes more complex when the career of the biographer or historian is tied to the issue, as when scholars write about their own disciplines.

When historians write about living persons, they are also faced with potential libel suits. As a general rule, historians are protected when writing about public officials or prominent individuals, unless actual malice is intended (Kelly 1968:451). The greatest problem comes from writing about the private lives of nonprominent individuals, where prosecution for libel or for invasion of privacy is more likely (Kelly 1968:451). Invasion of privacy is the disclosure of intimate private *facts* that hurt feelings or embarrass an individual, in other words, when the writer drags skeletons out of the closet (Neuenschwander 1985:4). Both invasion of privacy and libel were raised in reaction to Watson's *Double Helix* (Lewontin 1968).

The impact of the immediacy problem on the history of archaeology is that, although much of archaeology's past is still alive, certain aspects of it, generally falling into the category of personality or interpersonal relations, are off limits to discussion and analysis. Although 90% of the archaeologists who were ever alive are probably alive today, their accounts of the past must remain largely unwritten, or at least unpublished, until they or their subjects die.

The passage of time makes topics that were known by all but only discussed around dinner tables more acceptable (Schlesinger 1967:72). There is a gradation of decorum that allows more and more to be written about a person as time passes (Clifford 1968:70). Of course, death removes many constraints; one cannot libel or invade the privacy of a dead person (Kelly 1968:436). The revealing biography of Sir Mortimer Wheeler (Hawkes 1982) and the account of Louis Leakey in his wife's autobiography (Leakey 1984) reveal aspects of their characters and personal interrelations that, for reasons of discretion and good taste, would never have been published prior to their deaths.

The purpose of archaeological history is neither to publish dinner table gossip nor to conduct voyeuristic excursions into archaeologists' lives. Rather, it is to reveal why archaeology has taken the course that it has and how individual archaeologists have influenced this course. For example, Louis Leakey's physical and mental deterioration near the end of his life and his monumental ego are relevant to understanding his archaeological involvement at the supposed Early Man site at Calico, California, and to understanding other aspects of his career (Leakey 1984:143).

We cannot put off our investigations of sensitive aspects of archaeology's past, however, merely for propriety's sake because much information on interpersonal relationships will only be available while the participants are alive. We need to collect as much information as we can from living archaeologists with the understanding that some of it must remain sealed until the participants in the sensitive events die (Baum 1984:396). In some cases, researchers may collect and preserve information that they will not live to use.

The immediacy problem in writing the history of archaeology places limits on what we can write about during the last 50 years or so. For this reason, archaeologist-historians have chosen to write in most detail about periods or topics for which there are few or no living representatives. Thus, topics such as the Bureau of Ethnology's Mound Builder research and the first recognition of Paleolithic implements, and individuals such as Heinrich Schliemann and Frederic Ward Putnam have been written about to the point of tedium. They are safe. They are distant. The archaeologist-historian can take an outsider's viewpoint and avoid discussing issues that are currently sensitive.

There are, however, a number of alternative approaches to recent history that minimize the immediacy problem. The first is to write about living individuals, emphasizing the positive and avoiding villains and villainy. Such "goody-goody" history often has the dedicated scholar, contributing, by his hard work and brilliance, to archaeological knowledge. Such "history" appears most often in books having a didactic purpose and written for young readers (e.g., Poole and Poole 1968). This genre presumably had some value in attracting archaeologists to the discipline in the past, but the current overabundance of archaeologists now reduces the need for such literature.

The second approach to writing contemporary archaeological history is to emphasize ideas as they are expressed in publications (Trigger 1985: 222). This method considers who thought what and when, but it does not generally allow the historian to grapple with the details of the interesting who and why questions because those questions touch controversial interpersonal issues. Because it is easiest to research and because it fulfills important functions, this approach is the most common one used by historians of archaeology. As Gruber has indicated, however, "To describe the conflict or growth of ideas without describing the personal medium within which they grow is to deprive them of their human character" (1966: 21). A scholar's public and private lives are so intertwined that it is not possible to gain an understanding of one without considering the other (Leach 1984: 3, 22).

The third approach is a technique sometimes used by collectors of oral history in which the identities of individuals are hidden when potentially defamatory statements are made (Neuenschwander 1985: 5). Anonymous archaeological histories may be useful in some situations, but because the goal of most archaeological history is to understand known people and known events, hiding identities is virtually impossible.

A fourth approach, and one that will become more common in analyzing archaeology's past is a quantitative sociohistorical approach that examines change in various indicators. Rogge (1983) was able to consider the history of the Central Arizona Project (1968 to the present) without becoming involved in personalities, by examining change using various measures of funding, fieldwork intensity, and archaeological productivity. Citation analysis of the published literature is another way of using such an approach (Dyson 1985; Sterud 1978).

My principal point is that such human characteristics as discretion and self-preservation must lead archaeologist-historians to avoid writing recent archaeological history accurately when personalities and personal relationships are involved. Thus, for archaeology's recent past historians outside the discipline have an advantage; they can consider more sensitive issues without fear of harming their careers. The rarity of such scholars, however, means that much of archaeology's recent past will remain unstudied until time and death create sufficient distance to make it safe.

For this reason I encourage all archaeologists to keep records about their archaeological activities and those of their colleagues (see chapter 17). Archaeological oral history projects should be increased and expanded to include younger archaeologists, who are at the peak of their activity, as well as low-level personnel, such as laborers and lab workers who are not normally represented in the historical record. Although studying and understanding the prehistoric record requires more and more of archaeologists' time, I hope that they will still find the opportunity to keep records so that future archaeologists and other scholars, interested in why present-day archaeologists behave the way they do, will have the necessary information.

15

Methods of Relating Historical Collections of Artifacts and Associated Records to Known Sites and Current Research

Marvin D. Jeter

Artifacts are perhaps the most basic data available to archaeologists. Although it has been said that "American archaeology is anthropology or it is nothing" (Willey and Phillips 1958:2), one of my Arkansas colleagues once paraphrased this dictum, not completely in jest, by saying, "Archaeology is artifacts or it is nothing!" (Frank Schambach, personal communication 1983). To that statement I must add that various kinds of *records* are the vital connecting links between the artifacts and their contexts—between the collections and whatever we may wish to do with them. Here, I refer to records in the broadest sense, including not only detailed documents but also such minimal data as specimen numbers or cryptic codes written on the artifacts (or on ancient gummed labels falling off the artifacts) and sketchy field notes with corresponding lists of numbers.

Similarly, although my title refers only to collections of artifacts, I include "ecofacts," such as faunal and floral remains, and human skeletal materials. The reference to known sites should also be understood as including "knowable" sites, and I illustrate some cases wherein "lost" or forgotten sites have been relocated and reidentified, and misidentifications of sites have been corrected.

I also discuss some cases in which no artifacts, or only a few, were recovered during the early visits to sites—the main point here is to illustrate methods by which the historical records, in their turn, can be connected to known (or knowable) sites. Whether or not artifacts were recovered or saved, the principle is the same: the link to the sites must be made through the records. Artifacts cannot speak for themselves. Even if the records include fairly detailed site descriptions, sketch maps, drawings, or photographs, their connections with specific sites may be uncertain. It is common knowledge among archaeologists that sites are often difficult to relocate, even those found only a few years previously (Wauchope 1966:xii–xiii).

We begin with artifacts and end with sites. Both of these end points are in the realm of archaeological insiders. In general, documents and various methods of dealing with them are within the realm of outsiders such as historians, but these are archaeological documents, so they are partly insider material. The basic questions addressed here relate to identifying the specific locations of the sites, and beyond that, to identifying more specific proveniences within those sites.

Mine is not a general review of this subject but is essentially restricted to Arkansas examples. Although I attempt to provide an overview of outstanding historical collections from Arkansas sites that have been subjected to recent analyses, emphasis is on my own research of eastern Arkansas collections and related documents and of methods that have worked for me. I do not want to disclaim too much, though. I also want to *proclaim* that this sort of grass roots work is sometimes the key to writing accurate accounts of episodes in the history of archaeology. Some of these examples are of insiders' methods, some are of outsiders' methods. They are often most effective when used in combination.

Examples

Working Directly with Early Researchers

Perhaps the best means of relating historical collections to the present archaeological record and current research is to work directly with the people who made the historical collections and, in the process, to write a bit of archaeological history. I was fortunate enough to encounter such situations upon my arrival in southeast Arkansas in September 1978.

The interior of Arkansas's "delta" lands, which I call the Bartholomew-Macon region (Jeter 1982a:80, Figure 6.2), includes some very interesting late prehistoric and protohistoric sites along Bayous Bartholomew and Macon (Jeter 1982a:107–108, 1982b, 1986a). During the early 1880s, Edward Palmer made the first limited investigations here, representing the Mound Exploration Division, Bureau of Ethnology (Jeter 1981, 1989; Palmer 1917; Thomas 1894). In the early 1900s, C. B. Moore approached or skirted these localities but did not quite reach them.

Instead, the region was opened up by a homegrown pioneer of Arkansas archaeology, George P. Kelley (1902–1987). I met him in October 1978, when he showed me the artifacts he had donated to the nearby Arkansas City Museum. Almost all of them were ceramic vessels from a single low mound, which he had excavated in 1936. He also gave me four legal-size pages of typed, single-spaced notes on that 1936 excavation and showed me the site's former location. We called it the Kelley-Grimes site, and we found that his notes were good enough to serve as the basis of an article (Jeter et al. 1979). We concluded, primarily on the basis of ceramic comparisons, that the site was in use during the A.D. 1400s and perhaps the 1500s (1979:32–34). It is assigned to the Hog Lake mortuary complex or phase, which may represent a terminal prehistoric or protohistoric group of "Tunicans" (Jeter 1982a:107–108, 1986a:49–55, Figure 4.6).

While working on this report, I got to know George Kelley very well, and wrote a historical note (Jeter 1979) summarizing his pivotal role in the development of archaeology in southeast Arkansas. In 1924, he excavated a mass burial at the Gibson site near Bayou Macon (Jeter 1979:14; Lemley and Dickinson 1937:33–34), the first investigation of a Hog Lake phase site. In 1926, he excavated more than 50 burials and associated artifacts from Medley Mound A at the Hog Lake site itself (Jeter 1979:14; Jeter et al. 1979:38; Lemley and Dickinson 1937:19–20). During the early 1930s, he was visited several times by Harry J. Lemley (1883–1965), who lived in southwest Arkansas and was the major private collector in the state. This association led to an expedition in 1934 headed by S. D. Dickinson, whose family lived near the Lemleys.

Dickinson had studied archaeology at the University of Arizona, and he kept detailed records. He revisited the Gibson site and Medley Mound A. Then he excavated 12 burials and 10 vessels from the summit of Medley Mound B and worked at several other portions of the Hog Lake site. Kelley guided him to several other sites in this vicinity, including Bellaire (which had produced a Moundville-like stone pipe) and the Rohwer site, now known as Alma Brown (Lemley and Dickinson 1937).

Dickinson subsequently left archaeology to pursue journalism. Now retired, he retains an active interest in archaeology and ethnohistory (Dickinson 1980, 1982, 1986). I acquired copies of his unpublished field notes and drawings from the 1934 expedition, and I plan to use them and his personal communications in a reanalysis of the Hog Lake phase.

During the early and middle 1930s, Kelley corresponded with Samuel C. Dellinger (1892–1973), the director of the University of Arkansas Museum, and with John R. Swanton at the Smithsonian Institution. As a result of all these influences, he kept good notes during his 1936 excavation at the Kelley-Grimes site. In his later years, he became quite active in the Desha County Historical Society, which proved to be another useful source in my investigations.

A gray area in the history of archaeology consists of "data" from the highly variable records, or only from the memories, of local collectors. Arkansas archaeologists have a long tradition of salvaging information from this source by photographing collections and interviewing the collectors. An outstanding example is the work of Frank Schambach, who photographed thousands of vessels from collections in southwest Arkansas and nearby regions, providing invaluable data for his revisions of ceramic classifications in the trans-Mississippi South and the western margin of the lower Mississippi Valley (Schambach 1981; Schambach and Miller 1984). John

House (1986) has also worked with collector data from late prehistoric and protohistoric sites in the lower Arkansas Valley and east-central Arkansas, as have I (Jeter 1982b, 1986a) with such data from coeval sites in southeast Arkansas.

Working with Well-Documented Collections

In many cases, although the original collectors are deceased, the historical collections in question were well documented or had at least come from sites that are still known. Little has been done with Arkansas materials collected during the nineteenth and or early twentieth centuries, primarily because the materials were removed to institutions in the eastern United States and were not readily available to Arkansas archaeologists, but also because many of these collections were not well documented.

The first reasonably well-documented collections to remain within Arkansas were those made by Dellinger's field crews and students for the University of Arkansas Museum from northwest Arkansas bluff shelters between 1928 and 1935. Dellinger, alarmed at the prospect of foreign institutions "skimming off the cream" of Arkansas archaeology, obtained a Carnegie Foundation grant and set up a system for excavating sites and recording information (Hoffman 1981; Charles R. McGimsey, personal communication 1987).

Dellinger did not publish detailed site reports, but he did contribute to brief articles about specialized topics (e.g., Dellinger and Dickinson 1942). The materials recovered and their associated notes have become the basis for a long-standing tradition of theses by University of Arkansas graduate students. They have also been used in research projects by university faculty members, by Arkansas Archeological Survey station archaeologists, and, more recently, by contract archaeologists.

Dellinger also directed excavations in central and eastern Arkansas. An early example followed the work of a pioneering Arkansas amateur, James K. Hampson (1877–1956), who had begun intensive excavating, collecting, and mapping at the late Mississippian to protohistoric Nodena site on his property in northeast Arkansas in 1927. He eventually opened a museum (now operated by the state of Arkansas). Excavations were conducted at Nodena in 1932 by Dellinger's University of Arkansas Museum staff and, at the same time, by the University of Alabama Museum. Papers relating to these investigations were brought together in a volume edited by Dan F. Morse, who provided identifications for illustrations of selected artifacts (D. F. Morse 1973:Figures 5-10, 13, 18-21). Also, a dentist and Morse's father (a physician) analyzed the skeletal materials in Hampson's collection for pathological conditions (D. Morse 1973; Lowe 1973).

Also in 1932, Dellinger's students excavated 57 burials and 126 ceramic vessels from the protohistoric Quapaw phase Kinkead-Mainard site near Little Rock. No report was published on these materials, however, until they were reanalyzed by Michael Hoffman (1977).

In the middle Ouachita Valley from 1938 to 1941 Dellinger was in charge of WPA excavations, where major excavations were conducted at the Cooper and Means sites during 1939 and 1940. The huge collections from these sites were analyzed by Schambach, whose 1970 dissertation is the basis of the pre-Caddoan cultural sequence in the trans-Mississippi South. A third major WPA excavation, at the Poole site in the upper Ouachita Valley, was directed by Dellinger in 1940. Again, the materials remained largely unstudied, until analyzed by W. Raymond Wood (1963, 1981).

Another amateur pioneer of Arkansas archaeology, Thomas L. Hodges (1868–1953), accumulated a well-documented collection of more than 55,000 items, mainly from Caddoan and pre-Caddoan sites in the middle Ouachita Valley (Hodges and Hodges 1943a, 1943b, 1945). The Hodges collection has been acquired by Henderson State University in Arkadelphia (Early 1986) and provides an invaluable data base for studies of this region's prehistory (e.g., Early 1982).

Michael Hoffman's dissertation (1971), which established a Caddoan sequence for the Little River region of southwest Arkansas, was based in part on field notes, photographs, drawings, and maps provided by local collectors, plus interviews with them. He is currently working with collector data from 1960s excavations at two major Caddoan sites in the Red River valley (Hoffman 1984; personal communication 1987).

The tradition of University of Arkansas theses based on analyses of historical collections began with the work of Charles E. Cleland (1960, 1965), who analyzed faunal materials from 57 Ozark bluff shelters. Sandra Scholtz (1970, 1975) analyzed cordage, netting, basketry, and fabrics recovered from similar sites. Raab (1976) and Trubowitz (1980), in fulfillment of contract project requirements in the Pine Mountain–Lee Creek locality south of Fayetteville, restudied Dellinger's 1934 artifact collections from three nearby bluff shelters. More recently, Gayle Fritz (1984, 1986a, 1986b) analyzed floral remains from several of Dellinger's bluff shelter excavations.

In 1933, one of Dellinger's students excavated the Middle to Late Mississippian Hazel site in northeast Arkansas. The materials were analyzed decades later in a thesis project (Zinke 1975). At present, several graduate students are preparing theses based on materials in Dellinger's collections.

Working with Problematical Collections

There's many a slip 'twixt cup and lip, and many problems can interfere with a modern researcher's attempts to use historical collections. I encountered a number of such problems with Arkansas collections made by Edward Palmer in the 1880s (Jeter 1981, 1982b, 1986a, 1986b, 1989), and I draw most of my examples from these experiences.

Palmer (1830?–1911) was born in England, came to the United

States in 1849, and became perhaps the nineteenth century's greatest collector of botanical and natural history specimens (McVaugh 1956; Safford 1926). He also obtained ethnological and archaeological specimens for major museums, such as the Smithsonian and the Peabody. He worked primarily in the Southwest, California, and Mexico but from 1881 to 1884 was a field assistant for the Mound Exploration Division, Bureau of Ethnology, Smithsonian Institution, mainly in Arkansas (Jeter 1989; Palmer 1917).

Palmer's Arkansas documents are of three kinds (Jeter 1989): notes or diary entries, including "incidents of travel"; letters to Thomas and others at the Smithsonian; and monthly reports, which contain most of the archaeological data. In some cases, we have Palmer's original documents; in others, we have only copies made by unknown persons we call scribes. It is clear that Palmer worked closely with the scribes (at least some of the time), because in some cases, his handwriting interrupts that of a scribe. Some of Palmer's documents are undated but contain valuable bits of internal evidence, such as sequences of field specimen numbers, or references to previously visited sites or future plans, which permit at least relative sequencing and therefore restrict the geographical possibilities.

For two months Palmer was assisted in Arkansas by an black artist named Henry J. Lewis, who produced 36 drawings of mound sites. Most of these drawings remain unpublished in the National Anthropological Archives (but see Rolingson 1982:Figures 42–44), and some were converted to engravings by W. H. Holmes and published in the final report on the Mound Survey (Thomas 1894:Figures 135, 137, 147, 148, 149, Plate IX).

As Smith (1985:10–11) noted, Mound Survey artifacts often received three different specimen numbers. Palmer assigned his own field specimen numbers to artifacts or provenience lots of artifacts. When unpacked at the Smithsonian, they were given Bureau of Ethnology numbers, which Palmer called "Thomas numbers." Finally, since they were to be curated by the National Museum of Natural History, they were given its numbers, which Palmer called "Smithsonian numbers."

As neophyte archaeologists are warned, provenience data are especially at risk between the time artifacts come out of the ground and the time they are numbered and cataloged. Palmer did not always have time to catalog his specimens fully in the field, and later stated: "I therefore shipped the cases to Washington, hoping to unpack them there and to make a descriptive catalog of the specimens. In forwarding them I begged that the cases might be allowed to remain unpacked [sic] until my arrival, but my request met with a curt refusal from Mr. Cyrus Thomas . . ." (Jeter 1989; Safford 1926:480). I have not fully assessed the loss of provenience data that may have resulted. It is clear, though, that there are problems of provenience on the site level, even in cases of well-known sites. For instance, Rolingson (1982:83–84) noted that his collections from the Knapp (now called Toltec) Mounds may have become mixed with those from the nearby Thibault site.

There were other gremlins at work in the Smithsonian laboratories;

when James A. Ford (1961:161, Figure 11) examined Palmer's collections from the Menard site, he found that some of the reconstructed bowls had been pieced together with sherds from different vessels. When I examined some of the Palmer artifacts at the Smithsonian labeled "Stoneville, Lincoln County, Arkansas," I found it hard to believe that the artifacts had indeed come from that county in my southeast Arkansas research territory. No such site was mentioned in Palmer's Arkansas notes, and I could find no record of a Stoneville in that county. Later, I learned that Palmer had also visited the Leland Mounds near Stoneville, Mississippi, in the Yazoo Basin. Somehow, the collection had been mislabeled. (It is not yet clear whether these artifacts are from near Stoneville, Mississippi, or from a site in Lincoln County, Arkansas.)

There are also intrasite provenience problems, which may be solvable by close study of the original notes. For instance, Palmer found a large cache of ceramics at Menard in 1881. His monthly report to John Wesley Powell (Jeter 1989) plainly stated that the findspot was on a ridge connecting two mounds. But, this was before Thomas took over the Mound Survey. Thomas (1894:230–231), who may not have seen this report, confused this cache with other finds made by Palmer at Menard the next year. Phillips (1941) seems to have figured the situation out but worded his solution somewhat ambiguously. Ford (1961:160–161) added to the confusion, apparently by misreading Phillips, and concluded that the cache was found at the top of Mound B.

Palmer was by no means blameless. For one thing, he seems to have suffered from directional dyslexia at times. Also, it was necessary for me to become thoroughly immersed in his idiosyncratic style of writing notes. He often measured distances along section lines, east-west plus north-south, rather than in straight lines from one point to another. Ambiguities in his documents were sometimes converted by Thomas or by more recent researchers into errors that have become embedded in the literature and in site files.

A number of methods have proved useful in dealing with this situation. A beginning outsider's step is simple comparison of the documentary descriptions with contemporary historical maps. Moving on to inside information, we can check the Arkansas Archeological Survey's quadrangle maps that have site locations indicated. Such comparative methods recently revealed that Palmer's Gardner Mounds site was the important site now called Wallace, just north of Menard. The quadrangle map shows a "Gardner Cemetery" by the Wallace site. This connection also revealed that there had been a medium-size mound (in addition to the house mounds) at the Wallace site when Palmer and Lewis were there, although it seems to have been gone by the time of Moore's (1908) visit.

Turning to the smaller sites, many have been "lost" or "misplaced" over the decades, as landowners changed, rivers flooded and changed courses, and the land was made over in the image of agribusiness. The mound at Walnut Lake Station in western Desha County, Arkansas, visited by Palmer and Lewis in late 1882, is a good example. This community is now an agribusiness company town called Pickens. In 1983, the company's principal officer told me that he had lived there more than 60 years and had no memory of the mound. The only remnants from Lewis's drawing (Jeter 1989) were the railroad tracks and the foundations of the old water tank.

Indeed, many of the answers must be sought in the regions referred to in the documents. Landownership records are a very valuable supplementary resource. Although title searches cost money if you are buying property, I have so far had nothing but success in obtaining free information about specific periods of time, such as the 1880s, from title and abstract companies in county seat towns. In one critical county (Desha), where there are a number of lost and uncertain sites, the land records before 1903 were written in code. Fortunately, the clerks provided the key. Phyllis Morse (1981:20) used such records to show that the Stanley Mounds site, visited by Edwin Curtis on behalf of the Peabody Museum at Harvard University in 1879, was the site now called Parkin. Curtis's collections have not yet been studied, but now have the potential for adding to the Parkin data base.

Another method, which has a great deal of potential, is to work with local historians, amateur archaeologists, and landowners. There may also be some potential for enlisting the aid of scientists in other disciplines; for instance, Palmer was basically a botanical collector and sometimes added botanical notes to his archaeological observations. At the Arkansas City Cemetery Mound, he remarked on the abundance of *Ailanthus* trees. I took a botanist to the site 100 years later and found that this species (*A. altissima,* an Oriental import) was still flourishing (Eric Sundell, personal communication 1983).

The ultimate inside resource, though, is the accumulated knowledge and expertise of archaeologists who have had years or decades of experience in these regions. When I showed Dan Morse (who has been the Arkansas Archeological Survey's station archaeologist for northeast Arkansas for about 20 years) my hasty snapshots of the Smithsonian artifacts from Palmer's B. F. Jackson Mounds, Morse instantly protested that they were too late to have come from the modern Jackson Mounds site, which had been assumed to have been Palmer's site.

Closer scrutiny of Palmer's idiosyncratic description (Jeter 1989), plus a landownership records check, a visit with Morse to this northeast Arkansas site, interviews with local residents, and examinations of collections, led to the definite conclusion that Palmer's B. F. Jackson site was located about 10 miles southwest of the modern Jackson Mounds (Phillips 1970:Figure 447).

A counterexample, wherein unlikely artifacts lead to new insights, may be cited. The Morses originally regarded as improbable a few Parkin phase sherds in a Palmer collection from a site on Crowley's Ridge, well away from the usual St. Francis Valley locations for such materials (Morse

1981:Figure 19). However, their subsequent surveys produced a few more late artifacts from sites near Palmer's, verifying that minor use of this landform had continued into protohistoric times (Dan Morse, personal communication 1986).

Palmer's biggest find in southeast Arkansas was at the Tillar site, where he excavated a protohistoric charnel house (Jeter 1981, 1982b, 1989). When we wrote the Kelley-Grimes report, we based our comparative map (Jeter et al. 1979:Figure 1) on the Arkansas site files, which wrongly identified Palmer's Tillar site as a site we now call Tillar Farms. The Tillar Farms site was excavated in 1936 and 1938 by Judge Lemley's agents, who recovered 48 vessels, which are now at the Gilcrease Institute in Tulsa. I have made some preliminary studies of these collections (Jeter 1986a: 49–55), but unfortunately, their notes were sketchy.

In 1980, while analyzing the artifacts from Palmer's Tillar site, I found that his notes placed this site some five miles northeast of Lemley's site in an area where no sites were recorded. We checked the landownership records and found that the land described by Palmer had indeed been owned by Captain Tillar in 1882, as he had indicated, but that Lemley's Tillar Farms site had been owned by someone else. In 1983, I led local amateurs in an intensive survey that soon relocated Palmer's missing Tillar site. Both sites are part of the Tillar phase, which is closely related, if not identical, to the Hog Lake phase, and also appears to represent protohistoric "Tunicans" (Jeter 1986a).

My final example is Palmer's DeSoto Mound, which he said was surmounted by a Mr. DePriest's cabin. His description of its location was somewhat contradictory, but he did tie it to a nearby mound near an abandoned railroad track on J. P. Clayton's property and placed both in eastern Desha County near the Mississippi River (Jeter 1989). Nevertheless, Thomas (1894:242–243) confused the J. P. Clayton Mound with another Palmer site, the Powell Clayton Mound, 50 miles northwest in Jefferson County. Furthermore, Thomas (1894:243) also misplaced the DeSoto Mound in Jefferson County. This confusion was compounded in the Smithsonian's otherwise praiseworthy 1985 reprint of Thomas's 1894 report. Holmes's engraving (Thomas 1894:Plate IX), apparently made from a (now-lost or misplaced) Lewis drawing of the DeSoto Mound, was chosen as the cover illustration and, following Thomas, was mislocated in Jefferson County.

Historic maps of Arkansas (the Colton Sectional Maps) show that the rail line was indeed moved between 1878 and the year of Palmer's visit, 1882. A retired judge (James Merritt, personal communication 1986), who is a member of the Desha County Historical Society, provided an unpublished manuscript based on his detailed research into legal records, precisely dating the history of these railroads. The Colton maps also show a DeSoto community in the same section as the large Cook Mound. Decoded landownership records show that H. Y. DePriest owned a quarter section of low-lying land within one-eighth mile of the Cook Mound from 1880 to

1884 and that J. P. Clayton had owned land at the right distance from the Cook Mound. We had no site-form record of a mound on the J. P. Clayton property, but another society member, the late Gerald Hobson, had made a map of mound sites and had given a copy to the Arkansas Archeological Survey in 1980. It showed that a mound had formerly existed in the right place. Field investigations by the station archaeologist for southeast Arkansas (H. Edwin Jackson, personal communication 1986) verified that a mound had been in the mapped location but was bulldozed about 35 years ago. So, all the pieces fit together again, and the record has been corrected (Jeter 1986b:149, 1989).

Conclusions

Working with historical collections can provide many new insights and research ideas for archaeologists, and conversely, archaeologists can enlighten the museums that curate these collections. A positive feedback, synergistic relationship can and should be established. Analyses of historical collections and associated documents on the one hand and of better-controlled recent collections and data on the other can be mutually reinforcing and can lead to or guide new, problem-oriented fieldwork. Insiders and outsiders, archaeologists and historians, need each other's insights if well-rounded, enriched contexts are to prevail in accounts of archaeology's past.

16

Recording the Past: Capturing the History of Archaeology on Videotape

Michael Tarabulski

I credit my involvement with film to archaeologist Robert Salzer. In the autumn of 1980, the beginning of my senior year at Beloit College, I was reading film historian Kevin Brownlow's (1979) excellent book on silent documentary, *The War, the West, and the Wilderness*. In the course of discussing the book with Salzer, he told me that there were several reels of old film down in the storage area of the Logan Museum of Anthropology. He soon led me to the film, and I discovered that it documented the progress and discoveries of an American archaeologist with the peculiarly assonant name of Alonzo Pond.

Between 1925 and 1930 Pond directed excavations and extensive surface surveys in northeastern Algeria for the Logan Museum (Pond 1928, 1937). Pond and four of his associates had made the film as a visual record of their work, supplementing it with hundreds of photographs. It was black-and-white film, silent of course, some of it on familiar 16 mm stock and some of it on 35 mm nitrate stock. The passing of 50 years had made the 16 mm film brittle, and the very flammable nitrate had a poisonous, gunpowdery odor to it, but I managed to see enough of each to get an idea of the subject and the image quality. In addition, there were two photo albums with stills covering the same material and yellowed carbon copies of shot lists detailing the contents of each reel.

Salzer suggested that I do some work with the film for extra credit. I could, he added, go up to Minocqua, Wisconsin, 275 miles north of Beloit, and interview Alonzo Pond. According to Salzer, Pond, though 86 years old, had plenty of entertaining stories to tell about his African work.

The idea appealed to me. Brownlow had gathered material for his book almost wholly from interviews with the people who had made early documentaries and nonstudio films. I saw it as a chance to do the same, so I took up the challenge (put to me directly by Salzer and, through his book, by Brownlow) to get the old film restored and preserved and to gather as much information about it as I could from those involved in its production.

It seemed to me then, as it does now, that an archaeologist who would pass up an opportunity to save something from archaeology's past had little right to be out digging in other people's fields—a sentiment with which, probably because of the pun, Salzer agreed. At that time, I had no particular expertise in either film production or the history of archaeology. Had I known more about either I might not have taken on the work so readily. Use as an index of my undergraduate enthusiasm (i.e., naïveté) that I imagined I could finish this work by December 1981 at the latest and that I did not finish it until December 1986. However, and this should encourage those more experienced and thus more fearful than I, the Society for Visual Anthropology gave me an award for the documentary I produced. And this same documentary, *Reliving the Past: Alonzo Pond and the 1930 Logan African Expedition,* has been broadcast on Wisconsin Public Television and has been acquired by a distributor, so I must have done something right.

In this chapter I seek to encourage those with access to old archaeological films to preserve, document, and disseminate these materials. Beale and Healy state that "archaeological films continue to be produced in what is for all practical purposes a theoretical and methodological vacuum" (1975:889). Surely this is as true now as when Beale and Healy wrote their article, the dearth of archaeological films and writing thereupon being only a dozen years more overwhelming. Anyone planning to make an archaeological documentary, whether historically oriented or not, should use Beale's and Healy's piece and the accompanying review, as a starting point. Traditional histories or analyses of documentary and ethnographic film, such as Barnouw (1974), Heider (1976), and Jacobs (1979), provide general background on the documentary ethic and give an idea of the scope of film that has been produced. Any would-be documentarian, archaeological and otherwise, should review these texts and see as many of the films mentioned therein as possible. In the absence of anything more thorough than the Beale and Healy article, modeling work along established and praised lines, however idiosyncratically, will give it a certain amount of credibility. But these are aesthetic points and I am thus getting ahead of myself.

First Steps

The most important part of a project involving old film is getting the film stock on hand stabilized, preserved, and copied. If the film is on pre-1950 35 mm stock, it may be nitrate film. A glance along the edge by the sprocket holes, will reveal the stock type, as it will say either safety or nitrate every few inches. Even with proper storage, in cool areas with low humidity, nitrate film can destabilize and undergo spontaneous combustion (Weinstein and Booth 1977:189–192). Neither water, nor sand, nor ordinary fire extinguishers will put out a nitrate fire. Isolate such film immediately.

I now know that the United Parcel Service will handle nitrate film, but when I had to get about 20 pounds of it from Beloit to Washington, D.C., in the summer of 1982, there was no such option. More than I knew or desired, I was committed in body and soul to getting the Beloit film restored. Unable to take the film on public transportation, and having no car of my own, I arranged to borrow cars and rides from friends between Wisconsin and Washington. I hand carried the film to the Smithsonian Institution, and as I drove a borrowed 1972 Pinto through the hot August streets of Washington, D.C., I had visions of someone rear-ending me and creating a new metro entrance.

The Human Studies Film Archives (HSFA) in Washington, D.C., part of the National Anthropological Archives at the National Museum of Natural History, which helped my project along immensely, is the first place to contact about film preservation and copying problems. Not only did the people at the HSFA have the Beloit film restored and transferred to three-quarter-inch videotape they also sent a team of archivists to Minocqua to record the comments of Alonzo Pond and his wife, Dorothy, about the content of the films. These comments were recorded directly on the videotape transfers, thus synchronizing words and images.

This brings up the second important step in creating your documentary: amassing materials. As you would for an article or a book collect notes, letters, files, diaries, newspaper articles, and other written information that will help determine what is in the film you have now saved from dust and decay. Pay special attention to photographs, maps, and drawings that may be of use in your documentary. Interview anyone connected with the archaeological project or the production of the original film, assessing their appearance, mannerisms, and voices for later use in videotaping interviews.

I was fortunate to have had several intelligent, energetic, and articulate "eyewitnesses" around for interviews, Alonzo Pond foremost among them. His storytelling skills, honed by decades of travel-lecture work, are central to the structure of *Reliving the Past*. The very title is, in fact, the one he used in lecturing on the 1930 Algerian expedition.

I was lucky, too, in that Alonzo Pond and his wife, Dorothy, had kept and organized all the letters, notes, diaries, newspaper clippings, negatives, and photographs from this expedition, and from all their other work. I cannot praise their foresight and organization highly enough. They had even kept the gramophone records they had had with them on the 1930 trip. We used these records for the soundtrack of *Reliving the Past*. My coproducer and I thought that the scratchiness of the actual records added a special dimension to our documentary.

In the years leading up to the October 1985 reunion of eight members of the 1930 Logan African Expedition at Beloit College, I contacted all the surviving members of that expedition, and the families, friends, and colleagues of those who had died. This was exciting and rewarding work, and not in the least because I got to meet anthropologists Sol Tax and Lauriston Sharp, both of whom had been with Pond in Algeria in 1930 for their first fieldwork. Without exception the people I contacted were pleased about this attention to something they had been part of over 50 years ago. All retained vivid and pleasant memories of the experience, and most had photographs, newspaper clippings, and diaries to show me. Twelve of the original group of 21 were alive when I began the work in earnest. The hardest hit by mortality had been the archaeologists. Charles Nash, Ralph Brown, and Lloyd Wilford were all dead, as was John Gillin, who, with Tax and Sharp, had joined the combined Beloit College and University of Minnesota group from the University of Wisconsin-Madison.

As for published materials, Alonzo Pond had covered the work quite well (Pond 1928, 1931, 1937). Few scholarly and popular histories of archaeology mention Beloit College, the Logan Museum, or Alonzo Pond. Only Ceram (1971:263) makes any mention of Pond, and that in reference to Pond's (1930) book on stone-tool manufacture. Willey and Sabloff (1980:40) mention the work of Stephen D. Peet, son of a college founder and member of the first graduating class at Beloit, but they mention neither the college, founded in 1846, nor the Logan Museum, founded in 1893, thus ignoring an interesting thread of institutionalized American archaeology.

Production and Funding

Having seen to the preservation of the film, and having collected documentation, you are in the position of having a place to go and not being at all dressed up. If you know nothing about producing a film or a videotape, you will have to do some background reading and search for technical help. For background reading I refer you to the works on documentary and ethnographic film previously mentioned. Another helpful source, though its main subject is still photography, is *Visual Anthropology* (Collier and Collier 1986). Full of information from these books, and the films and photographs they refer to, you will be able to present yourself as if you know what you are talking about. You will be able to ask reasonably intelligent questions of your technical crew and understand their answers.

A technical crew can be assembled in any of several ways: watching documentary films and writing directly to their producers; talking to the people in charge of a local university communications department; or contacting state or local film boards for a listing of production people in your area. (Many states and large cities have film boards, which can probably be located though the board of tourism or the local chamber of commerce.)

I found my coproducer, Barry Teicher, at Beloit College in the summer of 1982 when he was on campus to show an Emmy-award-winning documentary he had worked on. We found our videography and editing crew from the University of Wisconsin–Stevens Point by asking around to see who did the best work at the lowest price.

I should say a few words about funding, an issue you will no doubt come up against. I will not bore you with tales of leads followed to no successful end, grant proposals that met with icy rejection, or the short-sightedness of certain highly placed individuals bent on stifling a major contribution to world history and cinematic art for want of a few thousand dollars. Suffice it to say that through much work by many, we eventually received a grant for 15,000 dollars from the Wisconsin Humanities Committee and Beloit College matched this figure. A grant for 1,000 dollars from the City of Madison, donations from Beloit alumni, and the generosity of family and friends made up most of the difference between what we budgeted and the actual cost.

We came out pretty close to our estimate, though the editing took two months longer than we had planned, and we did not get a distributor until some months after that. We made a major oversight in our budget, neglecting to figure the cost of royalties for the music we wanted to use, a total of 1,740 dollars. Keep royalties in mind if you want to use music that is not in public domain.

We decided to work with three-quarter-inch videotape because it is easy to handle and to edit and because, compared to 16 mm film, it is an inexpensive way to make a broadcast-quality production. The extensive interviews for *Reliving the Past* would not have been practical on 16 mm film, which would have doubled or tripled our costs, and we felt, quite justifiably, that we could not delay the interviews while trying to raise that additional money. Still, we prepared carefully for all the interviews; we went over questions and worked out rough scripts before turning on the camera. In most cases I had previously met with the individuals and had tape-recorded the interviews. We used the information on the cassette tapes to decide what questions we wanted to ask on videotape.

As we planned our documentary, my coproducer and I devised a film treatment to give ourselves a sense of the direction we wanted our production to take. We sent copies of it to all those we planned to interview and submitted copies as part of our grant applications. A film treatment is a scene-by-scene breakdown of a production, stating the purpose, narrational content, picture content, and additional sound or special effect for each scene (Table 16-1).

A film treatment is instructive in two senses. First, it serves as a model outlining a film, which as opposed to a piece of writing, has both diachronic and synchronic modes right up front for the world to see. Laid out in tabular form this way, one can follow the flow and observe the complexity of each moment at the same time. Second, and this is certainly true of *Reliving the Past*, the finished product may differ greatly from the film treatment. I estimate that we only made about half of what we planned to make. Note that we even changed the title. We dropped some material because of time restraints. (We had decided to keep the videotape under an hour in length, and we discovered that our original plan was too ambitious.) We dropped

TABLE 16-1. Film Treatment for *The Lost Expedition: Alonzo Pond and the Logan African Expedition of 1930*

Segment/Purpose of Segment	Summary of Picture Content	Summary of Narration
1) *The Reunion of the 1930 Logan African Expedition* Stimulate audience interest. Set up contrast between the past and present. Introduce people and places involved. Establish personal, historical, and scientific dimensions of the 1930 expedition. Introduce expedition leader, Alonzo W. Pond.	(Filmed in Beloit with additional interviews, archival film, and photos.) A montage of images from reunion and symposium (interviews, lectures, and informal shots) and from old film of expedition. Establishing shots of location and season, emphasis on Logan Museum. (Final shot: Fade from group on step of Logan Museum, 1985, to photo of same group in same place, 1930. Zoom in on face of A. Pond.)	Participants from expedition and speakers at reunion give statements about memories or analyses of the event. Comments are personal and scientific. Several individuals mention Alonzo Pond before we hear Pond himself. (Narrational montage complements visual montage; bits of it may show up later in film.)
2) *Alonzo Pond, Early Years* Convey background, character, and philosophy of Alonzo Pond. Show what led Pond to anthropology/archaeology. Explain connection between Pond and Beloit College (BC). Establish long tradition of anthropology at Beloit and links with Yale, Chicago, University of Wisconsin–Madison.	(From interviews done in Minocqua: 1982–1984. With old film and photos. Irrmann and Beloit campus, 1985.) Alonzo Pond, then and now. People and places mentioned. Robert Irrmann in his study. Indian mounds on BC campus. Photos of George Collie.	Pond on his career. Early interest in natural sciences. Going to Wayland Academy. On coming to BC: 1914–1920. Robert Irrmann, BC archivist, will give summary of archaeology and anthropology at Beloit: 1846–1914.
3) *Pond in Europe: 1921–1925* Explain how Pond became involved in archaeology in Europe and North Africa. Establish Pond's connections with other archaeologists and explorers. Lay groundwork for later Algerian expeditions.	(From interviews with Pond, archival film and photos.) Pond. Film and photos of people and places mentioned. Shots of artifacts Pond purchased for Logan Museum. Maps: France and Algeria.	Pond will tell how he obtained a scholarship to study on a Yale-sponsored field school, then went to school in Paris. This led Pond becoming a buyer for Logan Museum. Pond's first meeting with Roy Chapman Andrews and how Pond got into North African archaeology.
4) *The African Work, 1925–1929, in Context of the Period* Show work being done by other archaeologists and anthropologists in the 1920s. Establish existence of popular interest in anthropology	(From interviews with Pond in Minocqua, and interviews with others at Beloit. More old film and photographs, maps and newspaper items.) Pond. Film and photos from the Logan expeditions and other	Pond will discuss Logan-Sahara expedition of 1925, other trips to Europe and Algeria, working with Roy Andrews in the Gobi in 1928. Hinsley will talk about museum expeditionary work in archaeology in early twentieth century; patrons,

and archaeology in those years (e.g. museum sponsors like Frank G. Logan). Show why students of 1930 expedition might have been interested in going on a dig in Africa.	work done in that era. Shots from Egypt, the Gobi, Mexico, and Central America. Newspaper items about archaeology and exploration. Interview with Curtis Hinsley. Shots from documentary and narrative anthropological film of the 1920s.	sponsors, public interest. Popular interest in archaeology in 1920s, revolving around "King Tut," "missing link," and "cradle of mankind." Reference to Mound Builders in Midwest, Pueblos in Southwest.
5) *The 1930 Expedition* Establish connection between BC and other schools in Midwest, with particular emphasis on departments of anthropology. Show why it was decided that students should go on this trip and how some of those who went decided to go. Relate the atmosphere of camp and "dig" life. Provide information about methods and goals of work 1925–1930. Provide a modern assessment of this work and relate it to other work that had/has been done in the same region.	(Interviews with Pond from Minocqua. Interviews with students on expedition and with archaeologists who know about Logan African Expeditions and Algerian prehistory. Old film and photos, maps, newspapers.) Interviews with Pond and others intercut with shots of life in camp and archaeological work at various sites. Images of native workers, people in nearby towns, and places visited. Interviews with archaeologists David Lubell and Peter Sheppard intercut with shots from expedition, artifacts now at museum, various publications, and members making statements.	Pond, his wife, and students discuss some aspects of daily life in camp and at sites: housing and food, relations among group members, interactions with locals (Algerians and French), and archaeological work. Intercut with interviews of two archaeologists (at reunion in Beloit) giving a modern summation and analysis of methods used by Pond, goals of research in Northeastern Algeria, and Pond's work among that of others.
6) *Afterwards* Explain why work, including film, became lost (i.e., forgotten) and how work affected those involved. Demonstrate influence of Great Depression on careers of those involved in 1930 Logan African Expedition. (By extension, we see what the depression did to American anthropology.)	(From interviews filmed in Minocqua, Beloit, Memphis, Ithaca, and Chicago.) Interviews with Pond and men from expedition. Shots of various campuses where some of the men went: Chicago, Minnesota, C. H. Nash Museum in Memphis. Interviews with colleagues of some of those who became anthropologists.	Pond and others will discuss what happened to them immediately after the expedition: Why they dropped out of school, or how they stayed in. Colleagues of some of the deceased will talk about what happened to those men.
7) *The Reunion of the 1930 Logan African Expedition* Bring audience back to present. Recapitulate some of the ideas evoked by the film. Stimulate interest in preservation of history, specifically oral history and photographic materials.	(Filmed in Beloit with archival film and photos as in Segment 1.) Montage as in 1. Various scenes of the reunion intercut with the old footage and photographs. These will be "end" shots: end of lectures, end of reception dinner, and end of partially completed film as reunion group watches it. Title card from C. H. Nash's 1930 film of expedition: "The End."	Aural montage as in Segment 1, including members of expedition and guest speakers commenting on reunion. Close with Pond making comment about anthropology as a way of life.

other material for logistical or technical considerations. Alonzo Pond fell ill just at the time of the reunion and was unable to attend which obliged us to rethink our plan considerably. Nor did we have time to interview scholars, so we had to use footage of them presenting their papers at our October 1985 reunion and symposium. We also had problems with sound or lighting in scenes that we wanted to use and had to make substitutions. Such changes are standard in documentary production in which one has neither script nor control over events.

Interviews on videotape should be copied and transcribed. During production use the copy; save the original for editing. Transcribing allows you to see exactly what words you have to work with. By doing a shot-by-shot breakdown of the images in video transfers, stills, maps, graphics, and so on, you will have most of what you need to fill out the film treatment. The script you paste together from these materials will differ from the film treatment, and you will make more changes in editing, as sound and image dictate them. This all means much going back and forth between the scripts and the videotape.

A viewing of *Reliving the Past* would make evident both the way we fleshed out the parts of the film treatment we retained and the numerous changes we made. Then, too, I should note that the 45-minute version we made for distribution is 12 minutes shorter than the version my coproducer and I were happy with. Our distributor (Centre Productions, Inc., Boulder, Colorado) felt it wise to pare down the videotape to average class length, hoping by this reediting to reach a wider market in high schools and universities. This version, I will admit, speeds along where the 57-minute version drags, but it also leaves out much of the technical appraisal of Alonzo Pond's work that I labored hard to include.

Such internal and external influences on the shape of *Reliving the Past* should be viewed as an extension of the events that led to the original film, and Alonzo Pond himself, being shelved and virtually forgotten back in 1931. The message of the present chapter is that we should all work to preserve early films of archaeological endeavors and the words of those who made them.

Alonzo Pond died on Christmas day 1986, only a few months after we had finished editing our documentary. How many others like him might there be out there, with stories to tell and no one to listen? How much more film is facing decay for want of historians of archaeology who will attempt something new?

17

A Documentation Strategy for Archaeology

Edwin A. Lyon

An important archaeological resource is threatened with destruction unless archaeologists take action soon. Archaeologists have accepted responsibility for the preservation of sites and artifacts, but it is time to expand that responsibility to include records created by archaeologists. Unfortunately, concern for the records that archaeologists generate has been less than satisfactory. Some valuable documents have been lost in accidents. A fire at Carl Guthe's residence destroyed his papers, which probably included large amounts of information about research conducted in the 1930s and the early 1940s. Other records have simply disappeared. It was not uncommon for archaeologists to take records with them after they left WPA and other federal projects. James Ford, for example, took some of the Louisiana WPA records with him to Florida and New York to write site reports. Eventually some of these records have come under professional care at the National Anthropological Archives of the Smithsonian Institution. Some records have even been deliberately destroyed. After Robert Wauchope published his *Archaeological Survey of Northern Georgia* (1966), he disposed of his personal papers because he had no further use for them (see also Towne 1984:78).

While archaeologists are aware of the importance of field notes and laboratory records, these records are only part of the available material. The professional and personal correspondence of archaeologists must also be preserved. Archaeologists' correspondence not only contain valuable descriptions of surveys and excavations underway or planned but also include discussions about methodological developments, theoretical concerns, and site relationships. Archaeologists may see no value in their personal correspondence, but this material may provide the missing pieces to many puzzles in the history of archaeology, or may assist another archaeologist in studying a site excavated years ago (see chapter 15).

Archaeological documentation is important both in archaeological research and in writing the history of archaeology. Many undocumented collections will become more useful to archaeologists if missing records can be located. And, to reconstruct fully the history of archaeology, preservation of a full range of primary sources, including correspondence, is essential. Exclusive reliance on the published record will inevitably lead to an incomplete history.

A solution to this problem is to develop and implement a documentation strategy for archaeology—a new approach to dealing with archival problems.

> A documentation strategy is a plan formulated to assure the documentation of an ongoing issue, activity, or geographic area. . . . The strategy is ordinarily designed, promoted, and in part implemented by an ongoing mechanism involving records creators, administrators (including archivists), and users. The documentation strategy is carried out through the mutual efforts of many institutions and individuals influencing both the creation of the records and the archival retention of them [Samuels 1986:115].

Samuels sees two levels of analysis in developing a documentation strategy: "first, an analysis of the history and scope of a topic so that the purpose of the strategy and the issues to be documented can be defined; and, second, an analysis of the available sources of information so that an adequate record can be gathered for each issue" (1986:122). Other disciplines, notably physics and chemistry, have developed comprehensive and successful programs to document their disciplines by preserving records; archaeology can do the same.

Research in archaeology depends on effective use of a variety of documentary resources that provide data necessary for progress in the discipline. These resources include correspondence, field notes, laboratory records, photographs, maps, unpublished reports, machine readable records, and other materials. The purpose of a documentation project for archaeology is to preserve and make available for research documentary materials in archaeology in the United States. Over a period of time the project would locate records, encourage their deposit in appropriate repositories, develop a national data base of archaeological documentation, promote research and publication in the history of archaeology, encourage oral history of major developments in the history of archaeology, and help increase public understanding of the contributions of archaeology to society.

In this chapter I argue that a comprehensive view of archaeological documentation needs to be developed. While several efforts are underway to deal with parts of the problem, including unpublished reports and artifact curation, coordination between the projects is limited and the result will probably be fragmentation of effort. Cooperation between a variety of specialists on the comprehensive problem of archaeological documentation will prevent fragmentation and conflicting solutions.

The Problem: The Condition of Archaeological Documentation

The condition of archaeological documentation throughout the United States varies from records in excellent condition with outstanding access to material stored in deplorable conditions, unknown to archaeologists, and with severely limited access. The problems with archaeological records can be summarized under the categories preservation and access, which are primary considerations in planning a documentation strategy.

Preservation of archaeological documentation is influenced by the failure to understand the characteristics of records and the failure to realize their importance. Many archaeologists are unaware of the importance of unpublished documents when studying archaeological sites excavated many years ago. When site records have been lost, the unpublished reports submitted to the sponsoring institution can be valuable. For example, the WPA Quarterly Reports contain a wealth of data unavailable in some states where quarterly reports have disappeared. The unpublished Chickamauga Basin report written by Thomas M. N. Lewis and Madeline Kneberg (National Anthropological Archives, Smithsonian Institution) and similar documents from other states would be useful sources of data for contemporary archaeologists if they were more widely known.

The personal papers of archaeologists must be preserved. Traditionally, archaeologists have neglected preservation of personal papers and records, which is of particular importance for those belonging to senior archaeologists. Many of the current senior generation of North American archaeologists began their careers during the relief archaeology programs of the Great Depression in the 1930s. As they retire and die, there is a danger that their correspondence and records may disappear. And, in addition to archaeologists who continued to work in the discipline, others moved into new careers after the end of World War II. Some of these ex-archaeologists may have valuable archaeological records in their possession. It is unfortunate that the importance of correspondence is not generally recognized by archaeologists. Archaeological correspondence could be very helpful in understanding the activities of archaeologists when other records of excavations are incomplete. The history of archaeology will never be completely understood without preservation of the personal papers of archaeologists.

Of great importance is the lack of concern by some archaeologists for the preservation of site records. A number of horror stories could be told to illustrate this problem. Some archaeological records have been accidentally destroyed. For example, a fire at the University of Kentucky destroyed some WPA records. In the 1940s, archaeologists intending to complete reports on WPA projects, took records and artifacts to their new jobs. Some records were thus permanently separated from the artifacts they described.

Other records have simply disappeared; the notes of the Hooton Hollow excavation in Kentucky were borrowed by a graduate student during World War II and never returned. While some cases of lost documentation were probably unavoidable, others could have been prevented by improved security and preservation measures.

The problem of artifact curation is closely related to the problems of archaeological documentation. Archaeologists have tried to deal with the problem of curation for many years, but it remains unsolved. One study of curation and management of archaeological collections demonstrated the lack of concern. "The curation and housing of collected archaeological materials are almost always secondary considerations, following excavation activities or research interests" (Lindsay et al. 1979:93).

The National Park Service (NPS) is developing a regulation for curation of federally owned and administered archaeological collections. The proposed regulation defines a collection as the material remains from archaeological resources and the associated records that document the remains. Records are defined as any documents generated or copied during federally authorized archaeology: "site forms, field notes, drawings, maps, photographs, slides and negatives, films, video and audio cassette tapes, oral histories, artifact inventories, laboratory reports, computer cards, tapes, disks, diskettes and printouts, antiquities permits, reports" (National Park Service 1987:32745). In addition, copies of archival records and public records are included: birth, marriage, and death certificates; deeds; survey plats; historical maps; manuscripts; architectural and landscape plans; and diaries.

While archaeological documentation is a part of the issue of curation, the issue is really broader than curation and should be treated in a comprehensive manner apart from the management of archaeological collections. Curation is such a huge problem that it will not be resolved in the near future, but a documentation strategy for the records problem can be successfully implemented.

At the present time there is no national guide to archaeological records, which prevents archaeologists from easily finding records necessary to their research. For example, archaeologists trying to use New Deal archaeological records from the WPA, Tennessee Valley Authority (TVA), and NPS projects of the 1930s and early 1940s face several problems. One is that the documents are scattered across the country. For my own research on New Deal archaeology in the Southeast (Lyon 1982), I have consulted records in the National Anthropological Archives, in the National Archives, at the TVA, at the National Academy of Sciences, in the NPS Southeastern Archaeological Center, at the University of Chicago, at the Mound State Monument, at the University of Tennessee, at the University of Kentucky, and at Louisiana State University, and unfortunately, this research does not exhaust the sources for a history of New Deal archaeology in the Southeast.

In addition to the difficulty of locating records, in many cases, once the records have been found, the real problems begin. Many collections are not properly organized and lack useful finding aids to assist in identifying individual records of importance to the researcher. Many New Deal records have not been deposited in archives or libraries and have received no attention from professional archivists or historians. At the time of my research there were no finding aids available for the important collections of WPA and TVA records at the McKlung Museum of the University of Tennessee and at Mound State Monument in Alabama, the WPA records at Louisiana State University, or the NPS records at the Southeastern Archaeological Center. Fortunately, some collections of New Deal archaeological records are in archives and finding aids are available to facilitate their use. The papers of William Webb in the University of Kentucky Library are well organized as are Frank Setzler's papers in the National Anthropological Archives of the Smithsonian Institution. Both collections contain useful finding aids for locating individual documents.

Model Projects in Other Scientific Disciplines

Archaeologists can learn how to deal with their documentation problems from other scientific disciplines. Major documentation efforts are underway by the the Center for the History of Physics, the Center for the History of Chemistry (University of Pennsylvania), the Center for the History of Electrical Engineering (Institute of Electrical Engineering and Electronics), the Charles Babbage Institute, and by other organizations. If chemists, physicists, engineers, computer scientists, and other scientists can make progress on their documentation problems, archaeologists should be no less successful.

The documentation effort of the American Institute of Physics (AIP) has been an example of a successful program of preserving records of a science. The AIP is a coordinating organization of American associations in physics and astronomy representing approximately 60,000 individuals. In 1959 the AIP organized the Committee on History and Philosophy of Physics to deal with the problem of documentary resources in physics. The committee investigated the situation and concluded that, because physicists regularly destroyed their manuscript materials and archival programs did not collect in the area of modern physics, an immediate program to correct the problem was necessary. At that time the papers of only one twentieth-century physicist were in an American repository. The AIP soon established a program, later named the AIP Center for History of Physics, based on six basic principles: establish a close relationship with the community that produces the records; conduct educational activities designed to keep the program visible; cooperate with related programs; use expert advisors and an advisory committee of distinguished scientists and historians; focus attention on activities no one else is doing or should do; and develop documentation goals and strategies based on a knowledge of the national and even international scientific community (Warnow 1984 : 4−6).

The AIP Center has implemented these principles in a number of programs. The most important priority of the center was to save the personal papers of the most productive American physicists. An oral history program has interviewed more than 500 individuals. A special effort was made to document the field of quantum physics. Other three-year projects documented the fields of nuclear physics, astrophysics, and solid-state physics. A special documentation strategy was developed and implemented for the Department of Energy Laboratories, which has clearly been a great success. The AIP Center has been a model for many other history centers established since the 1960s. The AIP Center data base today includes information on the papers of approximately 2,500 physicists in repositories throughout the world.

Related Projects in Archaeology

These and other documentation programs in scientific disciplines illustrate that great progress can be made in dealing with documentation problems. Archaeology has much to learn from these successful programs, but the picture in archaeology is not entirely bleak. A number of archaeologists, historians, and archivists are interested in documentation problems, and efforts are already underway to manage the problem.

The recent publication of a guide to preserving field records by the University of Pennsylvania Museum is an example of a successful effort to assist anthropologists and archaeologists in preserving current records as they are generated but is not designed to handle the problem of older records. The museum recognized archaeologists' lack of knowledge about archival principles and argued to national organizations in anthropology, archaeology, and archives the need for a manual. An advisory committee was established consisting of representatives of the American Anthropological Association, the American Philosophical Society, the National Anthropological Archives, the Archaeological Institute of America, the Society for American Archaeology, the Society of American Archivists, and the Society for Historical Archaeology. Funding was obtained from the National Historical Publications and Records Commission. The manual, which describes archival techniques for anthropologists and archaeologists, begins with an overview of the formats of the records and contains chapters about preservation of paper records; film, tape, and video; machine-readable records; and storage (Kenworthy et al. 1985).

The National Anthropological Archives (NAA) of the Smithsonian Institution has made a substantial effort to collect and make available institutional records of archaeological organizations and the personal papers of archaeologists. The NAA has underway a five-year project to survey anthropological records in repositories in the United States and Canada. Because the focus of the project is anthropological records, it is a much larger job than just archaeological documentation. At the present time, the project has no financial support and uses personnel already employed at the NAA. There is little prospect of receiving monetary support or additional personnel from the Smithsonian. The project published notices in major periodicals announcing its goals and asking for information about records in repositories, and a larger number of responses resulted than the project personnel anticipated. James Glenn, director of the project, has expressed a desire to cooperate with an effort focusing on archaeological documentation and the assistance of the NAA would be of great benefit to this effort.

The Pacific Northwest Anthropological Archives at the University of Idaho has collected documentary materials in archaeology since it was established in 1975. Originally focusing on archaeology, with a grant from the National Endowment for the Humanities of 23,320 dollars, the archive has collected publications, papers, manuscripts, research reports and proposals, maps, films, tapes, slides, maps, notes, correspondence, and other material related to the Plateau and the Northwest Coast.

The University of Kentucky Museum with funds from the Kentucky Heritage Council has recently completed a review of the records of New Deal excavations in Kentucky. This project examined records in the University of Kentucky Library Archives, the University of Kentucky Museum of Anthropology, and the National Anthropological Archives. All relevant site documents were reviewed, notes were organized, and a cross-referenced file listing all documents relating to each site has been established (Milner and Smith 1986:3). In addition to a history of the University of Kentucky's New Deal archaeological activities, the report includes lists of sites excavated, supervisors, components found at each site, and other useful information. In a separate appendix, the numbers of museum documents are classified by feature forms, burial forms, profiles, field journals, field notes, and total papers. This project illustrates that a survey of records combined with an effort to organize and preserve records can be a valuable aid to archaeological research.

The gray literature of unpublished archaeological reports generated by cultural resource management projects is another area of concern to those interested in archaeological documentation. Several efforts are now underway or have been planned to deal with the problem of cultural resource management reports. One is the NPS National Archeological Database and another is the anticipated development of the Smithsonian Institution Cultural Resource Managment (CRM) repository project.

The NPS National Archeological Database was funded several years ago by Congress. This program, with a total budget of 400,000 dollars, was designed to compile two sources of information into one computerized data base: a bibliography of archaeology and CRM projects, including some general information about the projects and a data base of existing data bases. The goals of the project are

> To establish a central repository of information on archaeological and other cultural resource projects. To allow the users to avoid duplication of effort, particularly in the preparation of archaeological and cultural resource overviews, by altering them to existing work. To enhance the ability of the users to plan for necessary archaeological and cultural resource work by providing access to information on known resources. To allow the users to identify other data bases, which have more detailed information such as site or building inventories. To enhance the ability of the Department to fulfill the requirements in PL 93–291 and PL 96–95 to report annually to Congress on Federal archaeological activities and on archaeological and cultural resource investigations on public and Indian lands [Society for American Archaeology 1986:Section 5.1c].

The Solution: A Documentation Strategy for Archaeology

The discussion about a number of initiatives underway or in the planning stages to deal with specific problems of archaeological documentation indicates the substantial interest in the issue within the archaeological community. The difficulty is that each approach is limited to only a small part of a major problem. In this chapter I have argued that the individual projects are so closely related that they should be attacked by a comprehensive national project for documentation of archaeology. An integrated approach to the problem will allow the concept of archaeological records to be expanded so that appropriate documentation of activities of archaeologists may be preserved. Continuation of an uncoordinated, piecemeal approach will only allow significant archaeological resources to fall between the cracks of each separate project.

The solution to all of these related problems is to develop a documentation strategy for archaeology. The documentation strategy will have three major goals: identification of records of enduring value, encouraging preservation of records, and improving access to records (Society of American Archivists 1986). The program should be coordinated among the numerous individuals and institutions with an interest in archaeological records. The benefits of such a program as seen by the Society of American Archivists include "integration and coordination of collecting programs across individual repositories. Such strategies will enable archivists to study selected portions of the complex record which transcend the concerns of any one repository and to plan coordinated and cooperative retention programs" (1986:32).

The documentation strategy should begin with a comprehensive study of archaeological documentation. "The intent is to design an analytic process that guides selection and assures retention of adequate information about a topic or locale. Historical research and discussion at the beginning of a project will clarify the goals and identify the specific issues to be documented" (Samuels 1986:120). This study could build on the recently published guide to the records of science and technology (Haas et al. 1985) but customize the process for the unique characteristics of archaeological documentation. It guides archivists in deciding to acquire a collection of records, gives information helpful in appraising, arranging, and describing a collection, and assists records managers in developing retention guidelines.

After a thorough study of the nature of archaeological documentation, a survey of archaeological records using standard archival procedures could begin. Many records surveys have been completed that could serve as a model for archaeological records so archaeologists will not have to develop a new procedure for their records. To conduct an effective survey of archaeological records requires a clear operational definition of archaeological records and an identification of the archaeologists, institutions, and events to be documented. When planning the survey a decision must be made about its focus. Should the project limit its concern to archaeological records in the United States? Should the project limit its focus to the United States and Canada, or even the New World? Even if the limit of the survey is the United States, should all archaeological records be included or should only records relating to the archaeology of the United States be surveyed. In this case would records from other parts of the world, including those of classical archaeology, be excluded? To reach a decision about the geographic focus of the project, the focus of the project must be discussed with specialists in the archaeology of areas outside North America. Contacts could be established with Old World and classical archaeologists before a decision is reached.

My personal interest is documentation relating to the archaeology of North America. A viable project could focus on locating archaeological records in the United States, both professional and amateur. These records may be in archives, universities, museums, libraries, government agencies, private firms, professional associations, and private ownership. The survey would accumulate information on collections of papers and records, arrangements that have previously been made for the future deposit of collections in repositories, and information on materials that have been destroyed. Copies of available finding aids would be sought.

Planning for the survey will require an early decision on the sponsor of the survey and the funding agency. The Society for American Archaeology has recently organized a committee on the history of archaeology to sponsor the survey, but funding has not been obtained. A detailed statement describing the project should be developed not only to obtain funding but to serve as a basis for the cooperation between institutions—necessary if the survey is to be a success. Institutions and individuals with archaeological documentation would be identified using a variety of techniques. Archaeological records in known depositories are found in the *Directory of Archives and Manuscript Repositories in the United States* (National Historical Publications and Records Commission 1978), and the *National Union Catalog of Manuscript Collections* (Library of Congress 1962–present). Institutions now active or once active in archaeology would be contacted for information on their holdings. Manuscripts in private hands would be identified using a network of contacts with archaeologists and archivists. Statements describing the project would be placed in archaeological, anthropological, and archival publications to convince owners of materials to cooperate with the project. Letters to senior archaeologists would attempt to persuade them of the value of their papers and suggest that they deposit records in archives at their institutional home or in other repositories.

The survey could rely on questionnaires or field visits by project personnel. In either case the success of the records survey will depend on the owners of the records. "Cooperation by those who hold the records to be surveyed is a key element in every survey—whether the records holders provide information themselves or merely permit access by the field workers. Every survey project must consciously develop multiple sources of influence to secure this cooperation, including, perhaps, legal sanction, bureaucratic authority, self-interest, and professional obligation" (Fleckner 1977:8).

Once located, documents in danger of destruction must be preserved and made accessible to archaeologists, which will require an educational effort to convince archaeologists, the heirs of archaeologists, and other owners of archaeological records of the importance of archaeological documents. A similar educational effort will be necessary for the archival community. Archivists must understand the importance of the papers of archaeologists and be willing to commit the resources to acquire the records and produce useful finding aids to make this material available for archaeological research and historians of archaeology.

The design of the educational strategy should be modeled after the successful efforts of other scientific disciplines. One effective means of communication is to distribute a newsletter. The Center for History of Physics, Center for the History of Chemistry, and other institutions produce newsletters of varying degrees of sophistication. These newsletters communicate information about individual research projects in the history of the discipline, request information and cooperation, report activities at archives and museums, detail reports on meetings, review recent publications in the history of the discipline, and discuss funding opportunities.

Much information about the location of records would be accumulated during the survey and this information would have to be managed to ensure the preservation of these records. Archaeologists could emulate a successful strategy of the Center for History of Physics that uses data-base-management software on a microcomputer to track the process of preserving individual collections. Once collections of documents have been located, they are entered into the data base, then dates of follow-up actions are entered. Letters to scientists, families, and institutions are sent at appropriate times until the material is successfully preserved. Telephone calls and personal visits are used as necessary. Archaeologists have a well-developed network of personal and professional contacts throughout the discipline that could be used to influence preservation of personal papers.

To publicize the progress and needs of the documentation strategy, sessions in the history of archaeology and archaeological documentation should be held at major national and regional archaeological associations. Some successful sessions have been held, for instance at the fiftieth anniversary celebration of the Society for American Archaeology. Others are planned, including the fiftieth anniversary celebration of the Southeastern Archaeological Conference in 1988. But sessions should be held at other times in addition to special celebrations to develop relationships between archaeologists, archivists, and historians working in the history of archaeology.

The primary means of improving access to archaeological records will be to develop a national data base of archaeological documentation. Funding agencies are now willing to support development of computer data bases rather than a published guide to records. This relational data base should be capable of communication with the NPS National Archeological Database. Final decisions about the structure of the data base can be delayed until the project is funded, but preliminary decisions on the format of the data base will have to be a part of a funding proposal.

Conclusions

I have reviewed the current condition of archaeological documentation, examined several successful programs to preserve scientific documentation, and suggested a plan—a documentation strategy for archaeology. But this plan is a long-term solution to a big problem. What can we do now? What are the first steps to begin implementation of a documentation strategy for archaeology? Many of the elements of a documentation strategy for archaeology are already in place in the discipline. These existing elements should be combined into a workable, integrated program.

A committee or advisory board on archaeological documentation should be established as soon as possible. Successful development of a documentation strategy for archaeology must involve individuals and institutions in archaeology, archives, and history. John Fleckner, an authority on records surveys, sees several reasons to create an advisory board. "Advisory boards often have an important prestige function, affirming the project's legitimacy to those who must permit access to their records and to those who are asked to fund the project. Carefully chosen board members also may contribute technical expertise, scholarly perspective, personal contacts, or timely wisdom" (Fleckner 1977 : 6).

Statements of support by the major professional organizations should be forthcoming. The commitment of professional societies will legitimize the project and facilitate the involvement of archaeologists, archivists, historians, and funding agencies. While informal support for developing a solution to the problem has been expressed by some of the major professional associations, formal statements are now required.

Some archaeological organization or consortium of organizations should make a commitment to implement a documentation strategy for archaeology. Funding should then be sought to begin the project. Preliminary contacts with funding agencies including the National Science Foundation, the National Endowment for the Humanities, and the National Historical Publications and Records Commission have been uniformly positive. The funding is there if a viable program is developed that will produce a useful product in a reasonable period of time.

In conclusion, development and implementation of a documentation strategy for archaeology is a worthwhile and viable project. Future generations of archaeologists and historians will benefit from our action to save the documentation of archaeology.

References
Contributors
Index

References

Acuff, Lysbeth B.
1986 SAA Self Study–Interim Report. *Bulletin of the Society for American Archaeology* 4(5):3–5.

Agassi, Joseph
1981 *Science and Society.* D. Reidel, Dordrecht.

Akins, Nancy J.
1986 *A Biocultural Approach to Human Burials from Chaco Canyon, New Mexico.* Reports of the Chaco Center No. 9. National Park Service, Santa Fe.

Akins, Nancy J., and John D. Schelberg
1984 Evidence for Organizational Complexity as Seen from the Mortuary Practices at Chaco Canyon. In *Recent Research on Chaco Prehistory,* edited by W. James Judge and John D. Schelberg, pp. 89–102. Reports of the Chaco Center No. 8. National Park Service, Albuquerque.

Aldiss, Brian
1973 *Billion Year Spree: The True History of Science Fiction.* Doubleday, Garden City.

Alvarez, Manuel F.
1901 *Las Ruinas de Mitla y la Arquitectura Nacional.* Talleres Tipográficos de la Escuela de Artes y Oficios, Mexico City.

Angulo Iñíguez, Diego
1933–1939 *Planos de Monumentos Arquitectónicos de América y Filipinas Existentes en el Archivo de Indias,* 7 vols. Laboratorio de Arte, Universidad de Sevilla, Sevilla.

Ankersmit, F. R.
1983 *Narrative Logic.* Martinus Nijhoff, The Hague.

Arnove, Robert F. (editor)
1980 *Philanthropy and Cultural Imperialism.* G. K. Hall, Boston.

Aubrey, John C.
1685 *Monumenta Britannica.* Reprinted 1980–1982, Dorset Publishing, Sherborne.

A Woman Archaeologist
1895 *Scientific American.* August 10:83 (supplement 1023).

Bailey, T. A.
1968 The Mythmakers of American History. *The Journal of American History* 55:5–21.

Ballesteros Gaibrois, Manuel
 1960 *Nuevas Noticias Sobre Palenque en un Manuscrito del Siglo XVIII.* Universidad Nacional Autónoma de México, Mexico City.
Bancroft, Hubert H.
 1886 *The Native Races of the Pacific States of North America,* 5 vols. The History Co., San Francisco.
Bandelier, Adolph F. A.
 1884 *Report of an Archaeological Tour in Mexico, in 1881.* Papers of the Archaeological Institute of America. American Series, Vol. 2. Boston.
Barnes, Barry, and Steven Shapin (editors)
 1979 *Natural Order.* Sage, London.
Barnouw, E.
 1974 *Documentary: A History of the Non-Fiction Film.* Oxford University Press, New York.
Baron, Edward (editor)
 1976 *The Great Archaeologists.* Martin, Secker, and Warburg, London.
Bateman, Thomas
 1855 *Descriptive Catalogue of the Antiquities and Miscellaneous Objects Preserved in the Museum of Thomas Bateman at Lomberdale House, Derbyshire.* Privately printed, Bakewell.
Baum, Willa
 1984 The Expanding Role of the Librarian in Oral History. In *Oral History: An Interdisciplinary Anthology,* edited by David K. Dunaway and Willa K. Baum, pp. 387–406. American Association of State and Local History, Nashville.
Beale, T. W., and Healy, P. F.
 1975 Archaeological Films: The Past as Present. *American Anthropologist* 77:889–897.
Becker, Marshall
 1979 Priests, Peasants and Ceremonial Centers: The Intellectual History of a Model. In *Maya Archaeology an Ethnohistory,* edited by N. Hammond and G. R. Willey, pp. 3–20. University of Texas Press, Austin.
Beniger, James R.
 1986 *The Control Revolution.* Harvard University Press, Cambridge.
Bennett, John W.
 1943 Recent Developments in the Functional Interpretation of Archaeological Data. *American Antiquity* 9:208–219.
Bennett, Wendell C.
 1948 The Peruvian Co-Tradition. In *A Re-appraisal of Peruvian Archaeology,* edited by Wendell C. Bennett, pp. 1–7. Memoir No. 4. The Society for American Archaeology, Menasha.
Berger, Peter L., and Thomas Luckmann
 1966 *The Social Construction of Reality.* Doubleday, Garden City.

Bernal, Ignacio

1952 La Arqueología Mexicana de 1880 a la Fecha. *Cuadernos Americanos* 65(5):121–145.

1953 La Arqueología Mexicana del Siglo XX. *Memorias del Congreso Científico Mexicano* 11:235–262.

1961 La Arqueología Mexicana en 1960. In *Homenaje a Pedro Martínez del Río,* pp. 229–235. Instituto Nacional de Antropología e Historia, Mexico City.

1962 *Bibliografía de Arqueología y Etnografía.* Instituto National de Antropología e Historia, Mexico City.

1979 *Historia de la Arqueología en México.* Porrúa, Mexico City (English edition, *A History of Mexican Archaeology,* Thames and Hudson, New York, 1980).

Beyer, Bernd F.

1986 Cuatro Siglos de Interpretacíon de la Arquitectura Monumental Prehispánica del Valle de Oaxaca: 1580–1984. *Cuadernos de Arquitectura Prehispánica* 7:9–16.

Binford, Lewis R.

1962 Archaeology as Anthropology. *American Antiquity* 28:217–225.

1964 A Consideration of Archaeological Research Design. *American Antiquity* 29:425–441.

1977 General Introduction. In *For Theory Building in Archaeology,* edited by Lewis R. Binford, pp. 1–10. Academic Press, New York.

1981 *Bones: Ancient Men and Modern Myths.* Academic Press, New York.

1983a *In Pursuit of the Past.* Thames and Hudson, London.

1983b *Working at Archaeology.* Academic Press, New York.

1986 In Pursuit of the Future. In *American Archaeology: Past and Future,* edited by David J. Meltzer, Don D. Fowler, and Jeremy A. Sabloff, pp. 459–479. Smithsonian Institution Press, Washington, D.C.

Binford, Lewis R., and Jeremy A. Sabloff

1982 Paradigms, Systematics and Archaeology. *Journal of Anthropological Research* 38:137–153.

Binford, Sally R., and Lewis R. Binford (editors)

1968 *New Perspectives in Archeology.* Aldine, Chicago.

Boas, Franz

1907 Some Principles of Museum Administration. *Science* 25:921–933.

1955 *Primitive Art.* Dover, New York.

Boast, Robin B., Christopher Chippindale, and Fekri A. Hassan

1987 Proposal for a book on Grammars of Archaeological Design, submitted to Cambridge University Press.

Bourdieu, Pierre

1977 *Outline of a Theory of Practice.* Cambridge University Press, Cambridge.

Bozeman, Theodore Dwight
   1977 *Protestants in an Age of Science.* University of North Carolina Press, Chapel Hill.
Brasseur de Bourbourg, Charles E.
   1868 *Quatre Lettres Sur Le Mexique.* Maisonneuve, Paris.
Braverman, Harry
   1974 *Labor and Monopoly Capital.* Monthly Review Press, New York.
Brinton, Daniel
   1890 *Essays of an Americanist.* Porter and Coates, Philadelphia.
British Museum
   1866 *A Guide to the Exhibition Rooms of the Departments of Natural History and Antiquities.* Trustees of the British Museum, London.
   1868 *Guide to the Christy Collection of Prehistoric Antiquities and Ethnology.* Trustees of the British Museum, London.
Brown, Harold I.
   1977 *Perception, Theory and Commitment.* Precedent Publishing Company, Chicago. Reprinted by University of Chicago Press, Chicago.
Brownlow, Kevin
   1979 *The War, the West, and the Wilderness.* Alfred A. Knopf, New York.
Brunhouse, Robert L.
   1971 *Sylvanus G. Morley and the World of the Ancient Mayas.* University of Oklahoma Press, Norman. (Spanish edition 1973, *Sylvanus Morley y el Mundo de los Antiguos Mayas,* Editares Asociados, Mexico City.)
   1973 *In Search of the Maya: The First Archaeologists.* University of New Mexico Press, Albuquerque.
   1975 *Pursuit of the Ancient Maya.* University of New Mexico Press, Albuquerque.
   1976 *Frans Blom: Maya Explorer.* University of New Mexico Press, Albuquerque.
Bryan, Kirk
   1925 Date of Channel Trenching (Arroyo Cutting) in the Arid Southwest. *Science* 62:338–344.
   1941 Pre-Columbian Agriculture in the Southwest as Conditioned by Periods of Alluviation. *Annals of the Association of American Geographers* 31:219–242.
   1954 *The Geology of Chaco Canyon, New Mexico in Relation to the Life and Remains of the Prehistoric Peoples of Pueblo Bonito.* Smithsonian Miscellaneous Collections, Vol. 122, No. 7. Smithsonian Institution, Washington, D.C.
Burrow, John W.
   1966 *Evolution and Society: A Study in Victorian Social Theory.* Cambridge University Press, Cambridge.
Butterfield, Herbert
   1931 *The Whig Interpretation of History.* G. Bell, London.

Cairns, Dorion
1984 Philosophy as a Striving Toward Universal *Sophia* in the Integral Sense. In *Essays in Memory of Aron Gurwitsch,* edited by Lester Embree, pp. 27–43. Center for Advanced Research in Phenomenology and University Press of America, Washington, D.C.

Caldwell, Joseph R.
1958 *Trend and Tradition in the Prehistory of the Eastern United States.* Memoir No. 88. American Anthropological Association, Menasha.
1964 Interaction Spheres in Prehistory. In *Hopewellian Studies,* edited by Joseph R. Caldwell and Robert L. Hall, pp. 133–143. Scientific Paper No. 12. Illinois State Museum, Springfield.

Camp, John M.
1986 *The Athenian Agora.* Thames and Hudson, New York.

Campbell, Bernard G.
1985 *Humankind Evolving.* Little, Brown, Boston.

Cantwell, Anne-Marie, James B. Griffin, and Nan A. Rothschild (editors)
1981 *The Research Potential of Anthropological Museum Collections.* Annals of the New York Academy of Sciences 376.

Carmichael, Elizabeth
1973 *The British and the Mayas.* The British Museum, London.

Casasola, Luis
1975 Panorama General de la Arqueología en El Salvador. *America Indígena* 25:715–726.

Casson, Stanley
1934 *Progress of Archaeology.* McGraw-Hill, New York.
1939 *The Discovery of Man.* Harper & Brothers, New York.

Castañeda Paganini, Ricardo
1946 *Las Ruinas de Palenque.* Author's edition, Guatemala City.

Castillo Ledón, Luis
1924 *El Museo Nacional de Arqueología, Historia y Etnografía.* Museo Nacional, Mexico City.

Ceram, C. W. (Kurt W. Marek)
1971 *The First American.* Harcourt, Brace, Javonovich, New York.

Cerezo Dardón, Hugo
1957 Breve Historia de Tikal. In *Arqueología Guatemalteca,* pp. 155–166. Instituto de Antropología e Historia, Guatemala City.

Chang, Kwang-chih
1977 *The Archaeology of Ancient China.* Yale University Press, New Haven.

Chapman, William R.
1981 Ethnology in the Museum: A. H. L. F. Pitt Rivers (1837–1900) and the Institutional Foundations of British Anthropology. Ph.D. dissertation, Oxford University.
1983 The Pitt Rivers Collection 1874–1883: The Chronical of a Gift Horse. *Journal of the Anthropological Society of Oxford* 14:181–202.

1985 Arranging Ethnology: Augustus Pitt Rivers and the Typological Tradition. In *Objects and Others: Essays on Museums and Culture* edited by George W. Stocking, Jr., pp. 15–48. University of Wisconsin Press, Madison.

Childe, V. Gordon

1925 *The Dawn of European Civilisation.* Routledge and Kegan Paul, London.

1939 The Orient and Europe. *American Journal of Archaeology* 44: 10–26.

Chippindale, Christopher

1983 *Stonehenge Complete.* Thames and Hudson, London.

1986 Archaeology, Design Theory, and the Reconstruction of Prehistoric Design Systems. *Planning and Design* 13:445–485.

1987 Archaeology, Society and Evolution at the Invention of Prehistory, 1865–70, in press.

1988 The Invention of Words for the Idea of Prehistory. *Proceedings of the Prehistoric Society,* in press.

Christenson, Andrew L.

1980 Subsistence Change: Bibliographic Overview. In *Modeling Change in Prehistoric Subsistence Economies,* edited by T. K. Earle and A. L. Christenson, pp. 243–255. Academic Press, New York.

1983 The Archaeological Investigations of the Rainbow Bridge–Monument Valley Expedition, 1933–1938. In *Honoring the Dead: Anasazi Ceramics from the Rainbow Bridge–Monument Valley Expedition* by Helen K. Crotty, pp. 9–23. Monograph Series No. 22. UCLA Museum of Cultural History, University of California, Los Angeles.

1986 The Identification and Study of Indian Shell Middens in Eastern North America: 1643–1861. *North American Archaeologist* 6:227–243.

1988 Archaeological Exploration and Research in the Kayenta Anasazi Region: A Synoptic History. In *10,000 Years on Black Mesa, Arizona: Prehistoric Change on the Colorado Plateau,* edited by Shirley Powell, F. E. Smiley, and George J. Gumerman, in preparation.

Christy, Henry

1862 *Catalogue of a Collection of Ancient and Modern Stone Implements, and Other Weapons, Tools and Utensils of the Aborigines of Various Countries.* Printed Privately, London.

Clarke, David L.

1973 Archaeology: The Loss of Innocence. *Antiquity* 47(1):6–18.

Cleland, Charles E.

1960 Analysis of the Animal Remains in the Prehistoric Ozark Bluff-Dwellings of Northwest Arkansas. Master's thesis, Department of Zoology, University of Arkansas, Fayetteville.

1965 Faunal Remains from Bluff Shelters in Northwest Arkansas. *The Arkansas Archeologist* 6:39–63.

Clifford, James L.
1968 How Much Should a Biographer Tell? Some Eighteenth-Century Views. In *Essays in Eighteenth-Century Biography,* edited by Philip B. Daghlian, pp. 67–95. Indiana University Press, Bloomington.
1970 *From Puzzles to Portraits: Problems of a Literary Biographer.* University of North Carolina Press, Chapel Hill.

Cohen, Sande
1986 *Historical Culture.* University of California Press, Berkeley.

Cole, Douglas
1985 *Captured Heritage.* University of Washington Press, Seattle.

Collier, Donald, and H. Tschopik
1954 The Role of Museums in American Anthropology. *American Anthropologist* 56:768–779.

Collier, John, Jr., and Malcolm Collier
1986 *Visual Anthropology.* University of New Mexico Press, Albuquerque.

Cordier, Henri
1920 Les Origines de la Société de Américanistes de Paris: L'Evolution des Etudes Américaines depuis 1815. *Journal de la Société des Américanistes* 12:200–206.

Cuming, H. Syer
1860 On Old English Arrow-Heads. *Journal of the British Archaeological Association* 11:262–268.

Cutler, William, III
1984 Accuracy in Oral History Interviewing. In *Oral History: An Interdisciplinary Anthology,* edited by David K. Dunaway and Willa K. Baum, pp. 79–86. American Association of State and Local History, Nashville.

Damm, Charlotte
1986 An Appeal for Women in Archaeology. *Archaeological Review from Cambridge* 5:215–218.

Daniel, Glyn
1950 *A Hundred Years of Archaeology.* Duckworth, London.
1962 *The Idea of Prehistory.* Penguin Books, Harmondsworth.
1967 *The Origins and Growth of Archaeology.* Penguin, Middlesex, England.
1976 *A Hundred and Fifty Years of Archaeology.* Harvard University Press, Cambridge.
1981a Introduction: The Necessity for an Historical Approach to Archaeology. In *Towards a History of Archaeology,* edited by G. Daniel, pp. 9–13. Thames and Hudson, London.
1981b *A Short History of Archaeology.* Thames and Hudson, London.
1981c (editor) *Towards a History of Archaeology.* Thames and Hudson, London.

Daniel, Glyn, and Colin Renfrew
    1987 *The Idea of Prehistory,* new edition. Edinburgh University Press, Edinburgh.
Davis, Joseph B., and John Thurman
    1865 *Crania Britannica: Delineations and Descriptions of the Skulls of the Aboriginal and Early Inhabitants of the British Islands,* 2 vols. Privately printed, London.
Davis, Keith
    1981 *Désiré Charnay: Expeditionary Photographer.* University of Texas Press, Austin.
Dawkins, Richard
    1986 *The Blind Watchmaker.* Longmans, Harlow.
Dawson, Charles, and Arthur Smith Woodward
    1913 On the Discovery of a Palaeolithic Human Skull and Mandible in a Flint-bearing Gravel Overlying the Wealden (Hastings Bed) at Piltdown, Fletching (Sussex). *Quarterly Journal of the Geological Society of London* 69:117–124.
Deetz, James
    1988 History and Archaeological Theory: Walter Taylor Revisited. *American Antiquity* 53:13–22.
de la Borbolla, Daniel Rubín, and Pedro Rojas
    1956 *Honduras, Monumentos Históricos y Arqueólogicos.* Instituto Panamericano de Geografía e Historia, Mexico City.
Dellinger, Samuel C., and Samuel D. Dickinson
    1942 Pottery from the Ozark Bluff Shelters. *American Antiquity* 7:276–289.
Derrida, Jacques
    1982 *Margins of Philosophy.* Alan Bass, translator. University of Chicago Press, Chicago.
Desmond, Lawrence G.
    1983 Augustus Le Plongeon: Early Maya Archaeologist. Ph.D. dissertation, University of Colorado, University Microfilms, Ann Arbor.
    1988 Alice Dixon Le Plongeon: Mayanist Pioneer. Paper presented at the 87th Annual Meeting of the American Anthropological Association, Phoenix.
Desmond, Lawrence G., and Phyllis M. Messenger
    1988 *A Dream of Maya: Augustus and Alice Le Plongeon in Nineteenth Century Yucatan.* University of New Mexico Press, Albuquerque.
Deuel, Leo
    1977 *Memoirs of Heinrich Schliemann: A Documentary Portrait.* Harper & Row, New York.
de Vries, H., and Kenneth P. Oakley
    1959 Radiocarbon Dating of the Piltdown Skull and Jaw. *Nature* 184:224–226.

Dickinson, Samuel D.
1980 Historic Tribes of the Ouachita Drainage System in Arkansas. *The Arkansas Archeologist* 21:1–11.
1986 The River of Cayas: The Ouachita or the Arkansas River? *Arkansas Archeological Society Field Notes* 209:5–11.
Dickinson, Samuel D. (editor)
1982 *New Travels in North America by Jean-Bernard Bossu, 1770– 1771.* Northwestern Louisiana University Press, Natchitoches, Louisiana.
Donahue, A. A.
1985 One Hundred Years of the *American Journal of Archaeology. American Journal of Archaeology* 89:3–30.
Douglass, A. E.
1929 The Secret of the Southwest Solved by Talkative Tree Rings. *National Geographic Magazine* 41:763–770.
1935 *Dating Pueblo Bonito and Other Ruins of the Southwest.* Contributed Technical Papers, Pueblo Bonito Series, No. 1. National Geographic Society, Washington, D.C.
Dow, Sterling
1980 A Century of Humane Archaeology. *Archaeology* 33:42–51.
Duc de Loubat
1912 *Duc de Loubat 1894–1912.* Philippe Renouard, Paris.
Dunn, Robert
1867 Archaeology and Ethnology: Remarks on Some of the Bearings of Archaeology on Certain Ethnological Problems and Researches. *Transactions of the Ethnological Society of London* 5:305–317.
Dunnell, Robert C.
1971 *Systematics in Prehistory.* Free Press, New York.
1986a Methodological Issues in Americanist Artifact Classification. In *Advances in Archaeological Method and Theory,* edited by M. B. Schiffer, 9:149–207. Academic Press, New York.
1986b Five Decades of American Archaeology. In *American Archaeology: Past and Future,* edited by David J. Meltzer, Don D. Fowler, and Jeremy A. Sabloff, pp. 23–49. Smithsonian Institution Press, Washington, D.C.
Dyson, Stephen
1981 A Classical Archaeologist's Response to the "New Archaeology." *Bulletin of the American School of Oriental Research* 242:7–13.
1985 Two Paths to the Past: A Comparative Study of the Last Fifty Years of *American Antiquity* and the *American Journal of Archaeology. American Antiquity* 50:452–463.
Earle, Timothy K., and Robert W. Preucel
1987 Processual Archaeology and the Radical Critique. *Current Anthropology* 28:501–538.

Early, Ann M.

1982 Caddoan Settlement Systems in the Ouachita River Basin. In *Arkansas Archeology in Review,* edited by Neal L. Trubowitz and Marvin D. Jeter, pp. 198–232. Arkansas Archeological Survey Research Series No. 15. Fayetteville.

1986 Dr. Thomas L. Hodges and His Contribution to Arkansas Archeology. *The Arkansas Archeologist* 23–24:1–9.

Eastlake, Charles L.

1872 *A History of the Gothic Revival.* Longmans, Green, London.

Echánove Trujillo, Carlos

1975 *Dos Héroes de la Arqueología Maya: Teobert Maler y el Conde Waldeck.* Universidad de Yucatán, Mérida.

Edlund, Ingrid, Anna Marguerite McCann, and Claire R. Sherman

1981 Gisela Marie Augusta Richter (1882–1972): Scholar of Classical Art and Museum Archaeologist. In *Women as Interpreters of the Visual Arts, 1820–1979* edited by Claire R. Sherman and Adele M. Holcomb. Greenwood Press, Westport, Ct.

Embree, Lester

1980 Methodology is Where Human Scientists and Philosophers Can Meet: Reflections on the Schutz-Parsons Exchange. *Human Studies* 3:367–373.

1981 The History and Phenomenology of Science is Possible. In *Phenomenology and the Understanding of Human Destiny,* edited by Stephen Skousgaard, pp. 215–228. Center for Advanced Research in Phenomenology and University Press of America, Washington, D.C.

1987a Archaeology: The Most Basic Science of All. *Antiquity* 61: 75–78.

1987b Phenomenology of a Change in Archaeological Observation. Paper presented at Boston Colloquim for the Philosophy of Science.

1988 The Structure of American Theoretical Archaeology: A Preliminary Report. In *Critical Traditions in Contemporary Archaeology,* edited by Valerie Pinsky and Alison Wylie. Cambridge University Press, Cambridge, in press.

Evans, Joan

1949 The Royal Archaeological Institute: A Retrospect. *Archaeological Journal* 106:1–11.

1956 *The History of the Society of Antiquaries.* Oxford University Press, Oxford.

Evans, Nancy B.

1987 Frederick Starr: Missionary for Anthropology. Master's thesis, Department of Anthropology, Indiana University, Bloomington.

Fagan, Brian M.

1975 *The Rape of the Nile: Tomb Robbers, Tourists, and Archaeologists in Egypt.* Scribners, New York.

1977 *Elusive Treasure: The Story of Early Archaeologists in the Americas.* Scribner's, New York.
1978 *Quest for the Past.* Addison-Wesley, Reading.
1984a *The Aztecs.* W. H. Freeman, New York.
1984b *Precursores de la Arqueología Americana.* Fondo de Cultura Económica, Mexico City.
Fahnestock, Polly J.
1984 History and Theoretical Development: The Importance of a Critical Historiography in Archaeology. *Archaeological Review from Cambridge* 3:7–19.
Ferdon, Edwin
1955 *A Trial Survey of Mexican-Southwestern Architectural Parallels.* Monograph No. 21, School of American Research, Santa Fe.
Fernández, Justino and Pedro José Márquez
1972 *Sobre lo Bello en General y dos Monumentos de Arquitectura Mexicana.* Universidad Nacional Autónoma de México, Mexico City.
Feuer, Lewis S.
1975 *Ideology and the Ideologists.* Harper & Row, New York.
Figgins, J. D.
1927 The Antiquity of Man in America. *Natural History* 27:229–239.
Flannery, Kent V.
1968 Archaeological Systems Theory and Early Mesoamerica. In *Anthropological Archaeology in the Americas,* edited by Betty J. Meggers, pp. 67–87. Anthropological Society of Washington, Washington, D.C.
1976 A Plea for an Endangered Species. In *The Early Mesoamerican Village,* edited by K. Flannery, pp. 369–373. Academic Press, New York.
Fleckner, John
1977 *Archives and Manuscripts: Surveys.* Society of American Archivists, Chicago.
Ford, James A.
1954 Comment on A. C. Spaulding, "Statistical Techniques for the Discovery of Artifact Types." *American Antiquity* 19:390–391.
1961 *Menard Site: The Quapaw Village of Osotouy on the Arkansas River.* Anthropological Papers of the American Museum of Natural History, Vol. 48, Part 2.
Foucault, Michael
1973 *The Order of Things: An Archaeology of the Human Sciences.* Vintage, New York. (First published in 1966 by Tavistock, London.)
Fowler, Don D.
1987 Uses of the Past: Archaeology in the Service of the State. *American Antiquity* 52(2):229–248.
Freidel, David A., and Jeremy A. Sabloff
1984 *Cozumel: Late Maya Settlement Patterns.* Academic Press, New York.

French, Marilyn

1985 *Beyond Power: Men, Women, and Morals.* Jonathan Cape, London.

Frere, John

1800 Account of Flint Weapons Discovered at Hoxne in Suffolk. *Archaeologia* 13:204–205.

Frisbie, Theodore R.

1972 The Chacoan Interation Sphere: A Verification of the *Pochteca* Concept Within the Southwestern United States. Paper presented at the 37th Annual Meeting of the Society for American Archaeology, Bal Harbour.

Fritz, Gayle J.

1984 Identification of Cultigen Amaranth and Chenopod from Rockshelter Sites in Northwest Arkansas. *American Antiquity* 49:558–571.

1986a Dessicated Botanical Remains from Three Bluffshelter Sites in the Pine Mountain Project Area, Crawford County, Arkansas. In *Contributions to Ozark Prehistory,* edited by George Sabo III, pp. 86–97. Arkansas Archeological Survey Research Series No. 27. Fayetteville.

1986b Prehistoric Ozark Agriculture: The University of Arkansas Rockshelter Collections. Ph.D. dissertation, University of North Carolina, Chapel Hill. University Microfilms, Ann Arbor.

Fritz, John M., and Fred T. Plog

1970 The Nature of Archaeological Explanation. *American Antiquity* 35:405–412.

Gamio, Manuel

1959 Boas Sobre Cerámica y Estratigrafía. In *The Anthropology of Franz Boas,* edited by Walter Goldschmidt, pp. 117–118. The American Anthropological Association, Washington, D.C.

Gándara, Manuel

1978 *La Arqueología Oficial en México.* Thesis, Escuela Nacional de Antropología e Historia, Mexico City.

Gardin, J.-C., O. Guillaume, P.-O. Herman, A. Mesnard, M.-S. Lagrange, M. Renand, E. Zadora-Rio

1987 *Systèmes experts et sciences humaines; le cas d'archéologie.* Editions Eyrolles, Paris.

Garlake, P. S.

1982 Prehistory and Ideology in Zimbabwe. *Africa* 52(3):1–19.

Ghiselin, M. T.

1969 *The Triumph of the Darwinian Method.* University of California Press, Berkeley.

Giot, P.-R.

1971 The Impact of Radiocarbon Dating on the Establishment of the Prehistoric Chronology of Brittany. *Proceedings of the Prehistoric Society* 37:208–217.

Godoy, Ricardo
1977 Franz Boas and His Plans for the International School of American Archaeology and Ethnology in Mexico. *Journal of the History of Behavioral Sciences* 13:228–242.

Goguet, A. Y.
1761 The Ancient History of Mankind. Reprinted in *Man's Discovery of His Past,* edited by R. F. Heizer, 1969, pp. 13–23. Peek Publications, Palo Alto.

Goode, George Brown
1889 Museum-History and Museums of History. *Papers of the American Historical Association* 3:495–519. (Reprinted by Knickerbocker Press, 1889, pp. 253–275.)

Gossman, Lionel
1978 History and Literature. In *The Writing of History,* edited by Robert H. Canary and Henry Kozicki, pp. 3–39. University of Wisconsin Press, Madison.

Gould, Richard A.
1980 *Living Archaeology.* Cambridge University Press, Cambridge.

Gould, Stephen Jay
1977a Eternal Metaphors of Palaeontology. In *Patterns of Evolution as Illustrated by the Fossil Record,* edited by A. Hallum, pp. 1–26. Elsevier, Amsterdam.
1977b *Ontogeny and Phylogeny.* Belknap Press, Harvard University, Cambridge.
1979 Piltdown Revisited. *Natural History* 88(3):86–95.

Graham, Ian
1963 Juan Galindo Enthusiast. *Estuidos de Cultura Maya* 3:11–35.
1977 Lord Kingsborough, Sir Thomas Phillips and Obadiah Rich: Some Bibliographical Notes. In *Social Process in Maya Prehistory,* edited by N. Hammond, pp. 47–57. Academic Press, New York.

Graham, Loren, Wolf Lepenies, and Peter Weingart (editors)
1983 *Functions and Uses of Disciplinary Histories.* D. Reidel, Dordrecht.

Grayson, Donald K.
1983 *The Establishment of Human Antiquity.* Academic Press, New York.
1986 Eoliths, Archaeological Ambiquity, and the Generation of "Middle-Range" Research. In *American Archaeology: Past and Future,* edited by D. J. Meltzer, D. D. Fowler, and J. A. Sabloff, pp. 77–133. Smithsonian Institution Press, Washington, D.C.

Green, Sally
1983 *Prehistorian: The Life of V. Gordon Childe.* Moonraker, Bradford-on-Avon.

Greene, Mott T.
1986 History of Geology. In *Historical Writing on American Science:*

Perspectives and Prospects, edited by Sally G. Kohlstedt and Margaret W. Rossiter, pp. 97–116. Johns Hopkins University Press, Baltimore.

Griffin, James B.

1974 Forword to the New Edition. In *The Adena People,* by W. S. Webb and C. E. Snow, pp. v–xix. The University of Tennessee Press, Knoxville.

Griffin, James B. (editor)

1952 *Archeology of the Eastern United States.* University of Chicago Press, Chicago.

Griffin, William

1960 Juan Galindo: Central American Chauvinist. *Hispanic American Historical Review* 40:25–52.

Gruber, Jacob W.

1966 In Search of Experience: Biography as an Instrument for the History of Anthropology. In *Pioneers of American Anthropology: The Uses of Biography,* edited by June Helm, pp. 3–27. University of Washington Press, Seattle.

1975 Introduction. In *Toward a Science of Man: Essays in the History of Anthropology,* edited by T. H. Thoresen, pp. 1–13. Mouton, The Hague.

Gurwitsch, Aron

1974 *Phenomenology and the Theory of Science,* edited by Lester Embree. Northwestern University Press, Evanston.

Haas, Joan K., Helen W. Samuels, and Barbara T. Simmons

1985 *Appraising the Records of Modern Science and Technology: A Guide.* Society of American Archivists, Chicago.

Hacking, Ian

1981 Introduction. In *Scientific Revolutions,* edited by Ian Hacking, pp. 1–5. Oxford University Press, Oxford.

Hagen, Victor W. von

1974 *Search of the Maya: The History of Stephens and Catherwood.* Saxon House, New York.

Hall, Manly P.

1948 The Maya Empire. With special reference to the work of Augustus Le Plongeon. *Horizon* 7(4):23–35.

Hanfmann, George M. A.

1972 *Letters from Sardis.* Harvard University Press, Cambridge.

Harris, Marvin

1968 *The Rise of Anthropological Theory.* Thomas Crowell, New York.

Hassan, Fekri A.

1988 Prolegomena to a Grammatical Theory of Lithic Artifacts. *World Archaeology* 19:281–296.

Haven, Samuel F.

1856 *Archaeology of the United States.* Smithsonian Contributions to Knowledge 8(2). Smithsonian Institution, Washington, D.C.

Hawkes, Christopher F. C.
  1962 The British Museum and British Archaeology. *Antiquity* 36: 248–251.
Hawkes, Jacquetta
  1982 *Adventurer in Archaeology: The Biography of Sir Mortimer Wheeler.* St. Martin's, New York.
Hawley, Florence
  1934 *The Significance of the Dated Prehistory of Chetro Ketl, Chaco Cañon, New Mexico.* Monograph Series, Vol. 1. University of New Mexico, Albuquerque.
Hayes, Alden C.
  1981 A Survey of Chaco Canyon Archeology. In *Archeological Surveys of Chaco Canyon* by Alden C. Hayes, David M. Brugge, and W. James Judge, pp. 1–68. National Park Service Publications in Archeology 18A, Washington, D.C.
Haynes, C. Vance
  1982 Were Clovis Progenitors in Beringia? In *Paleoecology of Beringia,* edited by D. Hopkins, J. Matthews, C. Schweger, and S. Young, pp. 383–398. Academic Press, New York.
Heider, Karl G.
  1976 *Ethnographic Film.* University of Texas Press, Austin.
Heizer, Robert F.
  1969 *Man's Discovery of His Past.* Peek Publications, Palo Alto.
Heizer, Robert F., and Sherburne Cook
  1954 Comments on the Piltdown Remains. *American Anthropologist* 56:92–94.
Hempel, Carl
  1942 The Function of General Laws in History. *The Journal of Philosophy* 39:35–48.
  1965 *Aspects of Scientific Explanation and Other Essays in the Philosophy of Science.* Free Press, New York.
  1974 Reasons and Covering Laws in Historical Explanation. Reprinted in *The Philosophy of History,* edited by Patrick Gardiner, pp. 90–105. Oxford University Press, London.
Hewett, Edgar L.
  1936 *The Chaco Canyon and its Monuments.* University of New Mexico and School of American Research, Albuquerque.
Hinsley, Curtis, M., Jr.
  1981 *Savages and Scientists: The Smithsonian Institution and the Development of American Anthropology 1846–1910.* Smithsonian Institution Press, Washington, D.C.
  1985 Hemispheric Hegemony in Early American Anthropology, 1841–1851: Reflections on John Lloyd Stephens and Lewis Henry Morgan. In *Social Context of American Ethnology 1840–1984,* edited by

June Helm, pp. 28–40. American Anthropological Association. Washington, D.C.

1986 Edgar Lee Hewett and the School of American Research in Santa Fe 1906–1912. In *American Archaeology: Past and Future,* edited by D. J. Meltzer, D. D. Fowler, and J. A. Sabloff, pp. 217–233. Smithsonian Institution Press, Washington, D.C.

Hobsbawn, E. J.

1962 *The Age of Revolution, Europe 1789–1848.* World, New York.

1975 *The Age of Capitalism, 1848–1875.* Charles Scribner's Sons, New York.

Hodder, Ian

1984 Archaeology in 1984. *Antiquity* 58:25–32.

1986 *Reading the Past: Current Approaches to Interpretation in Archaeology.* Cambridge University Press, Cambridge.

Hodges, Dr. T. L., and Mrs. T. L. Hodges

1943a The Watermelon Island site in Arkansas. *Bulletin of the Texas Archaeological and Paleonotological Society* 15:66–79. (Reprinted in 1962 in *The Arkansas Archeologist* 3(3):9–16.)

1943b Possibilities for the Archaeologist and Historian in Eastern Arkansas. *Arkansas Historical Quarterly* 2:141–163.

1945 Suggestion for Identification of Certain Mid-Quachita Pottery as Cahinnio Caddo. *Bulletin of the Texas Archaeological and Paleontological Society* 16:98–116. (Reprinted in 1963 in *The Arkansas Archeologist* 4(8):1–12.)

Hoffman, Michael P.

1971 A Partial Archaeological Sequence for the Little River Region, Arkansas. Ph.D. dissertation, Harvard University.

1977 The Kinkead-Mainard Site, 3PU2: A Late Prehistoric Quapaw Phase Site Near Little Rock, Arkansas. *The Arkansas Archeologist* 16–18:1–41.

1981 The Father of Us All: S. C. Dellinger and the Beginning of Arkansas Archeology and Anthropology. Paper presented at University of Arkansas Anthropology Colloquium, Fayetteville.

1984 Treating with Mine Enemy: Pothunters, Collectors, Antiquities Dealers, and Archeological Responsibility; an Arkansas Case Study. Paper presented at the 49th annual meeting of the Society for American Archaeology, Portland, Oregon.

Holsinger, S. J.

1901 Report on the Prehistoric Ruins of Chaco Canyon, New Mexico, Ordered by the General Land Office Letter "P," December 18, 1900, 3 vols. Typescript on file at the National Anthropological Archives, Washington, D.C.

Hooton, Ernest

1954 Comment on the Piltdown Affair. *American Anthropologist* 56:287–289.

Hopkins, Clark
1979 *The Discovery of Dura Europos*. Yale University Press, New Haven.
Hosler, Dorothy, Jeremy A. Sabloff, and Dale Runge
1977 Simulation Model Development: A Case Study of the Classic Maya Collapse. In *Social Process in Maya Prehistory*, edited by Norman Hammond, pp. 553–590. Academic Press, London.
House, John H.
1986 The Mississippian Sequence in the Menard Locality, Eastern Arkansas. Paper presented at the 43rd annual meeting of the Southeastern Archaeological Conference, Nashville, Tennessee. Expanded version in possession of the author.
Hrdlička, Aleš
1907 Skeletal Remains Suggesting or Attributed to Early Man in North America. *Bureau of American Ethnology Bulletin 33*.
1912 Early Man in South America. *Bureau of American Ethnology Bulletin 52*.
1918 Recent Discoveries Attributed to Early Man in America. *Bureau of American Ethnology Bulletin 66*.
1927 The Neanderthal Phase of Man. *Journal of the Royal Anthropological Institute of Great Britain* 57:249–274.
Hudson, Kenneth
1981 *A Society History of Archaeology: The British Experience*. Macmillan, London.
Hull, David
1979 In Defense of Presentism. *History and Theory* 18:1–15.
Hunter, M. C. W.
1971 The Royal Society and the Origins of British Archaeology: I and II. *Antiquity* 65:113–121, 187–196.
Iguíñiz, Juan Bautista
1912 *Las Publicaciones del Museo Nacional: Apuntes Histórico-Bibliográficos*. Museo Nacional de Arqueología, Etnología e Historía, Mexico City.
Irwin-Williams, Cynthia
n.d. Women in the Field: The Role of Women in Archaeology. Unpublished manuscript in possession of the author.
Jackson, William H.
1878 Ruins of Chaco Cañon, Examined in 1877. In *10th Annual Report of the United States Geological and Geographical Survey of the Territories Embracing Colorado and Parts of Adjacent Territories*, edited by F. V. Hayden, pp. 431–450. U. S. Government Printing Office, Washington, D.C.
Jacobs, L. (editor)
1979 *The Documentary Tradition*, second edition. W. W. Norton, New York.

Jennings, Francis

1976 *The Invasion of America.* W. W. Norton, New York.

Jerdan, W.

1844 Suggestions for the Extension of the British Archaeological Association. *Archaeological Journal* 1:297–300.

Jeter, Marvin D.

1979 George P. Kelley and the Development of Archeology in Southeast Arkansas. *Arkansas Archeological Society Field Notes* 169:12–16.

1981 Edward Palmer's 1882 Excavation at the Tillar Site (3DR1), Southeast Arkansas. *Southeast Archaeological Conference Bulletin* 24: 57–59.

1982a The Archeology of Southeast Arkansas: An overview for the 1980s. In *Arkansas Archeology in Review,* edited by Neal L. Trubowitz and Marvin D. Jeter, pp. 76–131. Arkansas Archeological Survey Research Series No. 15. Fayetteville.

1982b The Protohistoric "Tillar Complex" of Southeast Arkansas. Paper presented at the 47th annual meeting of the Society for American Archaeology, Minneapolis.

1986a Tunicans West of the Mississippi: A Summary of Early Historic and Archaeological Evidence. In *The Protohistoric Period in the Mid-South: 1500–1700,* edited by David H. Dye and Ronald C. Brister, pp. 38–63. Mississippi Department of Archives and History Archaeological Reports No. 18.

1986b Review of "Classics of Smithsonian Anthropology" 1985 reprint of *Report on the Mound Explorations of the Bureau of Ethnology,* by Cyrus Thomas. *Southeastern Archaeology* 5:148–150.

1989 *Edward Palmer's "Arkansaw Mounds."* University of Arkansas Press, in press.

Jeter, Marvin D., David B. Kelley, and George P. Kelley

1979 The Kelley-Grimes Site: A Mississippi Period Burial Mound, Southeast Arkansas, Excavated in 1936. *The Arkansas Archeologist* 20:1–51.

Joussaume, Roger

1985 *Les dolmens pour les morts; le megalithisme a travers le monde.* Hachette, Paris.

Judd, Neil M.

1954 *The Material Culture of Pueblo Bonito.* Smithsonian Miscellaneous Collections Vol. 124. Smithsonian Institution, Washington, D.C.

1964 *The Architecture of Pueblo Bonito.* Smithsonian Miscellaneous Collections Vol. 147, No. 1. Smithsonian Institution, Washington, D.C.

Judge, W. James

1984 New Light on Chaco Canyon. In *New Light on Chaco Canyon,* edited by David Grant Noble, pp. 1–12. School of American Research, Santa Fe.

Judson, Horace F.
1984 Century of the Sciences. *Science 84* 5(9):41–43.

Keen, Benjamin
1984 *La Imagen Azteca*. Fondo de Cultura Económica, Mexico City.

Kehoe, Alice B.
1985 Modern Antievolutionism: The Scientific Creationists. In *What Darwin Began*, edited by L. R. Godfrey, pp. 165–185. Allyn and Bacon, Newton.

Kelly, Alfred H.
1968 Constitutional Liberty and the Law of Libel: A Historian's View. *The American Historical Review* 74:429–452.

Kemper, Robert V., and John F. S. Phinney
1977 *The History of Anthropology: A Research Bibliography*. Garland, New York.

Kendrick, Thomas
1954 The British Museum and British Antiquities. *Antiquity* 28:133–142.

Kennedy, K. A. R.
1985 The Dawn of Evolutionary Theory. In *What Darwin Began*, edited by L. R. Godfrey, pp. 3–23. Allyn and Bacon, Boston.

Kenworthy, Mary Anne, Eleanor M. King, Mary E. Ruwell, and Trudy Van Houten
1985 *Preserving Field Records: Archival Techniques for Archaeologists and Anthropologists*. The University Museum, University of Pennsylvania, Philadelphia.

Kerr, Robert
1871 *The Gentlemen's House*, 3rd ed. John Murray, London.

Kidder, Alfred Vincent
1924 *An Introduction to the Study of Southwestern Archaeology*. Papers of the Southwestern Expedition, No. 1. R. S. Peabody Foundation for Archaeology, Phillips Academy, Andover, Mass.
1936 Speculations on New World Prehistory. In *Essays in Anthropology*, edited by R. Lowie, pp. 143–151. University of California Press, Berkeley.

Kingsley, Charles
1863 *The Water Babies, a Fairy Tale for a Land-baby*. Macmillan, London.

Kintigh, Keith W.
1981 An Outline for a Chronology of Zuñi Ruins, Revisited: Sixty-five Years of Repeated Analysis and Collections. In *The Research Potential of Anthropological Museum Collections*, edited by A. M. Cantwell, J. B. Griffin, and N. Rothschild. Annals of the New York Academy of Sciences 376:467–487.

Klingender, F. D.
1968 *Art and the Industrial Revolution*. Schocken Books, New York.

Kluckhohn, Clyde

1940 The Conceptual Structure in Middle American Studies. In *The Maya and Their Neighbors*, edited by A. M. Tozzer, pp. 41–51. D. Appleton, New York.

Kluckhohn, Clyde, and Paul Reiter (editors)

1939 *Preliminary Report on the 1937 Excavations, Bc50–51, Chaco Canyon, New Mexico.* Bulletin 345, Anthropological Series, Vol. 3, No. 2. University of New Mexico, Albuquerque.

Knight, D.

1987 Background and Foreground: Getting Things in Context. *British Journal for the History of Science* 20:3–12.

Kohn, D. (editor)

1985 *The Darwinian Heritage.* Princeton University Press, Princeton.

Krieger, Alex D.

1944 The Typological Concept. *American Antiquity* 9:271–288.

Kristiansen, Kristian

1981 A Social History of Danish Archaeology. In *Towards a History of Archaeology*, edited by Glyn Daniel, pp. 20–44. Thames and Hudson, London.

1985 *Archaeological Formation Processes.* Nationalmuseet, Lyngby.

Kroeber, Alfred L.

1954 The Place of Anthropology in Universities. *American Anthropologist* 56:764–767.

Kuhn, Thomas S.

1962 *The Structure of Scientific Revolutions.* University of Chicago Press, Chicago.

1968 The History of Science. In *International Encyclopedia of the Social Sciences*, edited by David L. Sills, 14:74–83. Macmillan and Free Press, New York.

1977 *The Essential Tension: Selected Studies in Scientific Tradition and Change.* University of Chicago Press, Chicago.

1979 History of Science. In *Current Research in Philosophy of Science*, edited by P. Asquith and H. Kyburg, pp. 121–128. Philosophy of Science Association, East Lansing.

Kurtz, Royce D.

1979 Iowa Archaeology: A Social History, 1867–1920. *Journal of the Iowa Archaeological Society* 26:1–27.

Landau, Misia

1984 Human Evolution as Narrative. *American Scientist* 72:262–268.

Lange, Charles H., and Carroll L. Riley (editors)

1970 *The Southwestern Journals of Adolph F. Bandelier: 1883–1884.* University of New Mexico Press, Albuquerque.

Larrainzar, Manuel

1875–1878 *Estudios Sobre la Historia de América, Sus Ruins y Antigüedades*, 5 vols. Author's edition, Mexico City.

Laudan, Larry
    1981 *Science and Hypothesis.* D. Reidel, Dordrecht.
Layard, Austin H.
    1849 *Nineveh and Its Remains,* 2 vols. John Murray, London.
Leach, Edmund R.
    1984 Glimpses of the Unmentionable in the History of British Social An-
    thropology. *Annual Review of Anthropology* 13:1–23.
Leakey, Mary
    1984 *Disclosing the Past: An Autobiography.* Doubleday, New York.
Lears, T. J. Jackson
    1981 *No Place of Grace: Antimodernism and the Transformation of
    American Culture 1880–1920.* Pantheon, New York.
Lekson, Stephen H. (editor)
    1983 *The Architecture and Dendrochronology of Chetro Ketl, Chaco
    Canyon, New Mexico.* Reports of the Chaco Center No. 6. National
    Park Service, Albuquerque.
Lekson, Stephen H., William B. Gillespie, and Thomas C. Windes
    1984 *Great Pueblo Architecture of Chaco Canyon, New Mexico.* Na-
    tional Park Service Publications in Archaeology 18B, Washington,
    D.C.
Lemley, Harry J., and Samuel D. Dickinson
    1937 Archaeological Investigations on Bayou Macon in Arkansas. *Bul-
    letin of the Texas Archaeological and Paleontological Society*
    9:11–47.
Leone, Mark P.
    1986 Symbolic, Structural, and Critical Archaeology. In *American Ar-
    chaeology: Past and Future,* edited by David J. Meltzer, Don D. Fowler,
    and Jeremy A. Sabloff, pp. 415–438. Smithsonian Institution Press,
    Washington, D.C.
Le Plongeon, Alice Dixon
    1890 The Mayas. A lecture delivered at the Blavatsky Lodge, Theosophi-
    cal Society. *Theosophical Publishing Society, Theosophical Siftings*
    (London) 3(14):3–15.
Le Plongeon, Augustus
    1896 *Queen Móo and the Egyptian Sphinx.* Privately printed, New York.
    1913–1914 The Origin of the Egyptians. *The Word Magazine* 17–18.
Lesser, Alexander
    1981 Franz Boas. In *Totems and Teachers,* edited by Sydel Silverman,
    pp. 1–33. Columbia University Press, New York.
Levine, Joseph M.
    1987 *Humanism and History.* Cornell University Press, Ithaca.
Levine, Philippa
    1986 *The Amateur and the Professional.* Cambridge University Press,
    Cambridge.

Lewontin, Richard C.
1968 "Honest Jim" Watson's Big Thriller about DNA. *Chicago Sunday Sun-Times,* February 25. (Reprinted in *The Double Helix, by James D. Watson: Text, Commentary, Reviews, Original Papers,* edited by Gunther S. Stent, pp. 185–187. W. W. Norton, New York, 1980.)

Library of Congress
1962–present *National Union Catalog of Manuscript Collections.* Washington, D.C.

Lindsay, Alexander J., Jr., Glenna Williams-Dean, and Jonathan Haas
1979 *The Curation and Management of Archaeological Collections: A Pilot Study.* Heritage Conservation and Recreation Service, U.S. Department of the Interior, Washington, D.C.

Lister, Robert H., and Florence C. Lister
1981 *Chaco Canyon, Archaeology and Archaeologists.* University of New Mexico Press, Albuquerque.

Lord, Louis E.
1947 *A History of the American School of Classical Studies 1882–1942.* Harvard University Press, Cambridge.

Lothrop, Samuel
1926 Sculptural Fragments from Palenque: An Account of the First Old Empire Remains to Reach Europe. *Journal of the Royal Anthropological Institute* 59:53–63.

Lowe, Jere
1973 Nodena Dental Pathology as Reflected by the Hampson Skulls. In *Nodena: An Account of 75 Years of Archeological Investigation in Southeast Mississippi County, Arkansas,* edited by Dan F. Morse, pp. 61–64. Arkansas Archeological Survey Research Series No. 4. Fayetteville.

Lowenstein, J. M., T. Molleson, and S. L. Washburn
1982 Piltdown Jaw Confirmed as Orangutan. *Nature* 299:294.

Lubbock, John
1865 *Pre-historic Times, as Illustrated by Ancient Remains, and the Manners and Customs of Modern Savages.* Williams and Norgate, London.
1870 *The Origin of Civilisation and the Primitive Condition of Man.* Williams and Norgate, London.

Luján Muñoz, Luis
1972 Breve Historia de la Arqueología en Guatemala. In *Estudios Indigenistas,* pp. 1–17. Sociedad Mexicana de Antropología e Historia, Mexico City.

Lyon, Edwin A.
1982 New Deal Archaeology in the Southeast: WPA, TVA, NPS, 1934–1942. Ph.D. dissertation, Louisiana State University. University Microfilms, Ann Arbor.

Lysons, Samuel
1865 *Our British Ancestors; Who and What Were They?* London.

Madrid, Alfonso
1986 Archaeology in a Political Context: Examples from Four Latin American Countries. *Archaeological Review from Cambridge* 5:222–226.
Maine, Henry S.
1861 *Ancient Law.* John Murray, London.
Makagiansar, Makaminan
1984 Museums for Today and Tomorrow: A Cultural and Educational Mission. *Museum* 36:3–7.
Malinowski, Bronislaw
1954 Myth in Primitive Psychology. In *Magic, Science and Religion,* pp. 93–148. Doubleday, Garden City. (Originally published 1926.)
Mark, Joan
1980 *4 Anthropologists: An American Science in Its Early Years.* Science History Publications, New York.
Marshall, Michael P., John R. Stein, Richard W. Loose, and Judith E. Novotny
1979 *Anasazi Communities of the San Juan Basin.* Public Service Company of New Mexico and Historic Preservation Bureau, State of New Mexico, Santa Fe.
Martin, Paul S.
1971 The Revolution in Archaeology. *American Antiquity* 36:1–8.
Martin, Paul S., and John B. Rinaldo
1951 The Southwestern Co-Tradition. *Southwestern Journal of Anthropology* 7:215–229.
Martínez Gracida, Manuel
n.d.a Los Indios de Oaxaca y sus Monumentos Arqueológicos, 5 vols. Unpublished manuscript in the Genaro Vázquez Library, Casa de la Cultura, Oaxaca.
n.d.b Historia de la Fundación de Mitla. Unpublished manuscript in the Genaro Vázquez Library, Casa de la Cultura, Oaxaca.
Matos Moctezuma, Eduardo
1972 *Manuel Gamio: Arqueología e Indigenismo.* Sepsetentas, Mexico City.
Mayr, Ernst
1976 *Evolution and the Diversity of Life.* Harvard University Press, Cambridge.
1982 *The Growth of Biological Thought.* Harvard University Press, Cambridge.
McGregor, John C.
1965 *Southwestern Archaeology,* 2nd ed. University of Illinois Press, Urbana.
McKern, Thomas C.
1939 The Midwestern Taxonomic System as an Aid to Archaeological Culture Study. *American Antiquity* 4:301–313.

McNitt, Frank
  1966 *Richard Wetherill: Anasazi,* rev. ed. University of New Mexico Press, Albuquerque.
McVaugh, Rogers
  1956 *Edward Palmer: Plant Explorer of the American West.* University of Oklahoma Press, Norman.
McVicar, James B.
  1984 The History of Archaeology. *Archaeological Review from Cambridge* 3:2–6.
McVicker, Donald
  1986 Frederick Starr and the Walker Museum. *Council for Museum Anthropology Newsletter* 10:6–14.
  1987 Parallels and Rivalries: The Early Careers of Franz Boas and Frederick Starr. *Curator,* in press.
Medina, Andrés
  1976 Miguel Covarrubias y el Romanticismo en Antropología. *Nueva Antropología* 4:11–42.
Meek, Ronald L.
  1976 *Social Science and the Ignoble Savage.* Cambridge University Press, Cambridge.
Meltzer, David J.
  1983a The Antiquity of Man and the Development of American Archaeology. In *Advances in Archaeological Method and Theory,* edited by M. B. Schiffer, 6:1–51. Academic Press, New York.
  1983b Power, Prehistory and Politics in the Bureau of American Ethnology, 1879–1906. In *The Socio-Politics of Archaeology,* edited by J. M. Gero, D. M. Lacy, and M. L. Black, pp. 67–77. Research Reports No. 23. Department of Anthropology, University of Massachusetts, Amherst.
  1985 North American Archaeology and Archaeologists, 1879–1934. *American Antiquity* 50:249–260.
  1986 Pleistocene Overkill and the Associational Critique. *Journal of Archaeological Science* 13:51–60.
  1988 Late Pleistocene Human Adaptations in Eastern North America. *Journal of World Prehistory* 2:1–52.
Meltzer, David J., Don D. Fowler, and Jeremy A. Sabloff
  1986 Editors' Introduction. In *American Archaeology: Past and Future,* edited by David J. Meltzer, Don D. Fowler, and Jeremy A. Sabloff, pp. 7–19. Smithsonian Institution Press, Washington, D.C.
Meltzer, David J., and Bruce D. Smith
  1986 Paleo-Indian and Early Archaic Subsistence Strategies in Eastern North America. In *Foraging, Collecting and Harvesting: Archaic Period Subsistence and Settlement in the Eastern Woodlands,* edited by S. Neusius, pp. 1–30. Occasional Paper No. 6. Center for Archaeological Investigations, Southern Illinois University, Carbondale.

Mena, Ramón
1911 *La Ciencia Arqueológica en México desde la Proclamación de la Independencia Hasta Nuestros Días*. Author's edition, Mexico City.

Meritt, Lucey S.
1984 *A History of the American School of Classical Studies at Athens 1939–1980*. American School of Classical Studies, Princeton.

Merton, Robert K.
1979 *The Sociology of Science: An Episodic Memoir*. Southern Illinois University Press, Carbondale.

Miller, Edward
1973 *That Noble Cabinet: A History of the British Museum*. Andre Deutsh, London.

Miller, G. P.
1915 The Jaw of the Piltdown Man. *Smithsonian Miscellaneous Collections* 65(12):1–31.

Miller, R. Berkeley
1978 Anthropology and Institutionalization: Frederick Starr at the University of Chicago, 1892–1923. *Kroeber Anthropological Society Papers* 51–52:49–60.

Milner, George R., and Virginia G. Smith
1986 *New Deal Archaeology in Kentucky: Excavations, Collections, and Research*. Occasional Papers in Anthropology, No. 5. Program for Cultural Resource Assessment, University of Kentucky, Lexington.

Mindeleff, Victor
1891 A Study of Pueblo Architecture, Tusayan and Cibola. In *Bureau of American Ethnology, 8th Annual Report*, pp. 3–228. Smithsonian Institution, Washington, D.C.

Mitchell, S. Wier
1875 The Scientific Life. *Lippincott's Magazine*, pp. 352–356.

Molina, Augusto
1978 Palenque: The Archaeological City Today. In *Primera Mesa Redonda de Palenque*, edited by M. G. Robertson, Part 1, pp. 1–8. R. L. Stevenson School, Pebble Beach.

Moore, Clarence B.
1908 Certain Mounds of Arkansas and of Mississippi. Part 1, Mounds and Cemeteries of the Lower Arkansas River. *Journal of the Academy of Natural Sciences of Philadelphia* 13:481–563.

Moore, James A., and Arthur S. Keene (editors)
1983 *Archaeological Hammers and Theories*. Academic Press, New York.

Morgan, James R.
1977 Were Chaco's Great Kivas Ancient Computers of Astronomy? *El Palacio* 83:28–41.

Morgan, Lewis Henry
  1877 *Ancient Society.* World, New York. (Reprinted in 1985, University of Arizona Press, Tucson.)
Morse, Dan
  1973 Pathology and Abnormalities of the Hampson Skeletal Collection. In *Nodena: An Account of 75 Years of Archeological Investigation in Southeast Mississippi County, Arkansas,* edited by Dan F. Morse, pp. 41–60. Arkansas Archeological Survey Research Series No. 4. Fayetteville.
Morse, Dan F. (editor)
  1973 *Nodena: An Account of 75 Years of Archeological Investigation in Southeast Mississippi County, Arkansas.* Arkansas Archeological Survey Research Series No. 4. Fayetteville.
Morse, Phyllis A.
  1981 *Parkin: The 1978–1979 Archeological Investigations of a Cross County, Arkansas Site.* Arkansas Archeological Survey Research Series No. 13. Fayetteville.
Mosley, Oswald
  1851 Inaugural Discourse, Delivered at the Opening of the Derby Congress. *Journal of the British Archaeological Association* 7:179–190.
Mosse, W. E.
  1974 *Liberal Europe.* Thames and Hudson, London.
Mullins, Nicholas C., and Carolyn J. Mullins
  1973 *Theories and Theory Groups in Contemporary American Sociology.* Harper & Row, New York.
Mumford, Lewis
  1967 *Technics and Human Development.* Harcourt Brace Jovanovich, New York.
Murray, Stephen O.
  1983 *Group Formation in Social Science.* Linguistic Research Inc., Carbondale and Edmonton.
Nadaillac, Marquis de
  1883 *L'Amérique Préhistorique.* Mantoner Editeur, Paris.
Nadel, Ira Bruce
  1984 *Biography: Fiction, Fact and Form.* Macmillan, London.
National Historical Publications and Records Commission
  1978 *Directory of Archives and Manuscript Repositories in the United States.* Washington, D.C.
National Park Service
  1987 Curation of Federally-Owned and Administered Archaeological Collections. *Federal Register* 52:32740–32751.
Navarrete, Carlos
  1982 Otra vez Modesto Méndez, Ambrosio Tut y el Descubrimiento de Tikal. *Boletín Eucady* 52:21–24.

Nelson, Nels C.
 1914 *Pueblo Ruins of the Galisteo Basin, New Mexico.* Anthropological Papers Vol. 15, Pt. 1. American Museum of Natural History, New York.
 1916 Chronology of the Tano Ruins, New Mexico. *American Anthropologist* 18:159–180.
 1920 Notes on Pueblo Bonito. In *Pueblo Bonito* by George H. Pepper, pp. 383–390. Anthropological Papers Vol. 27. American Museum of Natural History, New York.
Neuenschwander, John N.
 1985 *Oral History and the Law.* Oral History Association, Pamphlet Series 1. Denton, Texas.
Norton, Charles Eliot
 1900 The Work of the Archaeological Institute of America: An Address. *American Journal of Archaeology,* second series, 4:1–16.
Oakley, Kenneth P.
 1953 Dating Fossil Human Remains. In *Anthropology Today,* edited by A. L. Kroeber, pp. 43–56. University of Chicago Press, Chicago.
 1959 *Man the Tool-maker.* University of Chicago Press, Chicago.
Oakley, Kenneth P., and C. R. Hoskins
 1950 New Evidence on the Antiquity of Piltdown Man. *Nature* 165:379–382.
Olavarría y Ferrari, Enrique de
 1901 *La Sociedad Mexicana de Geografía y Estadística.* Oficina Tipográfica de la Secretaría de Fomento, Mexico City.
Olsen, John
 1987 The Practice of Archaeology in China Today. *Antiquity* 61:282–289.
Palacios, Enrique Juan
 1930–1931 La Evolución de los Estudios Histórico-Arqueológicos de México. *Boletín de la Secretaría de Educación Pública* 6:234–276.
Palmer, Edward
 1917 Arkansas Mounds. *Publications of the Arkansas Historical Association* 4:390–448.
Patterson, Frank W.
 1979 *A Century of Baptist Work in Mexico.* Baptist Spanish Publishing House, El Paso.
Patterson, Thomas C.
 1986 The Last Sixty Years: Toward a Social History of Americanist Archeology in the United States. *American Anthropologist* 88:7–26.
Peñafiel, Antonio
 1890 *Monumentos del Arte Mexicana Antiguo. Ornamentación, Mitología, Tributos y Monumentos.* A. Asher, Berlin.
 1900 *Teotihuacan. Estudios Histórico y arqueológico.* Oficina Tipográfica de la Secretaría de Fomento, Mexico City.

Pendergast, David

1967 *The Walker-Caddy Expedition to Middle America.* University of Oklahoma Press, Norman.

Pepper, George H.

1896a Field notes. Ms. in possession of the author.

1896b Rooms 32 and 33, Pueblo Bonito. Handwritten manuscript on file at The American Museum of Natural History.

1896c Field diary. Typescript in possession of the author.

1897 Field notes. Ms. in possession of the author.

1898 Field notes. Ms. in possession of the author.

1899 Field notes. Ms. in possession of the author.

1909 The Exploration of a Burial-Room in Pueblo Bonito, New Mexico. In *Putnam Anniversary Volume,* pp. 196–252. G. E. Stechert, New York.

1920 *Pueblo Bonito.* Anthropological Papers Vol. 27. American Museum of Natural History, New York.

n.d. Typed notes on Pueblo Bonito. Typescript in possession of the author (typed ca. 1905 from notes made between 1896 and 1899).

Petty, William

1691 *Political Arithmetick.* Robert Clavel and Hen. Mortlock, London.

Phillips, Philip

1941 *The Menard Site on the Lower Arkansas River.* Special Report of the National Park Service, on behalf of the Central Mississippi Valley Archaeological Survey. (Excerpts reprinted in Ford 1961:160–161.)

1970 *Archaeological Survey in the Lower Yazoo Basin, Mississippi, 1949–1955.* Papers of the Peabody Museum, Harvard University, No. 60.

Pierson, Lloyd M.

1949 The Prehistoric Population of Chaco Canyon, New Mexico: A Study in Methods and Techniques of Prehistoric Population Estimation. Master's thesis, Department of Anthropology, University of New Mexico, Albuquerque.

Piggott, Stuart

1937 Prehistory and the Romantic Movement. *Antiquity* 11:31–38.

1976 *Ruins in a Landscape: Essays in Antiquarianism.* University Press, Edinburgh.

Pitt-Rivers, Augustus H. L. F.

1866 Objects of the Roman Period Found Near the Old London Wall. *Archaeological Journal* 24:61–63.

1867a Primitive Warfare. *Journal of the Royal United Services Institution* 1:612–643.

1867b A Description of Certain Piles Found Near London Wall and Southwark, possibly the Remains of Pile Buildings. *Journal of Anthropological Society of London* 5:lxxi–lxxxii.

1868 Primitive Warfare II. *Journal of the Royal United Services Institution* 12:379–439.

1869a Primitive Warfare III. *Journal of the Royal United Services Institution* 13:509–539.

1869b (editor) *Transactions of the Third Session of the International Congress of Prehistoric Archaeology.* International Congress, London.

1875 Excavations in Cissbury Camp, Sussex. *Journal of the Anthropological Institute* 5:357–389.

Plog, Fred T.
1974 *The Study of Prehistoric Change.* Academic Press, New York.

Pollard, Sidney
1971 *The Idea of Progress.* Penguin, Harmondsworth.

Pond, Alonzo W.
1928 *A Contribution to the Study of Prehistoric Man in Algeria, North Africa.* Logan Museum Bulletin Vol. 1, No. 2, Beloit.

1930 *Primitive Methods of Working Stone.* Logan Museum Bulletin Vol. 2, No. 1, Beloit.

1931 Suggestions on Technique in Archeology. *Wisconsin Archeologist* 10:46–53.

1937 *Prehistoric Habitation Sites in the Sahara and North Africa.* Logan Museum Bulletin Vol. 5, Beloit.

Poole, Lynn, and Gray Poole
1968 *Men Who Dig Up History.* Dodd, Mead, and Co., New York.

Powers, Robert P., William B. Gillespie, and Stephen H. Lekson
1983 *The Outlier Survey: A Regional View of Settlement in the San Juan Basin.* Papers of the Chaco Center No. 3. National Park Service, Albuquerque.

Price, Derek J. deSolla
1986 *Little Science, Big Science . . . and Beyond.* Columbia University Press, New York.

Prudden, Theophil M.
1897 An Elder Brother to the Cliff-Dwellers. *Harper's New Monthly Magazine* 95:56–63.

Raab, L. Mark
1976 *Pine Mountain: A Study of Prehistoric Human Ecology in the Arkansas Ozarks.* Arkansas Archeological Survey Research Report No. 7. Fayetteville.

Radford, C. A. Ralegh
1961 The Royal Charter. *Archaeological Journal* 118:1–6.

Rathje, William L., and Jeremy A. Sabloff
1973 Ancient Maya Commercial Systems: A Research Design for Cozumel, Mexico. *World Archaeology* 5:221–231.

Redman, C. L., M. J. Berman, E. V. Curtin, W. T. Langhorne, N. M. Versagg, and J. C. Wanser (editors)

1978 *Social Archeology: Beyond Subsistence and Dating.* Academic Press, New York.

Reinitz, Richard

1978 Niebuhrian Irony and Historical Interpretation. In *The Writing of History,* edited by Robert H. Canary and Henry Kozicki, pp. 93–128. University of Wisconsin Press, Madison.

Reiss, Timothy J.

1982 *The Discourse of Modernism.* Cornell University Press, Ithaca.

Renfrew, Colin

1967 Colonialism and Megalithismus. *Antiquity* 41:276–288.

1968 Wessex Without Mycenae. *Annual of the British School of Archaeology at Athens* 63:277–285.

1973 *Before Civilization: The Radiocarbon Revolution and Prehistoric Europe.* Jonathan Cape, London. (1979 edition, Cambridge University Press, New York.)

1982 *Towards an Archaeology of Mind.* Cambridge University Press, Cambridge.

1984 *Approaches to Social Archaeology.* Edinburgh University Press, Edinburgh.

Reyman, Jonathan E.

1970a Resource notes. Handwritten, in possession of the author.

1970b Southwestern Pueblo Conservatism: A New Look at an Old "Myth." Paper presented at the 35th Annual Meeting of the Society for American Archaeology, Mexico City.

1971a Astroarchaeology in the Anasazi Area. Paper presented at the 36th Annual Meeting of the Society for American Archaeology, Norman.

1971b Mexican Influence on Southwestern Ceremonialism. Ph.D. dissertation, Southern Illinois University. University Microfilms, Ann Arbor.

1976a Astronomy, Architecture, and Adaptation at Pueblo Bonito. *Science* 193:957–962.

1976b The Emics and Etics of Kiva Wall Niche Location. *Journal of the Steward Anthropological Society* 7:107–129.

1978 *Pochteca* Burials at Anasazi Sites? In *Across the Chichimec Sea: Papers in Honor of J. Charles Kelley,* edited by Carroll L. Riley and Basil C. Hedrick, pp. 242–259, 273. Southern Illinois University Press, Carbondale.

1980 The Predictive Dimension of Priestly Power (With a Note on Solar and Lunar Cycles by Harold J. Born). In *New Frontiers in the Archaeology and Ethnohistory of the Greater Southwest,* edited by Carroll L. Riley and Basil C. Hedrick, pp. 40–59. Transactions of the Illinois State Academy of Science, Vol. 72, No. 4, Springfield.

1982a A Deposit from Pueblo Bonito Having Possible Astronomical Significance. *Archaeoastronomy* 5:14–19.

1982b Review of *Archaeoastronomy in the Americas,* edited by Ray A. Williamson. *American Antiquity* 47:905–907.

1982c Southwestern Pueblo Architecture: Some Implications for Modern Housing Design. In *Desert Planning: International Lessons,* edited by Gideon Golany, pp. 105–112. Architectural Press, London.

1985 A Reevaluation of Bi-wall and Tri-wall Structures in the Anasazi Area. In *Contributions to the Archaeology and Ethnohistory of Greater Mesoamerica,* edited by William J. Folan, pp. 292–334. Southern Illinois University Press, Carbondale.

1987a Review of *Recent Research on Chaco Prehistory,* edited by W. James Judge and John D. Schelberg. *The Kiva* 52:147–151.

1987b The George H. Pepper Collections. In preparation.

1987c Pueblo Bonito Revisited. In preparation.

1987d George H. Pepper: Miscellaneous Southwestern Papers. In preparation.

Reyman, Jonathan E., and Martin K. Nickels

1987 The Burials of Pueblo Bonito. In preparation.

Rivet, Paul

1920 Le Movement Américaniste de 1914 a 1920. *Revue d'Ethnologie et des Traditions Populaires* 1:253–263.

Riviere, Peter

1978 Editor's Introduction to Reprint of John Lubbock, *The Origin of Civilisation and the Primitive Condition of Man.* University of Chicago Press, Chicago.

Roberts, Frank H. H., Jr.

1936 A Survey of Southwestern Archaeology. In *Annual Report of the Smithsonian Institution for 1935,* pp. 507–533. Smithsonian Institution, Washington, D.C.

1940 Developments in the Problem of the North American Paleo-Indian. *Smithsonian Miscellaneous Collections* 100:51–116.

Rogge, A. E.

1976 A Look at Academic Anthropology: Through a Graph Darkly. *American Anthropologist* 78:829–843.

1983 Little Archaeology, Big Archaeology: The Changing Context of Archaeological Research. Ph.D. dissertation, University of Arizona. University Microfilms, Ann Arbor.

Rolingson, Martha Ann

1982 Contributions to the Toltec (Knapp) Site Research by the Smithsonian Institution. In *Emerging Patterns of Plum Bayou Culture: Preliminary Investigations of the Toltec Mounds Research Project,* edited by Martha Ann Rolingson, pp. 71–86. Arkansas Archeological Survey Research Series No. 18. Fayetteville.

Ross, Dorothy

1979 The Development of the Social Sciences. In *The Organization of Knowledge in Modern America, 1860–1920,* edited by Alexander Oleson and John Voss, pp. 107–138. Johns Hopkins University Press, Baltimore.

Rudwick, M. J.

1985 *The Great Devonian Controversy.* University of Chicago Press, Chicago.

Ruz, Alberto

1978 Obras de Divulgacion Sobre la Cultura Maya. *Boletín del Instituto Nacional de Antropología e Historia,* third period, 21:26–40.

1982 *El Pueblo Maya.* Salvat, Mexico City.

Rydell, Robert W.

1984 *All the World's a Fair: Visions of Empire at American International Expositions, 1876–1916.* University of Chicago Press, Chicago.

Sabloff, Jeremy A.

1982 New Directions in Archaeological Methodology: Some Implications for Mesoamerican Archaeology. Paper presented at a meeting of the Sociedad Mexicana de Antropología in Zamora, Mexico.

1983 Classic Maya Settlement Pattern Studies: Past Problems, Future Prospects. In *Prehistoric Settlement Pattern Studies: Retrospect and Prospect,* edited by Evon Z. Vogt and Richard M. Leventhal, pp. 413–422. University of New Mexico Press, Albuquerque.

1985 Review of *Approaches to Social Archaeology,* by Colin Renfrew. *Antiquity* 49:70–71.

1986 Interaction Among Classic Maya Polities: A Preliminary Examination. In *Peer Polity Interaction and Socio-political Change,* edited by Colin Renfrew and John F. Cherry, pp. 109–116. Cambridge University Press, Cambridge.

Sabloff, Jeremy A. (editor)

1981 *Simulations in Archaeology.* University of New Mexico Press, Albuquerque.

Sabloff, Jeremy A., Lewis R. Binford, and Patricia A. McAnany

1987 Understanding the Archaeological Record. *Antiquity* 61: 203–209.

Sabloff, Jeremy A., Patricia A. McAnany, Bernd Fahmel Beyer, Tomas Gallareta N., Signa L. Larralde, and LuAnn Wandsnider

1984 *Ancient Maya Settlement Patterns at the Site of Sayil, Puuc Region, Yucatán, Mexico: Initial Reconnaissance (1984).* Latin American Institute, Research Paper Series No. 14. University of New Mexico, Albuquerque.

Sabloff, Jeremy A., and William L. Rathje (editors)

1975 *A Study of Changing Pre-Columbian Commercial Systems: The 1972–1973 Seasons at Cozumel, Mexico.* Monographs of the Peabody Museum, No. 3, Harvard University.

Sabloff, Jeremy A., and Gair Tourtellot

1987 Beyond Temples and Palaces: Recent Settlement Pattern Research at the Ancient City of Sayil. In *New Theories on the Ancient Maya,* edited by E. Danien. University Museum, University of Pennsylvania, in press.

Sackett, James
1981 From de Mortillet to Bordes: A Century of French Paleolithic Research. In *Towards a History of Archaeology*, edited by G. Daniel, pp. 89–99. Thames and Hudson, London.

Safford, William E.
1926 Edward Palmer: Botanical Explorer. Manuscript on file, National Anthropological Archives, Smithsonian Institution, Washington, D. C.

Sagan, Carl
1977 *The Dragons of Eden.* Random House, New York.

Salmon, Merrilee H.
1982 *Philosophy and Archaeology.* Academic Press, New York.

Samuels, Helen W.
1986 Who Controls the Past? *American Archivist* 49:109–124.

Sánchez, Jesús
1877 Reseña Histórica del Museo Nacional de México. *Anales del Museo Nacional,* first period, 1:1–12.

Saville, Marshall H.
1900 Cruciform Structures Near Mitla. *Bulletin of the American Museum of Natural History* 13:201–218.
1911 *The Work of the Loubat Expedition in Southern Mexico.* Privately printed. American Museum of Natural History, New York.

Sayce, A. H.
1875 *The Principles of Comparative Philology.* Trubner, London.

Schambach, Frank F.
1970 Pre-Caddoan Cultures in the Trans-Mississippi South: A Beginning Sequence. Ph.D. dissertation, Harvard University.
1981 A Description and Analysis of the Ceramics. In *The Shallow Lake Site (3UN9/52) and Its Place in Regional Prehistory,* by Martha Ann Rolingson and Frank F. Schambach, pp. 101–176. Arkansas Archeological Survey Research Series No. 12. Fayetteville.

Schambach, Frank F., and John E. Miller
1984 A Description and Analysis of the Ceramics. In *Cedar Grove: An Interdisciplinary Investigation of a Late Caddo Farmstead in the Red River Valley,* edited by Neal L. Trubowitz, pp. 109–170. Arkansas Archeological Survey Research Series No. 23. Fayetteville.

Schávelzon, Daniel
1983a Arqueología de una polémica: la pirámide de Cuicuilco. *Cuicuilco* 9:13–18.
1983b *La Pirámide de Cuicuilco: Album Fotográfico.* Fondo de Cultura Económica, Mexico City.
1983c La Contribución Científica de Ignacio Bernal: Bibliografía. In *Historia de la Arqueología en Mesoamérica: Homenaje a Ignacio Bernal,* edited by Daniel Schávelzon and Jaime Litvak. Universidad Nacional Autónoma de México, Mexico City, in press.
1984 Teorías e Historia de la Restauración de Edificios Arqueológicos en

Mesoamérica (1780–1980). Ph.D. dissertation, Universidad Nacional Autónoma de México, Mexico City.

1988 Las Excavaciónes en Zaculeu (1946–1950): Una Aproximación al Analisis de la Relatión entre Arqueología y Politica en América Latin. In *Recent Studies in Pre-Columbian Archaeology,* edited by Nicholas J. Saunders and Olivier de Montmollion, pp. 167–190. BAR International Series 421, Oxford.

Schávelzon, Daniel, and Jaime Litvak (editors)

1983 *Historia de la Arqueología en México: Homenaje a Ignacio Bernal.* Universidad Nacional Autónoma de México, Mexico City, in press.

Schelhass, Paul

1935 Fifty Years of Maya Research. *Maya Research* 2:129–139.

Schiffer, Michael B.

1976 *Behavioral Archaeology.* Academic Press, New York.

1987 *Formation Processes of the Archaeological Record.* University of New Mexico Press, Albuquerque.

Schlesinger, Arthur, Jr.

1967 On the Writing of Contemporary History. *Atlantic Monthly* 219(3): 69–74.

Scholtz, Sandra Clements

1970 A Structural and Comparative Analysis of Cordage, Netting, Basketry, and Fabrics from Ozark Bluff Shelters. Master's thesis, Department of Anthropology, University of Arkansas, Fayetteville.

1975 *Prehistoric Plies: A Structural and Comparative Analysis of Cordage, Netting, Basketry, and Fabric from Ozark Bluff Shelters.* Arkansas Archeological Survey Research Series No. 9. Fayetteville.

Schuyler, Robert L.

1971 The History of American Archaeology: An Examination of Procedure. *American Antiquity* 36:383–409.

Schwartz, Douglas W.

1978 A Conceptual Framework for the Sociology of Archaeology. In *Archaeological Essays in Honor of Irving B. Rouse,* edited by R. C. Dunnell and E. S. Hall, Jr., pp. 149–176. Mouton, The Hague.

Scott, Douglas P.

1972 The Nordenskiöld Campsite: A Test in Historic Archaeology. *The Kiva* 37:128–140.

Sheftel, Phoebe S.

1979 The Archaeological Institute of America 1879–1979: A Centennial Review. *American Journal of Archaeology* 83:3–17.

Silverberg, Robert

1974 *The Mound Builders.* Ballantine Books, New York.

Simpson, James H.

1850 *Journal of a Military Reconnaisance from Santa Fe, New Mexico to the Navaho Country Made in 1849.* Report, Secretary of War, 31st

Congress, 1st Session, Senate Executive Document No. 64, Washington, D.C.

Skidmore Liberal Studies Committee
1984 Guidelines for Liberal Studies Courses. Skidmore College, Saratoga Springs.

Smiles, Samuel
1859 *Self-help: With Illustrations of a Conduct and Preserverence.* London.

Smith, Bruce D.
1985 Introduction to the 1985 edition. In *Report on the Mound Explorations of the Bureau of Ethnology,* by Cyrus Thomas. Smithsonian Institution Press, Washington, D. C.

Smith, G. Elliot
1913 The Piltdown Skull. *Nature* 92:131.

Smith, Marian
1959 Boas' "Natural History" Approach to Field Method. In *The Anthropology of Franz Boas,* edited by Walter Goldschmidt, pp. 46–60. American Anthropological Association, Washington, D.C.

Society for American Archaeology
1986 *The Society for American Archaeology Briefing Book.* Washington, D.C.

Society of American Archivists
1986 *Planning for the Archival Profession: A Report of the SAA Task Force on Goals and Priorities.* Society of American Archivists, Chicago.

South, Stanley
1977 *Method and Theory in Historical Archaeology.* Academic Press, New York.

Spaulding, Albert C.
1968 Explanation in Archeology. In *New Perspectives in Archeology,* edited by Sally R. Binford and Lewis R. Binford, pp. 33–39. Aldine, Chicago.
1985 Fifty Years of Theory. *American Antiquity* 50:301–308.

Spencer, Frank, and F. H. Smith
1981 Hrdlička's Neanderthal Phase of Man. *American Journal of Physical Anthropology* 56:435–459.

Spencer, Herbert
1873 *Descriptive Sociology.* John Murray, London.
1876 *Principles of Sociology.* John Murray, London.

Stanzeski, Andrew J.
1974 The Three Beeches: Excavations in the House of an Archaeologist. *Bulletin of the Archaeological Society of New Jersey* 31:30–32.

Starr, Frederick
1894 *Notes on Mexican Archaeology.* Bulletin I, Department of Anthropology. University of Chicago, Chicago.

1907 *The Truth About the Congo: The Chicago Tribune Articles.* Forbes, Chicago.

Staudenmaier, John M.
1985 *Technology's Storytellers.* MIT Press, Cambridge.

Stent, Gunther S. (editor)
1980 *The Double Helix, by James D. Watson: Text, Commentary, Reviews, Original Papers.* W. W. Norton, New York.

Stephens, John Lloyd
1841 *Incidents of Travel in Central America, Chiapas, and Yucatán,* 2 vols. Harper & Brothers, New York.

Sterud, Eugene L.
1978 Changing Aims of American Archaeology: A Citation Analysis of *American Antiquity. American Antiquity* 43:294–302.

Stevens, Edward T.
[1867] *Some Account of the Blackmore Museum Salisbury.* Bell and Daldy, London.

Stevens, Frank E.
1947 *The Salisbury Museums, 1861–1947: A Record of Eighty-Six Years' Progress.* Salisbury and South Wilts. Museum, Salisbury.

Steward, Julian
1949 Cultural Causality and Law: A Trial Formulation of the Development of Early Civilizations. *American Anthropologist* 51:1–27.
1955 *Theory of Culture Change.* University of Illinois, Urbana.

Steward, Julian, and Frank Setzler
1938 Function and Configuration in Archaeology. *American Antiquity* 32:487–497.

Stewart, T. Dale
1951 Antiquity of Man in America Demonstrated by the Fluorine Test. *Science* 113:391–392.

Stocking, George W., Jr.
1968 *Race, Culture, and Evolution: Essays in the History of Anthropology.* Free Press, New York.
1971 What's in a Name: The Origins of the Royal Anthropological Institute. *Man,* new series, 6:69–90.
1974 *A Franz Boas Reader: The Shaping of American Anthropology, 1883–1911.* University of Chicago Press, Chicago.
1979a Anthropology as Kulturkampf: Science and Politics in the Career of Franz Boas. In *The Uses of Anthropology,* edited by Walter Goldschmidt, pp. 33–50. American Anthropological Association, Washington, D.C.
1979b *Anthropology at Chicago: Tradition, Discipline, Department.* University of Chicago Library. Chicago.
1985 Essays on Museums and Material Culture. In *Objects and Others,* edited by G. W. Stocking, Jr., pp. 3–14. University of Wisconsin Press, Madison.

1987 *Victorian Anthropology.* Free Press, New York.
Stoltman, James B.
   1978 Temporal Models in Prehistory: An Example from Eastern North America. *Current Anthropology* 19:703–746.
Stoltman, James B., and David Baerreis
   1983 The Evolution of Human Ecosystems in the Eastern United States. In *Late-Quaternary Environments of the United States,* Vol. 2, edited by H. Wright, pp. 252–268. University of Minnesota Press, Minneapolis.
Strong, William D.
   1935 *An Introduction to Nebraska Archaeology.* Smithsonian Miscellaneous Collections, Vol. 93, No. 10. Smithsonian Institution, Washington, D.C.
Susman, Warren I.
   1984 *Culture as History: The Transformation of the United States in the Twentieth Century.* Pantheon, New York.
Taylor, Reginald E.
   1932 The Humors of Archaeology, or the Canterbury Congress of 1844 and the Early Days of the Association. *Journal of the British Archaeological Association,* new series, 38:183–234.
Taylor, Walter W.
   1948 *A Study of Archeology.* Memoir No. 69. American Anthropological Association.
Thomas, Cyrus
   1894 Report on the Mound Explorations of the Bureau of Ethnology. *Twelfth Annual Report of the Bureau of Ethnology,* pp. 3–742. (Reprinted in 1985 by Smithsonian Institution Press, Washington, D.C.)
Thompson, Homer A.
   1980 In Pursuit of the Past: The American Role 1879–1979. *American Journal of Archaeology* 84:263–270.
Thompson, Michael W.
   1977 *General Pitt-Rivers: Evolution and Archaeology in the Nineteenth Century.* Moonraker Press, Bradford-on-Avon.
Thomsen, Thomas
   1937 The Study of Man. *American Scandinavian Review* 25:309–318.
Thurman, John
   1850 On Danish Tumuli and the Importance of Preserving Crania in Tumuli. *Archaeological Journal* 7:34–35.
Tomline, George
   1865 Inaugural Address Delivered at the Suffolk Congress, Held at Ipswich. *Journal of the British Archaeological Association* 21:1–5.
Towne, Arlean H.
   1984 *A History of Central California Archaeology, 1880–1940.* Archives of California Prehistory No. 1. Coyote Press, Salinas, California.
Trevelyan, S. M.
   1944 *English Social History.* Longmans, London.

Trigger, Bruce G.

1980 Archaeology and the Image of the American Indian. *American Antiquity* 45:662–276.

1981 Giants and Pygmies: The Professionalization of Canadian Archaeology. In *Towards a History of Archaeology,* edited by Glyn Daniel, pp. 69–84. Thames and Hudson, London.

1984 Archaeology at the Crossroads: What's New? *Annual Review of Anthropology* 13:275–300.

1985 Writing the History of Archeology: A Survey of Trends. In *Objects and Others,* edited by G. W. Stocking, Jr., pp. 218–235. University of Wisconsin Press, Madison.

1986 Prehistoric Archaeology and American Society. In *American Archaeology: Past and Future,* edited by D. J. Meltzer, D. D. Fowler, and J. A. Sabloff, pp. 187–215. Smithsonian Institution Press, Washington, D.C.

Trubowitz, Neal L.

1980 *Pine Mountain Revisited: An Archeological Study in the Arkansas Ozarks.* Arkansas Archeological Survey Research Report No. 23. Fayetteville.

Tylor, Edward B.

1865 *Researches into the Early History of Mankind and the Development of Civilization.* John Murray, London.

Valentine, Kermit

1959 *Charles Eliot Norton.* Harvard University Press, Cambridge.

Valentine, Lucia N., and Arthur Valentine

1973 *The American Academy in Rome, 1894–1969.* University of Virginia Press, Charlottesville.

Vaughn, Stephen (editor)

1985 *The Vital Past: Writings on the Uses of History.* University of Georgia Press, Athens.

Verneau, Réné

1920 L'Evolution des Études Américanistes depuis 1895. *Journal de la Société des Américanistes* 12:206–211.

Vivian, Gordon

1948 Memorandum for Superintendent McNeill, Chaco Canyon. Typescript on file, Chaco Culture National Historical Park, New Mexico.

Vivian, Gordon, and Paul Reiter

1960 *Great Kivas of Chaco Canyon and Their Relationships.* Monograph No. 22. School of American Research and the Museum of New Mexico, Santa Fe.

Wace, A. J. B.

1949 The Greeks and Romans as Archaeologists. Reprinted in *Man's Discovery of His Past,* edited by R. F. Heizer, 1969, pp. 203–218. Peek Publications, Palo Alto.

Warnow, Joan N.
  1984 Preserving Documentary Materials for the History of 20th Century Physics. Paper presented at the 5th Congresso Nazionale de Storia della Fisica, Rome.
Waterston, D.
  1913 The Piltdown Mandible. *Nature* 92 : 319.
Watson, Patty Jo
  1986 Archaeological Interpretation, 1985. In *American Archaeology: Past and Future*, edited by David J. Meltzer, Don D. Fowler, and Jeremy A. Sabloff, pp. 439–458. Smithsonian Institution Press, Washington, D.C.
Wauchope, Robert
  1962 *Lost Tribes and Sunken Continents*. University of Chicago Press, Chicago.
  1966 *Archaeological Survey of Northern Georgia, with a Test of Some Cultural Hypotheses*. Memoirs of the Society for American Archaeology, No. 21.
Way, Albert
  1844 Introductory Address. *Archaeological Journal* 1 : 1–6.
  1859 *Catalogue of Antiquities, Works of Art and Historical Scottish Relics, etc.* Constable, Edinburgh.
Weinstein, R. A., and Larry Booth
  1977 *Collection, Use, and Care of Historical Photographs*. American Association for State and Local History, Nashville.
Weitzner, Bella
  n.d. A Year-By-Year Summary of the Department of Anthropology 1871–1957—Based on the Annual Reports of the AMNH. American Museum of Natural History, New York.
Westropp, Hodder M.
  1866 On the Analogous Forms of Flint Implements Among Early and Primitive Races. *Anthropological Review* 4 : 208–213.
Westwood, John Obediah
  1858 Archaeological Notes of a Tour in Denmark, Prussia and Holland. *Archaeological Journal* 16 : 132–145, 236–252.
Wetherill, Richard
  1894 Snider's Well. *The Archaeologist* 2 : 288–289.
  1896 Field notes. In the possession of the author.
White, Hayden
  1973 *Metahistory*. Johns Hopkins University Press, Baltimore.
White, Leslie
  1940 *Pioneers in American Anthropology: The Bandelier-Morgan Letters 1873–1883*. University of New Mexico Press, Albuquerque.
  1959 *The Evolution of Culture*. McGraw-Hill, New York.
Wilkie, Nancy, and William D. E. Coulson (editors)
  1985 *Contributions to Aegean Archaeology: Studies in Honor of William*

A. McDonald. Center for Ancient Studies, University of Minnesota, Minneapolis.

Wilkins, Judith
1961 Worsaae and British Antiquities. *Antiquity* 35:214–220.

Willey, Gordon R.
1953 *Prehistoric Settlement Patterns in the Virú Valley, Peru.* Bureau of American Ethnology, Bulletin 155. Smithsonian Institution, Washington, D.C.

Willey, Gordon R. (editor)
1956 *Settlement Patterns in the New World.* Viking Fund Publications in Anthropology, No. 23. The Wenner-Gren Foundation, New York.

Willey, Gordon R., and Philip Phillips
1958 *Method and Theory in American Archaeology.* University of Chicago Press, Chicago.

Willey, Gordon R., and Jeremy A. Sabloff
1974 *A History of American Archaeology.* Thames and Hudson, London.
1980 *A History of American Archaeology,* second edition. W. H. Freeman, San Francisco.

Williams, Barbara
1981 *Breakthrough: Women in Archaeology.* Walker, New York.

Williamson, Ray A.
1981 North America: A Multiplicity of Astronomies. In *Archaeoastronomy in the Americas,* edited by Ray A. Williamson, pp. 61–80. Ballena Press, Los Altos.

Wills, Garry
1987 *Reagan's America: Innocents at Home.* Doubleday, Garden City.

Wilson, Daniel
1851 *The Archaeology and Prehistoric Annals of Scotland.* Sutherland and Knox, Edinburgh.
1865 *Prehistoric Man: Researches into the Origin of Civilisation in the Old and the New World.* Macmillan, London.

Wilson, Thomas
1892 Man and Mylodon: Their Possible Contemporaneous Existence in the Mississippi Valley. *American Naturalist* 26:628–631.
1895 On the Presence of Fluorine as a Test for the Fossilization of Animal Bones. *American Naturalist* 29:301–317, 439–456, 719.

Windes, Thomas
1984 A New Look at Population in Chaco Canyon. In *Recent Research on Chaco Prehistory,* edited by W. James Judge and John D. Schelberg, pp. 75–84. Papers of the Chaco Center No. 8. National Park Service, Albuquerque.

Wissler, Clark
1920 Foreword. In *Pueblo Bonito* by George H. Pepper, pp. 1–2. Anthropological Papers Vol. 27. American Museum of Natural History, New York.

1944 Marshall Howard Saville. In *Dictionary of American Biography,* vol. 11, Supplement 1, edited by Harris E. Starr, pp. 647–648. Charles Scribner's Sons, New York.

Wood, Neal
1983 *The Politics of Locke's Philosophy.* University of California Press, Berkeley.
1984 *John Locke and Agrarian Capitalism.* University of California Press, Berkeley.

Wood, W. Raymond
1963 The Poole Site: Components of the Fourche Maline and Mid-Ouachita Foci in Garland County, Arkansas. Ms. on file, University of Arkansas Museum, Fayetteville.
1981 The Poole Site, 3GA3. *The Arkansas Archeologist* 22:7–64.

Woodward, Arthur Smith
1948 *The Earliest Englishman.* Watts, London.

Woolley, Leonard
1953 *Spadework in Archaeology.* Philosophical Library, New York.

Worsaae, J. J. A.
1849 *The Primeval Antiquities of Denmark.* London.

Wright, Thomas
1866 On the Progress and Present Condition of Archaeological Science. *Journal of the British Archaeological Association* 22:64–84.

Wyman, Jeffries
1875 *Fresh-water Shell Mounds of the St. John's River, Florida.* Peabody Museum Academy of Science Memoir No. 4. Salem.

Zinke, Marjorie L.
1975 An Analysis of Mississippian Burial Components from the Hazel Site, Poinsett County, Arkansas. Master's thesis, Department of Anthropology, University of Arkansas, Fayetteville.

Contributors

SUSAN J. BENDER received her Ph.D. from the State University of New York at Albany in 1983 and is currently Assistant Professor of Anthropology at Skidmore College. She has supervised survey and excavations in the Grand Teton Mountains of northwestern Wyoming and has directed prehistoric and historic field projects in the upper Hudson Valley region of New York State. Her research interests focus on hunter-gatherer settlement systems and the transition to sedentary settlement in the Northeast, lithic procurement systems, and zooarchaeology. She is currently developing research into the history of women in Northeastern archaeology.

WILLIAM CHAPMAN received his Ph.D. in Anthropology from Oxford University in 1981 and currently teaches in the historic preservation program at the University of Georgia. He is involved with research on vernacular architecture and landscapes, architectural conservation, and the history of anthropology and archaeology. His fieldwork has centered on the Caribbean region, particularly the U.S. Virgin Islands, where he worked from 1979 to 1983.

CHRISTOPHER CHIPPINDALE is assistant curator for later archaeology in the Cambridge University Museum of Archaeology and Anthropology, Fellow of Girton College, Cambridge, and editor of *Antiquity*. He has particularly studied the history of Stonehenge, and has written *Stonehenge Complete* (1983) and *Who Owns Stonehenge?* (with Peter Fowler and others; in press). His research interests in archaeology are rock art and formal grammatical approaches to artifacts.

ANDREW L. CHRISTENSON received his Ph.D. in anthropology from UCLA in 1981. He is currently an adjunct faculty member at Prescott College. His interests are museum research and management, lithic and projectile technology, economic models, and the history of archaeology. Currently he is reanalyzing the collections and revisiting the sites of the Rainbow Bridge–Monument Valley Expedition. He is coeditor of *Modeling Change in Prehistoric Subsistence Economies* and coauthor of *Prehistoric Stone Technology on Northern Black Mesa, Arizona*.

LAWRENCE G. DESMOND received his Ph.D. from the University of Colorado–Boulder in 1983. He is currently a research associate in anthropology at the California Academy of Sciences in San Francisco and at the Mesoamerican Archive and Research Project at the University of Colorado. In addition to writing about the history of archaeology, he has done ethnographic and archaeological fieldwork in Oaxaca and Yucatán, Mexico.

STEPHEN L. DYSON received his Ph.D. in 1963 from Yale University and is currently professor of classics and history at Wesleyan University. His research has centered on the combination of archaeological and literary sources to write a more modern social and economic history of Rome. This approach is represented in his recent study *The Creation of the Roman Frontier*. The chapter in this volume is part of a larger comparative study of the development of classical archaeology in the United States, Britain, and Italy.

LESTER EMBREE received his Ph.D. from the New School for Social Research in 1972 and is now professor of philosophy and president of the Center for Advanced Research in Phenomenology, Inc., at Duquesne University. His research focus is the philosophy of the human sciences, particularly theoretical archaeology, and the philosophy of technology.

C. M. HINSLEY received his Ph.D. in American history from the University of Wisconsin–Madison in 1976 and currently is chair of the Department of History at Northern Arizona University. He has written extensively on the history of American cultural anthropology and archaeology. In 1985 he produced, with Melissa Banta of the Peabody Museum at Harvard, *From Site to Sight: Anthropology, Photography, and the Power of Imagery*, a catalogue and exhibit on the history of photography in the various fields of anthropology.

MARVIN D. JETER received his Ph.D. from Arizona State University in 1977. He has worked in Alabama, Tennessee, Louisiana, and especially Arkansas, where he is associate archaeologist/professor with the Arkansas Archeological Survey (Monticello) and the University of Arkansas. His major research interests are the late prehistoric to early historic remains of the lower Mississippi Valley and the history of archaeological investigations in that area. His publications include *Archaeology in Copper Basin, Yavapai County, Arizona* (1977), *Arkansas Archaeology in Review* (coeditor and contributor, 1982) and *Tunicans West of the Mississippi* (1986). His archaeohistorical book, *Edward Palmer's "Arkansaw Mounds,"* is scheduled for publication by the University of Arkansas Press in 1989.

ALICE B. KEHOE received her B.A. in anthropology from Barnard College, and her Ph.D. from Harvard University in 1964. She taught anthropology at the University of Regina, University of Nebraska (Lincoln), and has been at Marquette University, where she is professor of anthropology, since 1968. Her principal area of research is the prehistory and ethnohistory of the north-western Plains. Among her publications are *Francois' House, An Early Fur-Trade Post on the Saskatchewan* (1978), *The Ghost Dance: Ethnohistory and Revitalization* (1988), *North American Indians, A Comprehensive Account* (1981) and numerous articles including "The Ideological Paradigm in Tra-ditional American Ethnology," in *Social Contexts of American Ethnology, 1840–1984* (1985) (ed. J. Helm). In 1989 she will be a Visiting Research Fellow in the Institute for Advanced Studies in the Humanities, University of Edinburgh.

EDWIN A. LYON received his Ph.D. in history from Louisiana State Univer-sity in 1982. He is an archaeologist with the U.S. Army Corps of Engineers in New Orleans and an adjunct assistant professor in the Department of Geography and Anthropology at Louisiana State University. He is also a member of the History of Archaeology Committee of the Society for Ameri-can Archaeology. Much of his work focuses on the history of archaeology, including his dissertation, *New Deal Archaeology in the Southeast: WPA, TVA, NPS, 1934–1942*. His research interests include cultural resources management and historical anthropology.

DONALD McVICKER received his Ph.D. from the University of Chicago in 1969 and currently is associate professor of sociology and anthropology at North Central College. His research has concentrated on Mesoamerica, most recently on the Prehispanic murals of central Mexico. Previously he had studied the Tlacotepec collection from the Valley of Toluca, Mexico, at Field Museum of Natural History in Chicago. This research led him to trace the history of the collection and of the collector, Frederick Starr. Currently he plans to survey the site of Tlacotepec to provide an archaeological con-text for the museum's collection.

DAVID J. MELTZER received his Ph.D. from the University of Washington in 1984 and since that time has been on the faculty of the Department of Anthropology, Southern Methodist University. His research interests in-clude late Pleistocene hunter-gatherers (especially Paleo-Indians of North America), Quaternary paleoecology and Pleistocene extinctions, and the history of American archaeology.

JONATHAN E. REYMAN received his Ph.D. from Southern Illinois Univer-sity at Carbondale in 1971 and is currently professor of anthropology at Illinois State University. He has conducted archaeological and ethnographic fieldwork in Mexico, Ecuador, and several areas of North America. Since 1968 he has specialized in the American Southwest, working in the Anasazi region and among several Pueblos. Chaco Canyon and the early work of George Pepper and Richard Wetherill are focal points of interest, as are the issues of Mexican-Southwestern interaction, sociopolitical and cultural-econological adaptation, and ceremonialism.

JEREMY A. SABLOFF received his Ph.D. from Harvard University in 1969. He currently is university professor of anthropology and the history and philosophy of science at the University of Pittsburgh. He also is a research associate of the Carnegie Museum of Natural History, a Senior Fellow of the Center for the Philosophy of Science, University of Pittsburgh, and a Senior Fellow in Pre-Columbian Studies at Dumbarton Oaks. He is the author or editor of more than a dozen books and monographs, as well as numerous articles focusing on topics such as archaeological theory and method and the ancient Maya. He is a former editor of *American Antiquity* and president-elect of the Society for American Archaeology. He recently completed a five-year field project at the site of Sayil in Yucatán, Mexico.

DANIEL SCHÁVELZON received his Ph.D. from UNAM (Mexico) in 1983 and presently heads the Program of Urban Archaeology of the Buenos Aires National University, Argentina. His work is focused on prehispanic architecture and preservation of the cultural heritage in Latin America. His current research in historic archaeology is part of a global interest in the history of archaeology in Latin America. He has published several books, including *Arqueología y Arquitectura del Ecuador Prehispánico* (1981).

MICHAEL TARABULSKI received his M.A. in anthropology from Syracuse University in 1986 and is currently a masters candidate in the School of Library and Information Studies at the University of Wisconsin–Madison. Specializing in archives management, he has organized the papers of Alonzo Pond for the State Historical Society of Wisconsin. He has also participated in archaeological fieldwork in southeastern Minnesota.

Index